Work Appropriation of Low-Wage Workers in
the Service Sector

to Hannah Wayra

# Work Appropriation of Low-Wage Workers in the Service Sector

The Re/Production of Society

Antonia Kupfer

*Professor of Macrosociology, Institute of Sociology, Technical University of Dresden, Germany*

Cheltenham, UK • Northampton, MA, USA

This publication was produced as part of the author's placement as Professor of Macrosociology at Technische Universität Dresden, and has been supported financially by Technische Universität Dresden.

Published by
Edward Elgar Publishing Limited
The Lypiatts
15 Lansdown Road
Cheltenham
Glos GL50 2JA
UK

Edward Elgar Publishing, Inc.
William Pratt House
9 Dewey Court
Northampton
Massachusetts 01060
USA

A catalogue record for this book
is available from the British Library

Library of Congress Control Number: 2023952683

This book is available electronically in the **Elgar**online
Sociology, Social Policy and Education subject collection
http://dx.doi.org/10.4337/9781035321681

ISBN 978 1 0353 2167 4 (cased)
ISBN 978 1 0353 2168 1 (eBook)

Printed and bound in Great Britain by
TJ Books Limited, Padstow, Cornwall

# Contents

# Introduction to *Work Appropriation of Low-Wage Workers in the Service Sector*

Most people in the U.S. and in Germany buy their food and grocery goods in supermarkets. The COVID-19 pandemic increased global consciousness of the essential role supermarkets play in feeding populations. But despite the essential role of the supermarket sector, its workers and employees are mostly stuck in low-wage jobs insufficient for supporting families, and they operate in unfavorable working conditions characterized by part-time or fluctuating schedules. In contrast to other essential workers and employees who have received at least some public recognition since the pandemic, supermarket clerks mostly remain unseen and unrecognized. This book calls attention to a work sector that has largely been neglected: the people who order, unpack, stock, and sell the food and grocery goods most people rely upon for their existence. The voices of supermarket clerks therefore fill the pages of this book, which analyzes their perceptions of their work.

In both the U.S. and Germany, supermarket clerks form a large share of the workforce. For 2018, the U.S. Census Bureau counts 9.8 million retail workers, who account for 6.3% of the total U.S. labor force (U.S. Census Bureau 2023), and Ibisworld, an industry research company, reports that in 2023, U.S. supermarkets and grocery stores had 2,824,936 employees (Ibisworld 2023). According to this source, supermarkets and grocery stores are ranked first compared to clothes and other retail trade industries. In Germany, 1,345,852 employees are listed as being employed in food retail in the year 2020, with a revenue of 242,264 million Euros (Handelsverband Deutschland 2023). More women than men are employed in supermarkets in both countries, but the overrepresentation of women is higher in Germany than in the U.S. Supermarket clerks are crucial members of the workforce because they provide food for most people. This became apparent during the COVID-19 pandemic lockdowns, when other kinds of stores were closed, but supermarkets remained open. During these lockdowns supermarket clerks were given additional tasks, such as controlling the numbers of customers entering the supermarkets and ensuring that customers wore masks and abided by restrictions on the purchase of scarce products. These additional tasks had the effect of making supermarket clerks more visible to the public. In addition, the hierarchy between workers and customers shifted as customers were required to follow supermarket clerks' instructions. Before the pandemic, customers had not paid much attention to supermarket clerks, who formed a kind of invisible workforce. Their role had been to ensure that the processes of shopping went smoothly and without notable interactions. Most shoppers would not be able to recall the face of a cashier who had rung up their recent supermarket purchases. This study creates an opportunity to learn more about the people who form such a large share of our workforce yet remain largely invisible. The potential is high for new insights resulting from hearing how these workers think about their work.

In addition to the research interest in grocery and supermarket workers based on the size of the industry in which they work, another basis for studying workers in this sector is the unique tension between their relevance and their invisibility. How do these workers, who carry out essential jobs but go unrecognized and are poorly remunerated, think about their work? Do they suffer from the gap between their essential roles and perceived importance? Do they internalize these perceptions and on that basis refrain from demanding wage and salary increases? Other employees who carry out essential work, such as caregivers, are also paid poorly but generally receive more recognition than supermarket clerks. Thus, the discrepancy between the significance of their work and the degree of recognition they receive for the services they perform may differ between employees in these two sectors, and this gap may well lead to different work perceptions, even if some aspects of their attitudes toward their work may be similar. This book's aim is to focus on a group of employees for whom this tension between importance and visibility is strong.

For this study of work perceptions, two different countries are selected. The U.S. and Germany differ in their educational and labor market systems as well as in their welfare regimes. These differences can make it easier to address how social contexts impact and influence worker and employee perceptions of work. In particular, these two contexts will allow for a focus on whether the presence of a vocational education track (as in Germany) or its absence (as in the U.S.) makes a difference in the viewpoints of supermarket clerks.

As in other work sectors, supermarkets have introduced new technologies that are changing the nature of work. For example, automatization has altered ordering systems and resulted in less need for workers with knowledge and experience. Rationalization in the form of increasing the number of part-time workers has resulted in more compressed workdays and deteriorating working conditions. Studies on automation in other work areas have reported that moving to unskilled labor reduces workers' feelings of being challenged and increases boredom. In line with this research stream, this study also inquires about changes in working conditions as perceived by supermarket clerks.

The topic of workers' and employees' perceptions of work belongs to the subfield of the sociology of work that deals with subjective perspectives. This study belongs to that subfield. The first chapter sketches out an overview of the field of food retail, underlining the significance of food and grocery goods as well as supermarkets and calling attention to the dangers within current food systems in times of ecological destruction. Price increases resulting from armed conflicts pose a hardship to many people and necessitate that governments take measures to secure food for their populations. Food retail is a large industry in both countries studied here in terms of the number of employees and the amount of revenue involved. Thus, the first chapter offers an overview that touches on the important dimensions of this sector.

The second chapter outlines prior research findings in this field of study. Whereas early research on workers' perceptions focused on possible class struggles, more recent work deals mainly with employees' expectations of work in relation to personal realization and fulfillment. While debates on the subjectivization of employees' attitudes toward their paid work are connected with the development of many jobs in the knowledge sector, jobs in noncreative areas of work also require consideration in this context.

Since most workplaces are located outside of the knowledge sector, it was necessary to create a concept for the analysis of noncreative work expectations and experiences. The concept of work appropriation, which is explained in detail in the third chapter, serves as a theoretical framework for understanding and interpreting work experiences of so-called ordinary workers and employees. The term work appropriation encompasses the complexity of images and ideas workers and employees obtain before starting to work; it encapsulates their attitudes toward their work and ways of working as well as the processing of their work experiences. This new concept for the analysis of the whole process of conceptualizing one's work goes beyond catching a snapshot. Work appropriation as defined in this study accounts for workers' socialization through work. It therefore stretches from structural to subjective levels and contains three pillars: the structural level of the social status of the job; the core of the work, which is its use value; and the activity of working carried out by individuals. Work forms one of the major ways of social structuring of societies. Work is a social good that is highly regulated in terms of access, renumeration, and prestige. Carrying out work contributes largely to a person's social status. If access to a job is limited to those with particular educational credentials, for example, its prestige increases. Work is subject to social classifications (e.g., as physically hard or dirty, or as entailing responsibility). Classification of different types of work leads to different degrees of recognition and is thus socially contested. In terms of work appropriation, people acquire ideas about the social status of a given job, and that influences their attitudes toward the job. These ideas in turn are highly influenced by individuals' own social status. As a result, people tend to sort jobs into categories such as those that seem unreachable given their social or educational status, those they stand a good chance of acquiring, or those they tend to reject as beneath the status they have attained or aspire to. Socialization through work at least partly continues prior processes of socialization that occurred in schools and contributes to the perpetuation of social tiers. For this study on supermarket clerks in the U.S. and in Germany, differences between the social status associated with this occupation in the two contexts will prove a decisive factor in work appropriation differences, as the discussion will show.

The second crucial dimension of work appropriation is use value, which relates closely to workers' or employees' motivation to work and choose a particular occupation. Use value is closely connected to employees' interpretation of the meaning of work. Often, workers and employees relate their identity to the use value of their work, and since the use value determines the occupation's tasks and content, it is often introduced and acquired in apprenticeships or vocational education. As such, it forms a strong part of workers' or employees' work appropriation. Originally, I assumed that the existence of vocational education for supermarket clerks in Germany in contrast to the lack thereof in the U.S. would lead to a large difference in work appropriation with regard to use value. But the differences uncovered in the findings were rather small, as I will demonstrate below, and supermarket clerks in both countries expressed a strong concern with the use value of their work. As I will show later, impediments to carrying out tasks for realizing use value are often perceived as huge problems and are creatively overcome or fiercely resisted. Obviously, use value is also a relational category connected to recognition and the social status of an occupation. However, one cannot say that the more urgent the need for a particular service or good, the higher the recognition of those who provide it. In fact, quite the contrary is often true: basic fundamental human needs such as alimentation are often satisfied without according recognition to those whose work allowed this essential need to be filled. In some cases, supermarket clerks' consciousness that they were satisfying shoppers' need for food was enough motivation for them to perform high-quality work, despite shoppers' general lack of appreciation or consciousness of their work's importance.

The third dimension of work appropriation – activity – is important for understanding this study's particular usage of the concept of work appropriation, which is new and differs from the use of the term in other accounts. By activity, I refer to practices, actual work, or approaches to tasks in given situations and circumstances. Whether or not resources are sufficient or even present, workers and employees handle requests and produce changes through their activities. These activities, then, are understood as ways of appropriating work. Workers and employees might feel overwhelmed, insecure, or satisfied at work, depending on the differences they are able to make and the observable outcomes they can affect. Thus, although it is not always the case, activity can be associated with positive feelings. In some forms of work appropriation, workers and employees are not satisfied and must struggle to realize the use value of their work. Activity is an essential aspect of work appropriation that contributes to workers' perseverance at important tasks over long periods of time, even under deteriorating work conditions.

Altogether, the concept of work appropriation used in this study must not be confused with the Marxist concept of exploitation. Even though some forms of work appropriation could be categorized as exploitation, as I will demonstrate later, other forms of work appropriation create satisfaction among workers and employees. The concept of work appropriation developed for this study enables analysis of forms of work from subjective perspectives without imposing moral judgments. This allows for the analysis of cases in which workers or employees express feelings of satisfaction with their work even though they are aware of being exploited. The aim of the theoretical framework of work appropriation is first and foremost to enable an analytical perspective for the interpretation of workers' and employees' narrations. Any moral reflection on workplace exploitation that might lead to policy changes would follow from the study's results rather than the frame of analysis.

The methods by which the data are collected and analyzed are explained in the fourth chapter. I have conducted guided interviews with female and male supermarket clerks of various ethnicities and heterogeneous life contexts who work for a variety of grocery retailers in the U.S. and in Germany. Upon reading all of the interviews several times, I sorted them into main themes in the narrations about work perceptions in close connection to life contexts. Without providing a separate analysis of the social structures of the U.S. and Germany, I presume that both societies are characterized by discrimination-based hierarchies. Thus, in both contexts, aspects such as gender and "race" form the larger background of the supermarket clerks' life contexts. Additionally, structural features of specific contexts such as job ladders and management approaches are considered in the analysis of the interviews where they are crucial for understanding interviewees' work appropriations. The themes formed patterns, which I will explain below.

A crucial pattern concerning recognition and the social status of the occupation that could be detected in the sample is the difference in work appropriation among supermarket clerks working in the U.S. versus in Germany. This point is explained in more detail in the fifth chapter. The U.S. clerks expressed strong difficulties in identifying with the occupation. Their narrations conveyed an ongoing process of delegitimization of their jobs as "entry-level" work that should only be carried out for a short period in life. The devalued social status of the work they carried out led to a constant feeling that they needed to look for another job, a feeling of being in transition and thus not settled in the job. Only a few supermarket clerks, who considered themselves at the bottom of society because of struggles they faced, such as physical and mental health challenges, expressed feelings of belonging in their occupations. In contrast, in Germany, despite working in jobs associated with low social status, super-market clerks experienced work as offering legitimacy and enabling them to engage in a form of work appropriation that allowed them to settle into their profession over the long term. Despite the lack of status, their profession is accorded social legitimacy that allowed many of the sample's supermarket clerks in Germany to find contentment and settle into their jobs.

An important pattern among the supermarket clerks interviewed for this study and discussed in chapter six is work ethos. As mentioned, work appro-priation with regard to use value differed less than the social status of the job when the U.S. and Germany were compared. In both countries, many interviewees expressed an eagerness to perform high-quality work in order to create use value. One notable difference concerned the level of knowledge about products and business procedures: this was much higher among the supermarket clerks in Germany compared to their counterparts in the U.S. The two- or three-year vocational training required for retail professions in Germany translated into the employees' greater expectations of their work and knowledge-based critiques of some aspects and conditions. In this respect they differed from their U.S. colleagues. However, the motivation and eagerness with which supermarket clerks performed their work in the U.S. to satisfy customers' needs was keen. Despite being poorly paid and often looked down upon, in neither national context did supermarket clerks express indifference toward their work or the desire to slack off. Here another dimension of use value could be carved out: its contribution to feelings of self-worth. This became most apparent in cases in which customers and even bosses expressed no appreciation of supermarket clerks' work. Even in these cases, many inter-viewees expressed a need and commitment to perform well for the sake of their own self-worth and self-respect.

The analysis, in chapter seven, of interview responses about work activity examined a pattern that emerged around change versus continuity. With one exception, differences were apparent in the study's two national contexts. As explained above, the dimension of activity is one that enables the analysis of work appropriation over a long period of time and allows for experiences to be incorporated into practices. This is often a highly emotional process during which individuals may experience emotional pain, struggles, and disillusion-ment. The differences observed in the two national contexts could be explained by pointing to the occupation's professional status in Germany compared to its status as entry-level work requiring no vocational training in the U.S. A pro-fessional occupation creates higher expectations than a nonprofessional one. In vocational education, these expectations are partly met and create the basis for further expectations. Disillusionment with one's job might lead the employee to search for solutions within the institution, seeking change by climbing the career ladder. Systems that offer various institutional options allow their employees to avoid feeling stuck in a rut.

Finally, I tie together my research results. The first result is that the concept of work appropriation developed for this study was an effective tool for analyzing work attitudes, experiences, and practices from a comparative perspective. This theoretical framework highlights work appropriation as a form of socialization. It therefore proves useful for analyzing social structures from a subjective perspective. The second result is the finding that vocational education plays an important role in the subjective experience of work even in the case of occupations considered to be at the lower end of the social hierarchy. The comparison of work appropriation in the U.S. and in Germany uncovered several favorable conditions under which supermarket clerks were able to pursue ideas and expectations; the professional knowledge supermarket clerks in Germany acquired during their vocational training led to much more satisfaction than was observed among their American counterparts.

A third result is the surprising finding that a high work ethos was widespread among supermarket clerks in both countries. Despite being subjected to low pay and low social status, supermarket clerks in the study talked about the pursuit of quality in their work for the purpose of serving their customers well. This emphasis on the use value of their tasks was evident throughout the interviews.

The last finding strikes an encouraging note: the interviewees expressed their eagerness to perform high-quality work in order to satisfy the needs of their fellow workers. On a societal level, this finding could motivate further emphasis on the utility of work for the sake of social well-being. Putting utility at the center of work's aims and design could help to overcome the tendency to create jobs that cause damage or are pointless. Focusing on the use value of work could help to increase social cohesion.

This study would not have been possible without the cooperation of numerous supermarket clerks who gave their valuable time to talk about their work after long shifts or on their days off. My sincere thanks go out to them for taking the time to share their stories with me.

# 1. Food retail: outline of an essential sector

This chapter lays out the relevance of studying the food retail sector by first pointing to the vital role of supermarket clerks, who unload, stock, and sell goods and who also offer product advice to customers. The chapter first outlines the economic dimension of food retail to convey basic information on this field of research. Food retail is a large sector in both the U.S. and Germany, with links to the education and social welfare systems of each country that make it necessary to study it in light of the two countries' differences. For that reason, a comparative perspective is used to analyze the supermarket clerks' interview responses.

## SIGNIFICANCE OF FOOD AND GROCERY GOODS FOR DAILY LIFE

Fifty years after the Club of Rome's study titled "Limits to Growth" called attention to the developing crisis of limited ecological resources on earth, a team of social and economic scientists launched another warning, this time focusing on "global equity for a healthy planet" (Club of Rome 2022). The call for equity is the conclusion of another study for the Club of Rome in which scientists call for five turnarounds necessary for the survival of humans on earth (Dixson-Declève et al. 2022). The food system is one area of these required fundamental changes. The authors call for "transforming the food system to provide a healthy diet for people and the planet" (Dixson-Declève et al. 2022: n.p.) While it is obvious that people need food to survive, the need for a transformed food system for their survival arises from dominant social practices of cultivating, harvesting, processing, producing, and distributing food in ways that fail to nourish everyone. These dominant social practices not only lack material factors, to which I will return later, they also impact cultural and spiritual dimensions of food production. As a consequence of these disruptions, reflected in the global crises of both hunger and obesity, even those who get enough calories may lack access to nourishing food and good nutrition. An abundance of spiritual practices are related to food and nourishment, from burying the placenta after a birth to various forms of fasting. It matters whether what one eats is hand-made bread called "God's face" ("cara de dios," Zenobia

Zárate) or fast food from McDonalds. Many of my interviewees offered that they were eager "to take care" of their customers. One female salesclerk of color working at Trader Joe's (TJ), when asked what she meant by this, stated: "It's very important to just touch with honor and respect people's food. All kinds of emotions people are experiencing when they're buying their food" (Catherine Taylor, 57). The reduced cultural and spiritual dimensions in the modern food system shape how food is produced, transported, and delivered by the agricultural and animal industries. This is not a call for subsistence agriculture as a population of 8 billion requires social practices for producing a variety of foods. Nevertheless, the significance of food and grocery goods and the social practices connected with them cannot be understood without considering dimensions beyond the material production of food. As I will show later, (un)packing, shelving, and ringing up purchases in a store that resembles a small factory may result in different perceptions, activities, and evaluations of work among employees than would the same tasks if they were performed in a corner shop. While employees in a factory-like setting may become hardened to their jobs, those in a small shop setting may experience a high degree of satisfaction. As I will show later, an even greater satisfaction can come from working at a nonprofit organic foods cooperative, where the use value dimension of work appropriation is considerable.

While many people are poorly nourished despite access to food, millions more are malnourished due to a lack of food, and still millions more starve to death. World hunger results, in part, from ecological destruction in the form of disasters such as drought or floods. This is one major feature of dominant practices of the food system that I will come back to later. Death and suffering on the part of underpaid or even unpaid workers and employees in the food system (e.g., forced fishers off the shore of Thailand) must be taken into account in any comprehensive picture of the global food industry. I will also return to this point when touching on the topic of modern slavery. In short: supermarket clerks' work and labor take place in a food system that provides food at the expense of human beings and nature.[1] The stark nature of this trade-off varies. One major factor in differences in how the food system operates is the hierarchical relationship between the Global South and North. These relations influence supermarket clerks' perceptions of their work and labor as well as their position within the stores where they work, as this study demonstrates. Also, the social context of work is crucial. It makes a difference whether a migrated supermarket clerk without secure residency status has no better job opportunities than stocking shelves part time despite severe back pain and a lack of health insurance *and* does not earn enough to cover living costs or – on the other hand – the clerk is a native resident with vocational training and receives full-time wages and benefits such as health insurance. While it is important to take these and other differences into account, it is at the same time important not "to play both ends against the middle" but instead to understand the framework of the food system as an underlying problem that creates or contributes to these differences.

## Increasing Urgency around Food Production in the Face of Ecological Destruction

While the general significance of food and grocery goods has always existed, ecological destruction over the last few years has increased the urgency of addressing problems with the global food system. A growing world population is confronted with increasing difficulties involving land use and decreasing resources, such as water, that are crucial for growing food. Here, too, the Global South and North face different problems: the former has struggled longer and to a much larger extent with a lack of resources, whereas the latter has exploited resources while suffering less ecological destruction and while having at its disposal greater means to avoid the consequences of environmental challenges. At the same time, the need for ecologically produced food and grocery goods has increased. Within the current food system, sustainable foods and grocery goods are too expensive for most supermarket clerks and many others as well. Within the study's sample of interviewed supermarket clerks, the ones who worked at a cooperative or who received gift cards from their companies (sometimes) consumed ecologically produced food themselves. Alongside the existential threat of food shortages posed by increasing ecological destruction, pyramiding in agricultural sectors is leading to increased costs of food and grocery goods (Gilson & Kenehan 2019). Increasing social inequality means that an ever-growing share of the population cannot afford (adequate amounts of) food. We are witnessing a concurrence of two major and interrelated crises connected to the existing food system. By 2022, the COVID-19 pandemic had brought the twofold crisis to a head. I will return to this point after giving a brief background on the exploitation of ecological and social resources that has led to this moment. In the U.S. and West Germany, the period after World War II and into the 1960s was characterized by the development of a relatively large welfare state and middle class. Starting in the early 1970s (coinciding with President Nixon's 1971 policy of ending the convertibility of U.S. dollars into gold), the Fordist accumulation regime began its gradual transformation into neoliberalism. In both countries economic prosperity was predicated on the exploitation of natural resources and labor,[2] with a visible trend toward increasingly using human labor to work compressed hours for low wages,[3] as has been common in the retail sector. Many perceive the coincidence of the two crises as a sign that societies need to weigh whether social or ecological problems are more urgent and decide which ones should be addressed and resolved first. In the U.S., governments have tended to neglect both in favor of allowing the market to "solve" the crises. In Germany, governments have tended to prioritize social problems at the expense of ecological damage. At the time of writing this chapter (fall 2022), this preference has been clear in the way the U.S. and German governments have responded to the war in Ukraine, spending large amounts of taxpayers' money on financial aid to Ukraine's citizens at the expense of their own energy transition. In line with this tendency to prioritize the welfare and profits of a few over the health of the planet, we can point to other governmental policies and politics aimed at addressing the ecological crisis while stimulating the economy, a practice seen as essential for promoting social well-being (e.g., the Green New Deal of the European Union). Modifying consumption is viewed as a problem of consciousness and awareness, not only economics. Thus, initiatives such as channeling consumers' choices by informing them about the environmental impacts from food and grocery goods are being used increasingly to address the urgent food crisis (Clark et al. 2022). Michael Clark and nine other scientists estimated the environmental impacts of 57,000 grocery goods in the UK and Ireland and recommended adding an easily visible symbol to product labels to indicate the amount of environmental damage caused by each product's production. By evaluating the amount of greenhouse gas emissions, land use, water stress, and eutrophication potential associated with each product, along with a nutrition score, they were able to show that high nutrition often coincides with low environmental damage. This "could also help inform discussions with retailers, processors, producers, consumers, and policy makers on how trade-offs between the multiple types of capital may be mitigated" (Clark et al. 2022: 10). Here, a market tool is proposed as a means of addressing the perceived tension between meeting ecological and social needs.

On the other hand, analysis such as that of the Club of Rome (2022) in its newest publication (see above) demonstrates that the *distribution* of economic wealth is crucial for the environment, and that therefore the two crises cannot be solved independently from each other. In other words, weighting, by considering the respective importance of social and environmental concerns and prioritizing one or the other, does not work. Global social movements such as the Climate Justice movement and Degrowth policies and politics have created concepts for decelerating both crises and overcoming the practical constraint of weighting. According to these approaches, economic growth is the problem, not the solution (e.g., Kupfer 2023). Consequently, the current food system requires a transformation into a sustainable system in which living and destroying no longer go hand in hand. The food cooperative at which some of the interviewees in this book work influences their working conditions as well as their work perceptions and identities. Thus, their work appropriation might serve as an example of Degrowth since the cooperative's aim is not profit but functioning smoothly. (As I will explain later, this is an example of use value as opposed to exchange value.) Without going into further detail here, it is important to keep in mind that not only current problems but also fundamental social and environmental issues are at the center of attention once the significance of food and grocery goods is considered.

**Supermarket Clerks as Essential Workers and Employees during the COVID-19 Pandemic**

From March 2020 to February 2022, the German government enacted several ordinances to fight the COVID-19 pandemic (Bundesregierung 2022). Some of the regulations consisted of various forms of lockdowns of public and private organizations. Only three organizations were exempted from lockdowns during this period and remained open throughout the pandemic: hospitals, pharmacies, and supermarkets (Kunz 2022). Although these three kinds of organizations, along with providers of basic infrastructure like potable water, were already fundamental for meeting human needs before the pandemic, the necessity of keeping them functioning during the pandemic increased awareness of their significance. This awakening was manifest in the usage of the classification "essential" (denoted in German as "systemrelevant," suggesting that they are essential for the system currently in place, but also leaving open the possibility of imagining another system). This new widespread awareness led for a couple of weeks to the visibility of previously almost unrecognized workers and employees. Most of the public attention went to nurses and care staff: during the lockdowns citizens would stand on their balconies in cities or in their gardens in rural areas and applaud or bang on pots to express their appreciation for hospital and emergency workers at agreed-upon hours. But supermarket clerks also found themselves in the spotlight – although not as objects of public appreciation. They found themselves the subject of much negative attention as they took on additional tasks during the pandemic such as ensuring that customers wore masks and did not exceed their quotas of scarce goods such as toilet paper and certain food items. However, the new visibility of supermarket clerks did not lead to increased recognition for their importance as measured in better pay or better working conditions. In fact, empirical studies (e.g., Kupfer & Stutz 2022) offer evidence that during this time, female supermarket clerks especially took pay reductions so that they could care for their children. Even though in Germany these workers obtained the right to send their children to day care centers since they were classified as "essential staff," less "essential" workers received short-term allowances according to the wage agreements already in place (albeit at a reduced amount) in male-dominated jobs. In general, female workers and employees reduced their paid working time to carry out unpaid work to a larger extent than before the pandemic so that they could care for their own and their partners' parents and other family members and friends; this happened much more in the case of female workers and employees than it did in the case of their male counterparts (Kupfer & Stutz 2022; Miani et al. 2022). The second pattern of dealing with the crisis was that more female than male workers and employees took over unpaid care work in addition to their paid work.[4] This was more prevalent among low-wage workers than among higher-wage recipients. Overall, governments' approaches to dealing with the COVID-19 pandemic accelerated and increased social inequality and social disintegration, thus increasing the urgency and awareness of the fundamental significance of food and grocery goods sold in supermarkets.

To sum up the main points in this section, it is clear that the COVID-19 pandemic called attention not only to the dangers of climate change and the ecological damage our planet faces but also to the weaknesses and inadequacies of the dominant economic models on which our societies are based. Nevertheless, research on government policies and politics during the COVID-19 pandemic has shown that there has been no fundamental change in economic policies or politics. Apart from becoming visible for a short moment and being classified as "essential," supermarket clerks, as workers on a highly contested and increasingly long list of essential workers and employees (Grenz & Günster 2022), have still not received recognition in the form of better pay and better working conditions. I now turn to a fourth aspect of the significance of food and grocery goods: price increases triggered in part by the war in Ukraine and other armed conflicts.

**Increasing Cost of Food and Grocery Goods due to Armed Conflict have Increased the Importance of Supermarkets for Sustaining the Population**

Given the fundamental significance of food and grocery goods, the destruction of agricultural land and disruptions in agricultural practices and distribution resulting from climate change and the COVID-19 pandemic have put pressures on the entire food industry. In this section, I turn to another pressure faced in the Global North (including Germany and the U.S.): the need to secure the livelihoods of millions of people despite rising food prices. It could be observed that high food prices become a topic in countries of the Global North only when their own populations are affected, whereas millions of people starving from hunger in countries of the Global South receive little attention in the news media of the Global North. However, among my interviewees in the U.S., many were migrants from countries of the Global South. Therefore, in order to understand their perceptions of work, it is necessary to apply a global perspective. For that reason, I start with some very brief remarks on armed conflicts around the world before I explain the increased significance of supermarkets for feeding the populations of the U.S. and Germany. A second reason for starting with a global view on armed conflicts is the fact that the destruction of agriculture due to climate change and other environmental disasters often leads to armed conflicts, and during the COVID-19 pandemic lockdowns the number of affected people grew much more in the Global South. Data from the World Food Programme (WFP), an organization of the United Nations, provide evidence of this (e.g., WFP 2020, 2022). At the same time, the livelihoods of people in the Global North are clearly also affected, as the war in Ukraine illustrates.

Somalia is one of many countries where armed conflicts have been taking place for years. It should be named here as one of many countries whose history is linked to the U.S. and Germany (Federal Foreign Office 2022; U.S. Department of State 2022). Starting in the 20th century, after more than 20 years of suppression of one part of the country by the other one, a civil war started in 1991. Its agents and agendas changed, but armed conflicts continued. Somalia's economy is based mainly on livestock and agriculture. As mentioned, Somalia is also a country suffering severely from climate change and from the COVID-19 pandemic, so food insecurity is at crisis levels. "As of August 2022, 7.1 million people cannot meet their daily food requirements today and require urgent humanitarian assistance" (WFP 2022: n.p.). Another example of the culmination of pressure on food security due to the named factors is Liptako-Gourma, a region in West Africa comprising the three countries Burkina Faso, Mali, and Niger (WFP 2020).

While only one of many conflicts, the aftermath of Russia's invasion of Ukraine on February 24, 2022, is highly relevant for this study as it takes place in Europe, and the U.S. and Germany are involved in support for Ukraine through economic sanctions on Russia and arms and materials for infrastructure. With regard to food security and the fundamental significance of food and grocery goods, this war is important as Ukraine is the fifth-largest wheat exporter in the world; consequently, the already insufficient food production for a growing world population faces additional impediments. Increasing droughts in the U.S. and Europe (e.g., in Germany and France in 2022) also put alimentation and the livelihoods of people in the Global North at risk. The threat takes several forms, including lack of water, caused not only by climate change but also by consumption at unsustainable levels. For example, in Brandenburg, the federal state in Germany surrounding the city-state of Berlin, the company Tesla consumes large amounts of water to produce electric cars. This depletes the water resources needed for potable water in the capital city of Berlin. The water is also needed to grow wheat and other agricultural products and to maintain water levels in rivers (e.g., the Rhine) for the transportation of goods such as coal (which in turn is needed for production). One result of this reduction in available water for these uses has been shortages of flour in supermarkets in parts of Germany in 2022. In a market economy, reduced supply leads to price increases. As of the time of this writing, the U.S. and EU economic sanctions against Russia have not induced it to stop its invasion of Ukraine and end the war. In September 2022, Russia stopped providing gas to Germany, and the German government has succeeded in acquiring liquefied natural gas (LNG) from countries such as Qatar and Norway. LNG is more expensive to produce than Russian natural gas, so prices for heating and production have gone up. Also, some companies have taken advantage of energy shortages to make a profit. The resulting inflation in turn devalues wages and salaries.

Without going into further detail, it is easy to make the case that the fundamental significance of food and grocery goods has increased under the current conditions of worsening climate change, impacts from the COVID-19 pandemic, and disruptions from armed conflicts. In addition, it is important to remember that these factors leading to what many would call crisis conditions are interrelated. Their impact on supermarket clerks and their customers, and therefore the majority of the population in the U.S. and in Germany, is clear.

## THE ECONOMIC DIMENSION OF (FOOD) RETAIL

Part of the brief description of the need for this study on supermarket clerks is the economic dimension of (food) retail. In the previous sections I have outlined the significance of food and the increasing vulnerability of the food supply due to climate change, the COVID-19 pandemic, and the price increases related to armed conflicts and trade disruptions. This section focuses on laying out the significant place of food retail and the work and labor of supermarket clerks in (national) economies. Furthermore, it outlines the contexts and specific features of both countries to clarify how the economy of (food) retail is embedded globally and also how the extreme exploitation of the workforce, which could be called a form of modern slavery (Graf & Kupfer 2015), is one important factor in how these economies are construed. I apply a Marxist perspective, which means that the economic analysis is embedded in an analysis of societal reproduction and therefore includes the unpaid reproductive labor mainly carried out by women. Thus, a key aspect of my analytic model is the division of labor. Focusing on labor division along the lines of gender relations, ethnic relations within one nation and also globally, and relations between national states can bring to light significant aspects of working conditions. This is fruitful as the economy of food retail is shaped by an unequal share of female and male employees, with a larger share of women at the lower-end clerk positions and men at the upper-end, managerial positions. In the U.S., as my data will show later, many ethnic minorities and migrants are employed as clerks in supermarkets. This is no accident, but rather an expression of the business model based on creating profits with the help of a low-wage, precarious workforce. The global division of labor with regard to the economy of food retail is also crucial for keeping profits high as local farmers and fishers worldwide are often paid very little for their products, and in some cases they are coerced to work, as studies on modern slavery demonstrate (Stein 2019). In addition to the division of labor, the state as an institution is also crucial for societal reproduction. Its legislative and executive power sets conditions for means of reproduction. Social policies and education are key areas for understanding economic contexts, and in the case of the two countries under consideration here I will first address their differences by outlining their specific systems as contexts for the economy of food retail and the work of supermarket clerks.

## THE LIBERAL WELFARE REGIME OF THE U.S. AND THE CONSERVATIVE WELFARE REGIME OF GERMANY

For a comparison of social policies, I turn to Gøsta Esping-Andersen's welfare regime typology as the one most suited to my study.[5] In a large team with several major funders,[6] Esping-Andersen developed this model over many years, starting in the 1970s. According to Ann Shola Orloff, "He noticed women's employment behaviors, how state policies in the provision of services mediated the impact of shifts from industrialism toward service-dominated economies, and considered how gendered employment patterns might shape political conflicts. This took him squarely onto the intellectual terrain that had been tilled by feminists without acknowledging that work" (Orloff 2009: 319). In addition to taking women's employment behaviors into account, his typology is based on measures of the degree of (de)commodification, which is also highly significant for my study of supermarket clerks. "It was the commodity status of labor that lay at the heart of the nineteenth-century debates and conflicts over the 'social question' or, as it was commonly termed in Germany, the 'Arbeiterfrage'" (Esping-Andersen 1990: 37). What makes the focus of commodification so crucial is the fact that in modern societies characterized by labor power as a commodity, "people's rights to survive outside the market are at stake" (Esping-Andersen 1990: 35). Today, as was also true in previous decades, increasing numbers of people are not surviving, but are starving and dying of exposure in rich welfare states like the U.S. and Germany.

Over the course of working on his welfare regime typology, Esping-Andersen changed his understanding of decommodification by lowering its political content.[7] The now-classic definition of decommodification is "the degree to which individuals, or families, can uphold a socially acceptable standard of living independently of market participation" (1990: 37). This redefinition is applicable to my study on supermarket clerks because it allows work appropriation to be understood along the dimension of use value (as one of the three conceptualized dimensions of work appropriation, as I will explain in more detail in the theory chapter). The degree of (de)commodification is crucial for the dimension of use value as – one might say – the more a welfare system is decommodified, the greater the possibility of orientation toward use value, while – in turn – the more a welfare system is commodified, the greater the possibility of orientation toward exchange value. Since use value orientation seeks to satisfy human needs, it is inextricably linked with social and ecological reproduction. This in turn requires policies and politics of sustainability with regard to human and nonhuman natural resources. The U.S. and Germany[8] instead build their systems with an orientation toward perpetual growth and wealth creation. I will develop this point further in the theory chapter, where I discuss the dimension of use value as one of three concepts of work appropriation. The problem I underline here is that needs are created in capitalist societies in order to seek profit or wealth for some. Therefore, decommodification cannot be equated with use value per se, but it can serve as a yardstick for measuring it.

Having explained why I selected this typology, I will now briefly describe the two cases I use for modeling them – the U.S. and Germany. The U.S. is considered a liberal welfare regime because the role of the state in securing conditions for living outside of the market is seen as minimal compared to other countries, especially the Scandinavian ones. Typical features of the U.S. welfare state are means-tested assistance to targeted low-income citizens following strict entitlement rules and guaranteeing only a minimum of benefits. In the U.S., private welfare organizations and wealthy individuals are seen as bearing some responsibility for caring for the needy through donations. In contrast, Germany's welfare state is labeled as conservative because the state's policy aim is to preserve individuals' social rights to live according to the status they have already attained. Thus, most welfare money stems from insurance-based schemes to which people contribute depending on their income position. As a result, already privileged employees, such as those working full time who have earned a (vocational) educational degree, receive more than part-timers with no or lower (vocational) educational degrees. In addition, the German welfare regime is seen as patriarchal as it rewards mothers for caring for their children while fathers earn the family income. The role of the state is much stronger compared to the U.S. as it is considered a so-called "Soziale Marktwirtschaft" (welfare market economy). Compared to Germany, the U.S. has a low level of state policies and politics geared toward securing employment. Hence, people's survival is more closely tied to the labor market than to political mechanisms. In Germany, there are more political mechanisms and a politically hard-earned "social partnership" between employers on the one hand and workers and employees on the other operating on the foundation of juridical regulations. A common practice in both countries is to ensure that supermarket clerks' working and living conditions are pretty much commodified as part-time work with an income below the existential minimum. While the U.S. level of decommodification is classified as low, Germany's is higher. The highest level of decommodification is in the Scandinavian states, which are labeled as social-democratic welfare regimes.

One might argue that Esping-Andersen's (1990) welfare regime typology is outdated due to several changes within and between national states. According to Powell et al. (2019), who conducted a literature review of texts dealing with the welfare regime typology on the occasion of the thirtieth anniversary of the classic book, a convincing argument in favor of the welfare regime typology was made by Arts and Gelissan, who argued that the theoretical quality of this typology is vastly superior to alternative typologies, many of which lacked a firm theoretical foundation. Powell et al. (2019) concluded "that the country classification seems to show less consensus than previous reviews, with fewer pure nations" (84). I return to this interesting finding in my last chapter. Here I simply offer a preliminary argument supporting it: since about the 1990s, countries have become more internally diverse and less homogeneous, partly due to neoliberal policies and politics and the resulting increase in social inequalities, and partly as a continual process of differentiation.

## EDUCATIONAL SYSTEMS IN THE U.S. AND GERMANY

Education is another key institution of societal reproduction that helps to create a context for economic analysis. Broadly speaking, education equips people with the skills and knowledge they need for work and their lives beyond work. According to Pierre Bourdieu and Luc Boltanski (1977), in addition to the first function of the education system, which they call "technical reproduction" (62), education has a second function of "reproducing the positions of the agents and their groups within the social structure (the function of social reproduction) – positions which are relatively independent of strictly technical capacity" (62). Both kinds of educational reproduction are relevant for my study of supermarket clerks, whose perceptions and evaluations of their work are also constituted by their skills and knowledge as well as their perceptions of and responses to how their jobs are positioned within society. In both areas of educational reproduction, the U.S. and Germany differ. According to Jutta von Allmendinger (1989), who used degree of standardization and stratification to measure the comparison of educational systems, vocational education is unstandardized and stratified in the U.S. and standardized and unstratified in Germany.[9] With regard to the vocational education of supermarket clerks, this takes place mainly in on-the-job-training in the U.S., while in Germany an approved, certified apprenticeship requires two or three years of training.

In the U.S., working as a supermarket clerk is seen as an entry-level job that could be carried out by anyone. In Germany, supermarket clerks can either decide on a two-year apprenticeship (to become a "Verkäufer/Verkäuferin") or a three-year one, enabling them to learn how to run a shop (to become a "Kaufmann/Kauffrau im Einzelhandel"). Apprenticeships take place in the so-called dual system of vocational education at two sites: the company and a vocational school in which apprentices learn both specific knowledge in the area of their occupation (in the case of supermarket clerks, they learn commodity economics – "Warenkunde") and general education, which includes areas such as English and political education. For decades, the occupation "Kaufmann/Kauffrau im Einzelhandel" has been very popular. In 2021, it was ranked third, and the occupation of "Verkäufer/Verkäuferin" was ranked ninth (Statistisches Bundesamt 2022a). In that year the share of male apprentices of "Kaufmann im Einzelhandel" was higher than the share of female apprentices, while the numbers were almost identical in the occupation of "Verkäufer/Verkäuferin." One reason why this occupation is nevertheless classified as one of the "feminized" occupations is the high share of temporary workers filling these positions. Many of these are working "Minijobs," which means they must keep their hours below a certain threshold (since October 2022, that threshold has been 520 Euros per month; previously it had long been 450 Euros). Above this threshold, jobs are subject to social insurance contributions. In Germany, about a third of all employees in retail are so-called "Minijobbers." In 2021, the share of women in retail overall was 67% and the share of men was 33% (Handelsverband Deutschland 2022).

To sum up, in both countries, a vocational education for the occupation of supermarket clerk is ranked lower in comparison to a general education taking place at higher education institutions. Nevertheless, while in the U.S. the occupation of supermarket clerk is ranked very low on the social scale, in Germany it is classified as a profession – albeit one at the lower end of the hierarchy of professions. This difference is crucial for supermarket clerks' perceptions and evaluations of their work, as I will demonstrate later.

## KEY INFORMATION ON EMPLOYEES, REVENUES, AND WAGES IN THE U.S. VERSUS GERMAN FOOD RETAIL INDUSTRIES

In both countries, workers and employees in food retail form a large share of the workforce. In 2021 in the U.S., 9.7% of all employees worked in the retail trade (Bureau of Labor Statistics 2022). This was 15,396.0 (in thousands of jobs). For a rough description of major characteristics of retail workers, I quote a study by Anderson and Laughlin (2020: 12):

> The majority of retail workers had a younger age profile, were less likely to hold a bachelor's degree, and were less likely to work full-time, year-round when compared with the total labor force. Of retail workers, women on average earned less than men, and also were less likely to serve in supervisory positions. Black and Hispanic workers were overrepresented in cashier jobs, which were the lowest paying jobs in retail. In contrast, non-Hispanic White retail workers were overrepresented in supervisory retail positions, the highest-paying jobs in retail (albeit declining over the past decade). Although health insurance coverage was common for retail workers, cashiers were more likely to receive Medicaid (a government-based health insurance plan for low-income people), which could be attributed to the fact that cashiers were more likely to work part-time and more likely to have incomes below the poverty threshold. Retail occupations are among the lowest-paying jobs, with limited opportunities for advancement.

According to Ibisworld, supermarkets and grocery stores constitute the largest sector of the retail trade industry. Total U.S. grocery store sales in 2021 were $803.05 billion, and sales of retail food and beverage stores came to $880.3 billion (Statista 2022). Following a report by the National Retail Federation (2020), 7.7% of the 2018 GDP in the U.S. came from the retail industry. For the first two quarters of 2022, according to the Federal Reserve Economic Data (FRED 2022), retail made up 5.8% of the GDP.

In Germany, the number of employees in the food retail industry for 2019 was 1,382,113, and the revenue of that industry was 225.730 million Euros (Handelsverband Deutschland 2022). Food retail's share of the GDP was 4.8% in 2019 (EHI Retail Institute GmbH 2022). For 2021, revenues came to 182 billion Euros, of which the largest share belonged to discounters, with 79.5 billion Euros (EHI Retail Institute GmbH 2022). For a brief description of the workforce in the German retail sector, I follow Dorothea Voss-Dahm (2008: 253–254), who compared Germany and the U.S.:

> In both countries, low wages are considerably more prevalent in the retail sector than in the economy as a whole ... More than half of retail workers in Germany are part-timers, many of them employed in marginal part-time jobs called "mini-jobs", whereas in the United States the share of full-timers is much higher. There are also considerable differences in the level of institutional support for employment relationships. More than three-quarters of all employees in German retailing have completed a two- or three-year vocational training course, whereas American retail workers have little formal training. Another difference is that, in Germany, the basic working and employment conditions, such as pay and working time, are regulated by industry-wide collective agreements. Moreover, employees in Germany enjoy a higher level of social protection than their counterparts in the United States. In Germany all part-time and full-time employees in jobs subject to social insurance contributions are covered by the social security system.

Since this study, the coverage of employees under collective bargaining agreements declined. *Handelsblatt* (2022), a German trade newspaper, stated that less than 30% of employees in retail are paid according to collective agreements.

I end this section on the economic dimension of food retail by pointing to a crucial source of revenue for large companies in the industry: modern slavery. Often, especially among discounters, supermarket clerks sell products that are made by extremely low-wage workers, often migrants. Recent media discourse on the meat industry in Germany during COVID-19 lockdowns alerted a wide public audience about extremely exploitative working and living conditions (Friedrichsen 2020; Soric 2020). One salient point was the fact that seasonal laborers received extraordinary travel permission to enter Germany for harvesting asparagus during lockdowns in 2020 (Tagesschau 2020), at the same time that other workers and employees were denied passage over national borders within the Schengen area. This case shows how closely food production and the exploitation of migrants are intertwined. The public is more aware of the use of migrant workers, mainly from West Africa, for picking fruits in Italy and Spain, a practice that predates the pandemic (Scaturro 2021; Strohschneider & Gerlof 2019). Modern slavery practices have enabled retailers to earn high revenues while selling products cheaply, mainly in discount stores. Before inflation started to climb sharply over the course of 2022, grocery goods were relatively cheap in Germany compared to other European countries and the U.S. In light of decades-long stagnation and in some cases even falling real wages (Statistisches Bundesamt 2022b), low-priced grocery goods contributed to the maintenance of living standards, or its rather slow decrease. Modern slavery is part of a food system that functions at the expense of humans and nature.[10] It is also important to realize its global dimensions in the food retail industry workforce. In the Global North, low-wage supermarket clerks are both the exploited and the exploiters of other workers because of the high demand for low-priced grocery goods across all income levels. The fact that exploited workers and employees are themselves exploiters is important to note (Graf & Kupfer 2015). Jan-Christoph Marschelke (2015) calls these links in the chain of exploitation "indirect profiteers" serving within the "imperial mode of living" (Brand & Wissen 2021). Although the working classes are part of this arrangement, that does not reduce the responsibility of the privileged for upholding this system. It remains to be seen whether policies and laws against human workforce exploitation can bring about real change. In Germany, the "Gesetz über die unternehmerischen Sorgfaltspflichten in Lieferketten" (Bundesgesetzblatt 2021) will become effective in 2023. It obliges companies with more than 3,000 workers or employees to end any violation of human rights occurring within the scope of their business practices. If suppliers violate human rights, companies in Germany are obliged to implement a model for monitoring and avoiding modern slavery and can otherwise be fined. In 2023, the European Parliament passed and the European Council is expected to pass the Corporate Sustainability Due Diligence Directive and amend the Whistleblower Directive 2019/1937 (European Union 2022), which the European Commission passed in February 2022. The EU directive goes farther than existing German legislation in obliging companies with over 500 workers or employees to ensure compliance with legal requirements for themselves, their subsidiaries, and all suppliers along the entire value chain. In addition to obliging companies not to accept violations of human rights, it also obliges them to accept restrictions on activities that can cause damage to biodiversity or the environment. Apart from fines, companies could face claims for damages. However, small and medium-sized companies are exempt, and they constitute the large majority in the European Union. The declaration refers only to established trade partnerships and could therefore create incentives to make frequent changes to trade relations; moreover, the threshold for lodging complaints against affected companies is high as companies' violations must be proven. In the U.S., a federal tariff act prohibits importation of all goods and merchandise produced with forced labor (Congressional Research Service 2022). The law empowers the U.S. Customs and Border Protection agency to investigate domestic companies that use forced labor in the supply chain.

To sum up, this chapter has outlined fundamental dimensions of the significance of food retail. It pointed to a dynamic of accelerating urgency to study this sector and the food system. The chapter has also sketched out the national contexts of food retail in the U.S. and Germany, the countries under focus in this study. Equipped with basic information on the field of supermarket clerks' labor, the following chapter offers an overview of the state of research on the topic.

## NOTES

1. The reference to nature is intended to mean biological, chemical, and physical processes both independent from human beings and in constant exchange with humans and highly affected by them (see Kupfer 2023). It is also true that supermarket clerks' work and labor take place within a food system that offers them employment and incomes. I will discuss this at more length in the section on economic dimensions.
2. Exploitation of labor differs along the lines of gender, perceptions of race/ethnicity, world region, and many other factors.
3. Neoliberalism has numerous other features, such as an increase in the control of labor through subjectification, for example.
4. There is no consensus on a clear distinction between the notions of work and labor. In this book, I use both terms according to their respective subtexts and customs.

5.    For an overview of definitions of welfare states and different concepts of categorizing welfare states, see Greve (2009).

6.    Swedish Delegation for Social Research, the Bank of Sweden Tercentennial Foundation, and the German Marshall Fund of the U.S. (Esping-Andersen & Korpi 1987).

7.    In a publication co-authored with Walter Korpi, Esping-Andersen defined decommodification as "the extent to which needs are to be satisfied through the labor market, or, as an alternative, through political mechanisms. It measures the strength of entitlements to welfare based on social citizenship in contradistinction to market earnings, or perhaps kinship and community altruism ... the degree of de-commodification – can be empirically determined by examining the degree to which entitlements are unconditional, the extent to which normal human needs are satisfied via social programs, and the degree to which an adequate standard of living is politically guaranteed" (Esping-Andersen & Korpi 1987: 40–41).

8.    The socialist policies and politics of the former German Democratic Republic did not lead to a more sustainable society. The GDR may have relied less on human and nonhuman exploitation than did Western capitalist states, but it can hardly be called a success in this respect. This is one reason why I refrain here from singling out capitalist societies (which the U.S. and Germany obviously are).

9.    Here I do not discuss the varieties of capitalism (Hall & Soskice 2001; Estébez-Abe 2005) in which the different vocational education systems are focused for the comparison of capitalist societies because I do not consider it crucial for understanding food retail and supermarket clerks. However, this discussion does focus on the different societal levels of vocational education in the U.S. versus Germany. Broadly speaking, vocational education is valued less in a U.S. context than in a German one, but in both countries general education is valued more than vocational training.

10.   Here I refer to industrialized agriculture at the expense of nature in terms of soil health, biodiversity, contributions to climate change, and ecological destruction as outlined above.

# 2. State of the research: Literature review

The topic of supermarket clerks' perceptions of their work in the U.S. and Germany touches on many areas within sociology. This chapter helps to embed this study within existing traditions and debates and offers an overview of the main research results of studies with similar research questions, relating them to the research of this field in both countries. However, as my own approach is located in the German research tradition, the main focal point will be the German context. Nevertheless, I intend to touch upon major American research findings as well.

Because the discipline of sociology developed differently in the U.S. and Germany, studies of workers or employees and how they perceive their work have also differed. In the context of German sociology, Karl Marx has been a major influence for studies on paid workers and employees. Because he theorized during a time of rapid industrialization, much of his work centered on issues of social inequality, and inquiries about workers' perceptions of labor were often linked to questions of social structure and class. In addition, the political power of the workforce was a point of much interest to Marx. These topics are still detectable in current research traditions in Germany. In contrast, early American sociology was much more concerned with questions of behavior and sociality, for which Charles H. Cooley and George H. Mead, and later the Chicago School and cultural-anthropologist functionalist approach, were key. In the area of labor research, U.S. sociologists focused largely on the meaning of work by asking workers and employees to describe the meaning work has for them.

My book's subject and research interest are located within the area of the sociology of work as it relates to both research contexts. In their textbook on the sociology of work, Steven P. Vallas et al. (2009) give an overview of occupational structures and the social categories of class, gender, ethnicity, and issues of migration. Their focus on social inequality relates directly to my study as I set out to learn more about work perceptions of a largely disregarded part of the low-wage workforce. Vallas et al. (2009) characterize the occupational area of service jobs as one in which employment relationships are changing and globalization is making jobs increasingly precarious. This is largely true of the food retail sector, as the first chapter has outlined and as the narratives of employees in this study will illustrate. One additional feature of Vallas et al. (2009) is their emphasis on the category of the "emotional proletariat," borrowing an idea coined by Cameron L. Macdonald and Carmen Sirianni (1996) in their textbook. Workers and employees belonging to an emotional proletariat are tightly regulated by their employers and are expected to "do deference," meaning they subordinate themselves to customers, whom corporate managers declare to be "always right." Later, I will go into more detail by referring to Barbara Ehrenreich's work (2011 [2001]), where she relates her own experiences as an undercover salesperson at Walmart and in other occupations. Ehrenreich lists some of the features of subordination in service jobs: uniforms, name tags (often with first name only, leading to asymmetrical interactions), and tips (although waitresses and waiters rely on these for securing their existence).

Gertraude Mikl-Horke (2007) offers a different approach to the sociology of work. Coming from within the German-speaking sociology tradition, she explicitly starts with industrial society but later divides the sociology of work into three strata: organizations, society, and humans. This structure somehow demonstrates that the sociology of work touches on the macro, meso, and micro sociological levels, which are inseparable. Her textbook serves as a useful introduction to my study as I offer insights on all three levels and agree with Mikl-Horke's claim that the sociology of work should be understood as a contribution to societal analysis. This resonates with another major introduction to the sociology of work by Fritz Böhle et al. (2018). Their volume starts with the "phenomenon of work," stretching from work as a foundation of human existence, and then focuses on the design and development of work processes. Next, it identifies societal agents and institutions of work – such as labor markets, professions, political regulations of work and care, and the informal sector – as key areas of the sociology of work. Later, in presenting my empirical findings, I will identify anthropological elements of work closely related to work as a foundation of human existence, and I will also consider societal institutions such as professions and political participation. Böhle et al.'s textbook also offers key introductions to the research field in which my study is grounded. All three together provide a good orientation for research traditions and areas in the sociology of work and connections to the topic of supermarket clerks' perceptions of their work.

With regard to the Anglophone research tradition, Vallas (2012) distinguishes four schools of thought in the sociology of work: Marxist, interactionist (from the Chicago School of Sociology; Randy Hodson 1951), feminist, and institutionalist (Meyer & Rowan 1977; Di Maggio & Powell 1983; Meyer & Scott 1992). However, as I have already mentioned, the interactionist and institutionalist approaches seem to be the most widespread.[1] In relation to research on the perceptions of work among low-wage workers, Labor Process Theory (LPT) plays a significant role. According to Vallas (2012), a central concern of LPT was the problem of managerial control over work and workers. The key question was: "How has it been possible for employers to maintain their control over labor in spite of the deeply conflicting interests that capital and labor bring to bear on the labor process?" (Vallas 2012: 38). Vallas mentions Harry Braverman's influential study *Labor and Monopoly Capital* (1974), in which he gave rise to a debate over the "de-skilling" of work by focusing on Taylorism (or scientific management). Daniel Bell and later Peter Drucker pushed the idea of the "Knowledge Society" in asserting that a so-called post-capitalist society is characterized by dissolving productive forces of labor and increasing productive forces of knowledge. In contrast, Braverman made two arguments. One was that employers were able to save labor costs by employing "cheap" labor forces as unskilled. The other, according to Vallas et al. (2009: 28), was the following:

> By utilizing unskilled labor, managers were able to reduce their reliance on subordinate-level employees, since workers who lacked skill and production expertise were often unable to exercise independent control over the methods or pace of their work. The long-term result, Braverman concluded, was an historical "degradation of labor," in which more and more jobs were cheapened, emptied of their former skill, and increasingly controlled from above.[2]

A second influential study in the tradition of LPT was Michael Buroway's *Manufacturing Consent*, published five years later, in 1979. Following Jeffrey J. Sallaz (2013: 122), "Its overarching thesis is that regimes of labor control are effective to the extent that they provide workers with meanings and challenges. Management, in this perspective, is like the designer of a game, and employees the players." As I will explain in the chapter on the theoretical framework for my analysis of the interviewees' responses, my understanding goes beyond reading their behavior as constituting that of players. Instead, I will outline how serious and often desperate, but also occasionally satisfied and proud, supermarket clerks perceive their work. As I did not interpret my data from the perspective of LPT, here I will only point to Paul Thompson's (1983) introduction to the debates on the labor process and his subsequent contributions to the LPT debate in the UK (Thompson 2021).

Another important contribution to this literature in the UK is an empirical study on retail by Paul du Gay (1996). It falls within the research strand of behavior and identity mentioned above. Du Gay presents findings from a collection of empirical data consisting of over 100 semi-structured interviews from employees at four companies (albeit none of them food retailers). Reproaching Marx for having left subjective experience out of his concept of alienation and accusing Braverman of an "objectivist concept of alienation" (15), Du Gay describes a specific identity at work as a consequence of managerial discourses that is reflected in the German coinage by Hans Pongratz and G. Günter Voß (1998) "Arbeitskraftunternehmer." Another contradictory lived experience in service work is outlined by Marek Korczynski (2009), who captures employees' contradictory experiences of customers as sources of satisfaction on the one hand and of humiliation and pain on the other. He conceptualizes this experience as a *"customer-oriented bureaucracy"* (78, italics in original). This concept conveys the idea of systematically rationalizing service work while at the same maintaining customer orientation as a means of keeping up with fierce competition from other companies. Du Gay suggests that "store managers and shopfloor employees within retailing are increasingly being reconceptualized as 'enterprising' subjects: self-regulating, productive individuals whose sense of self-worth and virtue is inextricably linked to the 'excellent' performance of their work and, thus, to the success of the company employing them" (Du Gay 1996: 119). In a paper with co-authors (Kupfer et al. 2019), I have made a slightly different argument, interpreting supermarket clerks' references to their excellent performance as a way that they can construct their own self-worth by relating to the widely legitimized, and thus recognized, normative value in capitalist societies – the value of chasing profits – even though those profits are not the workers' own.

Du Gay's approach coincides with what Vallas (2012) calls ways in which work organizations have effectively begun to colonize workers' identities. In Germany, Martin Baethge (1991) started the research strand on subjectivization, which has since then taken on different forms (e.g., following a Foucauldian perspective of governmentality in analyzing management strategies, as do Boltanski & Chiapello 2003 in France or Bröckling 2007 in Germany; or "artist criticism" ["Künstlerkritik"], as explained by Kleemann & Voß [2018 (2010)] and Voswinkel [2012]).

One strand of the subjectification debate that is important for my own study requires some explanation. I am following Frank Kleemann and G. Günter Voß (2018 [2010]) in seeing people as both constructed by society and partly autonomous. According to them, normative subjectivity is a productive force. They evaluate the ambivalence of subjectivity: on the one hand, it is seen as a chance for self-realization, and on the other it is a management technique (see Matuschek 2010 for an overview) for the benefit of corporations. This resonates with several of my empirical findings. Among my interviewees, there were many who spoke about "giving their all" at work, "working with great ethos," "serving customers as best they can," and "performing [their] best." For the most part, these efforts aimed to meet customers' needs, ensuring that work processes were functioning. But there were also cases in which supermarket clerks referred to their high motivation to perform their best as a way to support their self-esteem in a context in which they generally receive little appreciation or recognition for their work. Here, subjectification goes beyond management techniques and is employed by workers and employees themselves in their specific social contexts. Cameron Lynne Macdonald and

David Merrill (2009) suggest an intersectional approach to the analysis of discrimination in service work. By tying into Hochschild's (1983) category of emotional labor in their analysis of employers' hiring preferences, they find gendered and racialized stereotypes of employees that resonate with one case from my sample in particular, in which a supermarket clerk from Ethiopia reports that her boss expresses a preference for Ethiopian women as cashiers because of their reputation for being polite, customer friendly, and hard working. This kind of subjectification also goes beyond Studs Terkel's (2004 [1972]) assertion after having interviewed 129 employees in a large variety of jobs that workers see more in work than just earning money. Referring to work ethos as a way to uphold self-esteem in a world that dismisses one's occupation appears to be a mental survival strategy. Later I will go into more detail about this phenomenon.

   In addition to LPT and subjectification, a third research strand moves in a "more cultural direction" by emphasizing "the symbolic or normative controls that workers typically encounter at work" (Vallas 2012: 38). Without going into this strand in any depth, I mention it only in passing. This study belongs mainly within a Marxist research tradition that is also informed by conceptualization of the subject in terms of subjectification. Unlike the Foucauldian or Weberian accounts of subjectivity, the Marxist tradition treats workers' perceptions as relevant for what they reveal about social positioning. Thus, I will now turn to studies in the field of workers' and employees' consciousness.

## WORKERS' AND EMPLOYEES' CONSCIOUSNESS STUDIES

In German sociology publications, it has become standard to start state of research overviews on workers' and employees' subjectivity with the classic study by Heinrich Popitz, Hans Paul Bardt, Ernst August Jüres, and Hanno Kesting (1972 [1957]), *Das Gesellschaftsbild des Arbeiters. Soziologische Untersuchungen in der Hüttenindustrie* (Concepts of society of the worker. Sociological studies in the iron and steel industry). Within the German research tradition, this study represents empirical evidence for a "dichotomous concept of society" (237) of the West German worker in the 1950s.[3] Authors define "concept of society" as something that goes beyond one's own experiences. A closer look at the study reveals that the so-called evidence of a prevailing dichotomous concept of society among West German workers in the 1950s is problematic for two reasons. First, a dichotomous concept of society was already presupposed in the questions being asked of 600 workers at an iron and steel company in West Germany. Workers were interviewed about their professional paths, their learning, their bosses and coworkers, technical innovations, workers' participation in management, and "the higher ups." The second problematic aspect of this study and its dichotomous perspective is that a rather low share of interviewees held such a view – only 38% of the sample – while 20% held no apparent concept of society at all. The remaining group of 35% held a concept of society as a structural framework whereby the structure was not explicitly worded as a dichotomous one. Despite this problematic interpretation of the data, Popitz et al. (1972 [1957]) describe workers' consciousness as consisting of a consciousness of performance and of collectivity ("Leistungs- und Kollektivbewusstsein"). The consciousness of performance is linked to physical labor. Added to it is a consciousness of collectivity that comes with being part of the workforce. Part of the consciousness of collectivity is the interviewees' own history of being part of the industrial workforce and their experience that workers remain workers.

Despite the problematic assertion of a dichotomous perspective, Popitz et al. (1972 [1957]) is still relevant for my study. The authors' motivation differs from mine, but the topics of their interviews were similar to mine, as I will show later. Also, my interviewees located themselves at the lower end of societal hierarchics and explicitly reflected upon their performance ("wir schmeißen den Laden" – we run the show). But in contrast to Popitz et al., I did not find evidence of a consciousness of collectivity among the supermarket clerks I interviewed. This ties in with Klaus Dörre et al.'s (2013) research findings on industrial workers in a reunited Germany, discussed later in this chapter. The reasons for the lack of a collective consciousness among these workers undoubtedly include the neoliberal policies and politics prevailing since the 1970s, as a result of which supermarket clerks and other workers and employees suffered from deteriorating working conditions and the decline of collective agreements in light of diminishing union power and membership, especially in Germany, as described in the first chapter. In the U.S. context, the lack of recognition for supermarket clerks and salespeople in general forms another reason for the lack of consciousness among supermarket workers of being part of a collective. There are more reasons as well, as I will show in the chapters below on the empirical findings of my study.

Other important research on workers' perceptions of their work and societal position includes the seldom-mentioned study by Friedrich Fürstenberg (1969), *Die Soziallage der Chemiearbeiter. Industriesoziologische Untersuchungen in rationalisierten und autmatisierten Chemiebetrieben* (The social position of chemical workers: Industrial-sociological studies in rationalized and automatized chemical companies.) Fürstenberg argues for the considerable surplus value chemical workers contribute to the German economy and selects this group for that reason. Representing a perspective in which causal constellations are crucial, he analyzes the organizational labor system as embedded in a social structural framework. This means that his topic of interest, processes of rationalization, needs to be analyzed from the perspective of consequences for the fabric of social relations within a company. "The social position of workers therefore cannot be one-sidedly analyzed with regard to technological conditions and changes in their labor. Each social practice of the labor process and the structural framework in which it is embedded needs to be taken into account as well" (Fürstenberg 1969: 81). Fürstenberg's approach applies to the current study of supermarket clerks' perceptions, which also requires knowledge of social contexts – in this case, the German and U.S. welfare regimes and educational systems outlined in the previous chapter. Fürstenberg (1969) argues that workers' subjective consciousness of their workload is crucial for understanding their attitudes toward rationalization. As I will later explain, this relates to interviewees' welcoming self-checkout cash registers due to their high workloads. Overall, Fürstenberg's study is crucial for pointing to the importance of analyzing subjective attitudes toward work with regard to the system in which work is carried out. My comparative study of two different countries and their labor systems takes this into account and analyzes interviewees' responses within the social contexts in which they are embedded.

Moving chronologically, I come to the next important study for this analysis and one that is considered a classic: Horst Kern and Michael Schumann's (1977 [1970]) research on the influence of technological developments on industrial work and workers' consciousness. The study edition of this work contains an authors' foreword in which they reflect on their own study and describe the development toward prosperity ("Wohlstandsentwicklung") since the second half of the 1950s, which led them to formulate the thesis that workers have aligned with the rest of the increasingly middle-class society in terms of living standards. John H. Goldthorpe, David Lockwood, Frank Bechhofer, and Jennifer Platt (1971 [1968]) apply this thesis in the context of the UK in their widely cited two-volume study, which despite its critical reception was found by Gudrun Axeli Knapp (1981) to contain methodological errors and epistemic shortcomings.[4] Kern and Schumann analyze workers' integration into society, which they clearly equate with the middle class,[5] with the objective of learning whether the labor process changes with technological changes. They arrive at two main findings. First, there is not an automatic parallel between technological changes and the quality of work conditions. The relation is characterized by non-coincidence and contradictions (Kern & Schumann 1977 [1970]). Second, Kern and Schumann see tendencies that work against the development of collective consciousness among workers. Their interviews of 981 workers collected from April 1965 to September 1967 in eight industrial branches (from automobile to textile) and nine companies revealed a shift from leftist perspectives to more right-wing views.

In addition to the two findings above, Kern and Schumann state, "the current technological change in the area of industrial work is generally not linked to hard problems around worker qualifications. Reserves of qualified industrial laborers are usually sufficient to meet the skill and knowledge requirements in case of technological changes" (Kern & Schumann 1977: 316). Still, technological changes carry requirements for workers: above all, a high degree of flexibility. The required flexibility could not be accomplished with practical on-the-job training, and this in turn would lead to worker replacement and destabilized labor groups. In answer to their research question about the impact of technological change on workers' perceptions of their social status, they therefore find that technological change does not result in workers' perception of themselves as belonging to the middle class: "The danger of downward mobility persists in their thinking; because these labor groups do *not* develop a consciousness of experts with recourse to their own, not easily replaceable qualifications and allows for a confident presence" (Kern & Schumann 1977: 318, emphasis in original).

Kern and Schumann's large-scale study is relevant for my research on supermarket clerks in the service sector since most recent technological changes have taken place in this sector (e.g., automated ordering systems and self-checkout registers), and the majority of people, both in the U.S. and Germany, now work in services rather than in manufacturing. The extent to which the introduction of automated ordering systems and self-checkout registers might reduce supermarket clerks' qualifications and replace cashiers remains an open question. However, interviewees' descriptions of tasks suggest that disqualification is indeed taking place. As I will show later, interviewees for my U.S. sample localized themselves in low positions of the social scale because they worked in "entry-level jobs" not even requiring high school degrees, not to mention vocational or higher education. In addition, their self-localization made reference to their minimum-wage earnings, as regulated by their state of residence (Massachusetts). In Germany, vocationally trained, professional, certified supermarket clerks working the floor at their shops showed a tendency to locate themselves within the lower middle class, not as working class or as being temporary jobholders (so-called minijobbers earning up to 450 Euros of untaxable income). I will offer much more detail on their responses below; here it is enough to mention that in both countries, supermarket clerks often referred to feeling undervalued by their bosses (in the U.S.) and by customers (in both countries) and localized themselves at the lower end of the social structure.

A second study by Kern and Schumann, published in 1984, is titled *Das Ende der Arbeitsteilung? Rationalisierung in der industriellen Produktion* (The end of labor division? Rationalization in industrial production). In this book, less subjective perceptions of workers and employees are collected, and the main thesis predicts the development of a so-called knowledge society in which a transition would take place in the automobile, toolmaking, and chemical industries and more qualifications would be required, disadvantaging less-qualified workers. Above all, it predicted, the number of unemployed would rise. Some of the foreseen developments did indeed occur, such as the decline in labor union memberships and an increase in unemployment, but this came only in the early 1990s, in the wake of unforeseeable events related to Germany's reunification, which shut down major parts of the former German Democratic Republic's economy and organizations.

In 2013 Klaus Dörre and his team studied industrial workers' consciousness in a reunified Germany, but for the period between the late 1980s and 2010s research on the sociology of work in Germany took a different direction, about which I will say more below.

A 2013 anthology edited by Klaus Dörre, Anja Happ, and Ingo Matuschek, titled *Das Gesellschaftsbild der LohnarbeiterInnen* (Wageworkers' perception of society), comprises quantitative and qualitative analysis of empirical data collected in various different research projects, mostly by the editors themselves, conducted between 2006 and 2012. The core data used is from an international automobile group in southwestern Germany (after cleansing data from 880 quantitative surveys and 100 qualitative interviews) and one traditional optical group in Thuringia, eastern Germany (459 quantitative surveys, 403 qualitative interviews, and 130 cases). The surveys were administered by a company commissioned by the Friedrich Schiller Universität Jena, and the responses consisted of open statements by 82 people on their consciousness of society ("Gesellschaftsbewusstsein").[6] The large and diverse body of empirical data is both rich and confusing. The approaches vary widely, from quantitative descriptions to analyses of latent structures of meaning. Topics and research questions varied too, touching on workers' and employees' perceptions of their work, company, and society and focusing on whether these perceptions amount to the emergence of a new "Unterschicht," or "underclass" (281).[7] Like Richard Sennett (1989), Dörre et al. (2013) also condense empirical data, but in contrast to Sennett they offer many interview quotes and thus a much more profound scientific analysis. Here I will describe the main findings from their research that are important in the context of my study on supermarket clerks. They sum up their findings with the coinage "good company, bad society" ("guter Betrieb, schlechte Gesellschaft"). Workers and employees, according to Dörre et al. (2013), insist upon their demands concerning the quality of work content and conditions, including wages or salaries and job security, despite feeling devalued at work. Nevertheless, workers and employees lack a conceptual framework ("intellektuelles Bezugssystem") that could pool their attitudes politically, so while they criticize society, they identify positively with their company without drawing a connection between the two. Even in times of financial crisis, no radical protests take place. According to Dörre et al. (2013), there are three reasons for this: first, the social welfare state and support measures, such as the short-term social insurance program, are still strong in Germany (compared to France); second, the deconstruction of the framework for organized labor has been much more advanced in Germany (compared to France); and third, the anti-capitalist attitudes among workers and employees are much less advanced among elected politicians and union representatives. Finally, Dörre et al. (2013) emphasize in their conclusion a "surprising finding" (242), which I have also encountered in many of my interviews:

> The fact that high-quality, subject-centered work demands are an important motivator for individual action can be seen, as paradoxical as this may seem, predominantly in the lowest segments of society, among those who experience employment precarity or are unemployed Hartz IV recipients. The persistency with which social welfare beneficiaries make demands concerning qualitative, subject-oriented, content-related and social-communicative aspects of work is the surprising result of our seven-year investigation. (242–243)

Later, I will return to this research result and offer an interpretation of this finding.

To my knowledge, the most recent study in this stream of research on the sociology of work was conducted by a team of four sociologists, Nick Kratzer, Wolfgang Menz, Knut Tullius, and Harald Wolf (2015), and titled *Legitimationsprobleme in der Erwerbsarbeit. Gerechtigkeitsansprüche und Handlungsorientierungen* (Problems of legitimization in paid work. Justice claims and possibilities of action). The authors' motivation was to find out about ways and problems of legitimization of the capitalist system by their interviewees. Thus, their research tied in with Popitz et al. (1972), who also aimed at enquiring about possibilities of class struggle. Kratzer et al. (2015) offered the first study on workers' and employees' consciousness that included empirical data from the service sector collected between 2012 and 2014. The empirical data came from 207 interviews with workers and employees (of which 42.5% were from the service sector) and 19 group discussions (of which five included workers in the service sector) about subjective perspectives. Also included were 53 expert interviews on the organizational level and nine on the supra-organizational level. One novelty of this study was that 34% of the participants were female. Apart from research by Regina Becker-Schmidt and her team on female pieceworkers in factories of the early 1980s, it is unusual to have such a high percentage of women represented in the data. Most of the interviewees were between 35 and 54 years of age and had been working longer than ten years in the same organization; 85% were employed full-time, 95% had German citizenship, about 10% had a migration background,[8] and 13% came from the former GDR. The most important result was that the workers indicated a widespread expectation of being rewarded according to level of work performance. Specifically, the interviewees formulated statements about what they considered adequate performance and the degree to which they were willing to perform to expectations. For their efforts, they expected recognition from their bosses and colleagues as well as adequate wages and salaries. Statements to this effect were made by interviewees from all areas – electricians; workers in the chemical and construction industries; and workers in public administration, retail, the finance sector, and knowledge-intensive services. However, in two areas this legitimization structure displayed stress fractures: first, the end of remuneration linked to work performance, and, second, flexible employment contracts. Remarkably, these fissures have not intensified toward a crisis of legitimacy for capitalism or for neoliberal policy or politics. Instead, "certain demands and expectations which could go unfulfilled are no longer even placed on the workplace or socioeconomic system. The system thus lost its legitimacy, but its normativity nevertheless goes unchallenged" (Kratzer et al. 2015: 395). It would be interesting to know if workers and employees posed demands also in other directions such as politics, and if so, what became of them. In some sociological studies, right-wing social movements are interpreted as a consequence of a lack of expectations of organizations and the socio-economic order. For a discussion on what draws individuals to right-wing politics, see Arlie Russell Hochschild (2016) and Karina Becker et al. (2018). Kratzer et al. (2015) assert that the experience of an economic crisis (e.g., the global crisis in 2008) can lead to a downward shift of comparisons of social positions. Thus, in retail, for example, employees observe that their younger coworkers and colleagues start at lower wages and salaries than they once obtained, despite an increasing cost of living. This dynamic is similar to Dörre et al.'s (2013, see above) description of two industrial companies' workers and employees. The authors conclude (resonating with Dörre et al.) that there are no signs of a class struggle because of an erosion of normative comparisons that would allow for a broader context, as a result of which demands and expectations would be relativized. This finding requires more investigation since taken on its face it could mean that knowledge, empathy, and solidarity could lead to a deterioration of one's own social positioning. It is more likely that other factors are also at play, such as fewer union memberships, increased workloads, cuts in social welfare, one-sided information policies and politics, and so forth. An overall increase in pressure and fewer mechanisms for action may restrict possible responses. Without being able to go deeper into these issues, I will simply note here that Kratzer et al.'s (2015) findings resonate largely with my analysis of responses from supermarket clerks in the U.S. and in Germany. Within my sample, only one workers' council member claimed to be without any kind of expectations after long years of commitment to the job, and a few U.S. supermarket clerks were simply shut down and unable to make any demands or set any expectations, as I will show later.

# BRIEF INTERIM CONCLUSION

Dörre et al. (2013) once summed up the state of research on workers' consciousness in Germany as "from collective consciousness to identification with the company" ("vom Kollektivbewusstsein zur Betriebsidentifikation"). This is a concise description that may serve its purpose relating to the production sphere, but in the case of the service sector, my findings in the present-day context suggest something different. My empirical data, as I will show later, provide more evidence of identification with coworkers and colleagues as well as with work content and tasks. However, I have also found differences depending on the prestige of the supermarkets. For example, "Edeka Simmel is the Mercedes Benz among supermarkets," as one German interviewee put it, and U.S. interviewees who worked at Trader Joe's and Whole Foods reported recognition by their relatives and friends for the simple fact of their employer – regardless of their position within the company. Thus, in highly prestigious supermarkets, identification with the company also occurred. Nevertheless, claims about "running the shop" with immediate coworkers and colleagues, which led to identification and pride, were dominant, along with a widespread and strong identification with serving customers. In other words, use value orientation emerged as a crucial part of workers' and employees' identification. This is not a new finding. Some research has provided evidence of this kind of worker and employee identification, and, overall, studies on worker and employee consciousness have tended to show low levels of political commitment or readiness for strikes or other actions. While the reasons for this in the production sector may relate to the "middle-classness" of these workers and employees, who live in relatively secure and comfortable material circumstances, employees in the service sector have much more precarious employment conditions, as outlined in the first chapter. Their reasons for not taking political action thus differ, and as I will argue, their often-desperate living conditions may even impede them from any attempts to unite and fight for better conditions or pay.

Before I start an overview of the research stream on use value orientations, upon which my own work builds, I first present a brief excursus on yet another research tradition that aims at giving an extensive overview: research on professions and biographies of workers and employees. Because this part of the literature does not tie in with my study, I present it briefly and without detail.

## EXCURSUS: RESEARCH ON PROFESSIONS[9] AND BIOGRAPHIES OF WORKERS AND EMPLOYEES

For some workers and employees, their profession is an important dimension of their perception of work. Some have gone through years of vocational and professional education and training, which became an important part of their socialization and forms part of their identity at paid work and beyond. For many workers and employees, their professional training informs their work expectations, and discrepancies between learned content and actual working conditions are a source of conflict and unease. Later, I will present findings that confirm this same dynamic among the supermarket clerks I interviewed. One's choice of profession is a very strong indicator of one's expected or perceived social position. The sociology of professions deals largely with how professions relate to issues of social inequality. In his textbook *The Sociology of the Professions*, Keith M. Macdonald (1995) offers an overview of professions and social stratification. With the example of law and medicine, Macdonald shows differences in cultural contexts of professions from a comparative perspective. Since medicine and law are closely related to state regulations, the state receives attention too, and because part of social stratification has to do with gender relations, his textbook contains a chapter on patriarchy and the professions. Crucial for my study of supermarket clerks is the difference between the American and German contexts in terms of whether these workers perceive their occupation as a profession. In the American context, supermarket clerks are not considered part of a professional group, but in Germany they are. This marks a difference in work appropriations between the two countries. The social status of the occupation of supermarket clerk and its classification as simply a job in the U.S. but a profession in Germany influenced the ways in which supermarket clerks related to their work and positioned themselves in the two societies. In general, Germany is known for its system of vocational education below the tertiary level. Many of the interviewees in the U.S. were surprised to learn that supermarket clerks in Germany are certified professionals with a two- or three-year vocational education. Because of these contextual differences, the next section of the literature review will focus on the German research stream in its a chronological account of studies relating to workers' perceptions of their professions.[10]

A large-scale Munich collaborative research initiative (Sonderforschungsbereich, or SFB), funded during the period 1972–1986,[11] was crucial for the development of work on professions and biographies. Ulrich Beck and Michael Brater, research assistants on the project, published the 1978 book titled *Berufliche Arbeitsteilung und soziale Ungleichheit. Eine gesellschaftlich-historische Theorie der Berufe* (Professional division of labor and social inequality: A societal-historical theory of professions). It contains five chapters, of which three are reprints from papers (and two have a third author, E. Tramson) and two are original chapters. The book is an attempt to tie together various aspects of the study of professions under the overall aim of the SFB initiative: to establish a subjectivity-oriented sociology of work aimed at finding out about the social and individual significance of divisions of labor, as Karl Martin Bolte, spokesman of this SFB, points out in his preliminary remarks in the volume. One chapter, published in a journal two years earlier in a slightly different version, is discussed here as it deals explicitly with use value.[12] Beck and Brater (1976) expressed surprise at workers' and employees' orientation toward work content and willingness to make demands; they argued that the workers' orientation could not be explained with reference to structural interests resulting from their social positions or by the interests of the capitalist system – instead, their attitudes appeared to work against these interests. Beck and Brater (1976) follow Offe in their contention that subjective work-content-related demands are necessary for maintaining dominant structures of production-oriented societies even though they infringe upon this same structure of production. Unfortunately, they ignore Karl Marx and others (e.g., Pierre Bourdieu), whose theory of power relations offers answers to Beck and Brater's confusion: workers and employees carry out use value production but are at the same time exploited because they do not have the power to decide about production and service objectives and do not participate in decisions about the use of profits from their labor. In this context, instrumentalist work attitudes directed exclusively at renumeration (if they emerge) are self-undermining in the sense that emancipation from a disappointing system comes at expense of one's own motivations and demands. While Beck and Brater (1976) fail to grasp the state of research and give an inadequate description of workers' and employees' difficult position, they end with an important (albeit old) political warning: if unions do not raise work-content-related demands but leave these up to companies and organizations, they leave all work-related action and decisions with the companies (209). Thus, their suggestion that unions serve as conscious representatives of corporative and societal processes is still crucial and especially resonates with the findings of Dörre et al. (2013) and Kratzer et al. (2015) that the politicization of workers and employees is diminishing. Beck and Brater's (1976) analysis of the social conditions of use value orientation leads them to the insight that the human need for work content demands is exploitable, as is workers' and employees' need for the satisfaction of carrying out meaningful work. This research finding is crucial for my study and will later tie in with my analysis of supermarket clerks and the extent to which their content-oriented demands benefit the corporations they work for.

The next publication from the SFB and in this research stream by some of the same authors is the monograph by Beck et al. (1980) *Soziologie der Arbeit und der Berufe* (Sociology of work and professions), a classic textbook in German sociology dealing with issues around work and professions. Two of the three authors (Beck and Brater) studied sociology at the University of Munich and were professionally socialized within the larger research initiative (SFB 101). Thus, their book follows the research project's perspective, which is interested in the creation of structures of personality, interest, and action through professional labor in different organizations. The authors presuppose a union between person and profession and focus on meanings of the social phenomenon of a profession for particular workers. Their perspective is subject related, but that does not mean their account is socio-psychological, interactionist, or action-oriented (Beck et al. 1980). Rather, this book focuses on societal structures and their objective consequences as related to individuals' professions. Beck et al. (1980) discuss different concepts of professions, taking into account the history and shortcomings of various concepts. In particular, they are interested in grasping and analyzing what they consider to be the union between person and profession, a dimension left out of other concepts of profession. Thus, they define "professions" as "*subject-related*" and entailing "*complex, institutionalized pooling of marketable [marktrelevant] work abilities of people*" (19, emphasis in original). Their account regarding professions informs my comparative study of U.S. and German contexts, in only one of which supermarket clerks obtain a vocational education and professional title.

Another product of the same large research initiative is the detailed empirical study by Ditmar Brock and Hans-Rolf Vetter (1982) on the introduction of computer technology in the printing industry, replacing lead typesetting at four West German newspaper firms during the period 1978–1979. This was also a time when telemarketing ads were introduced. Brock and Vetter (1982) were research associates on the project whose aim was to discover "subjective constellations" (15) with help of current forms of industrialization – namely, the replacement of lead typesetting with computer-generated print. Their special focus was on worker biographies, so in contrast to earlier work on workers' consciousness, the new focus was on the impacts of new techniques on daily lives. Their empirical data collection was realized through 108 biographical interviews, nine expert interviews, and six observations of workplaces; 36% of the interviewees were women, many of whom were employed in nonspecialist positions in new areas.

In four steps, beginning with protocols of the recorded but not transcribed interviews, Brock and Vetter "sifted" through the data[13] and arrived at a list of "structural types of vocational socialization" (25) that go beyond biographical analysis. The types they identified are more abstract and general than biographical and can be summed up in terms of degree of alienation from labor and engagement in other areas of life. This observation was interesting in light of my study since one of my initial hypotheses was that I might find this kind of engagement beyond paid work among U.S. supermarket clerks and more commitment to paid work among their German counterparts, but as it turns out, this was not the case. Brock and Vetter (1982) find little commitment to paid work among German workers because of an extensive social safety net. This hypothesis aligns with the brief discussion of use value above. One conclusion to draw is that the focus on daily life, to be taken systematically into account for the analysis of workers' and employees' perception and evaluation of their work, is an important extension of existing research that is now established as belonging to the sociology of work.

Another research associate of the SFB initiative was G. Günter Voß, a renowned sociologist of work especially known for studying subjective perspectives on work in Germany. In 1983 he published the paper "Bewußtsein ohne Subjekt? Zur Differenzierung des Bewußtseinsbegriffs in der Industriesoziologie" in the comprehensive volume edited by Karl Martin Bolte and Erhard Treutner and titled *Subjektorientierte Arbeits- und Berufssoziologie* (Subject-oriented sociology of work and professions). Voß's text offers insights into the objective of this large research project: to present an alternative perspective to Marxist accounts of consciousness. He ties his analysis in with Brock and Vetter's emphasis on daily life engagement as crucial for understanding workers' and employees' attitudes toward and perceptions and evaluations of their paid work. Most important for my study, Voß (1983) deliberates on a "subjective-oriented notion of consciousness" (344) that is independent from any criteria of objective truth and therefore does not directly reflect societal relations. However, while Voß (1983), without elaborating, holds that consciousness is more than collective thinking, Knapp (1981), drawing on psychological research, has offered a concept of the fundamental relationship between consciousness, societal structures, and workers' and employees' actions, thus explaining sources of practical changes. My concept of work appropriation ties into Knapp's and Becker-Schmidt's theories and seeks to develop them further.

Hans-Georg Brose (1983) offers a rich and dense study based on analysis of 170[14] long and intensive interviews with workers in the construction and electrical industries in West Berlin and West Germany between 1972 and 1974. He assumes that the reconstruction of professional-biographic developments and experiences must include the objects of experiences, which are the specific conditions of industries, companies, and occupations. Thus, the guided interviews included questions on changes in work organization and on experiences over time. Generally, the interviews were spread out over three three-hour sessions. The interviews were recorded, transcribed, and interpreted in relation to interview protocols. From the interviews, Brose discerns three types of bio-graphical patterns: (1) further qualifications and changes in qualifications, (2) continuity, and (3) precarious and threatened stability. Brose links these three patterns to his interpretations of work-related action patterns. Especially when asked about pressures resulting from work situations in addition to conflicts, variability of performance levels, and methods of relieving stress, Brose found mainly two action patterns: workers who focus on reasons and workers who focus on consequences. In linking the three types of biographical patterns with the two types of work-related action patterns, Brose argues that workers with biographies of further qualifications and changes in qualifications who focus on reasons show signs of actively coping with work situations, while workers with biographies characterized by continuity and by precarity and threatened stability tended to focus on the consequences of strain at the workplace. According to Brose, the latter group were more instrumentally oriented. They faced the problem of not being able to control conditions for action. While workers whose biographies were dominantly characterized by continuity tried to secure incalculable consequences by long-term inclusion and incorporation in workplaces or working groups and through increased self-control and self-discipline, workers whose biographies were characterized by precarity and threatened stability were constantly faced with unsolvable problems. Brose himself refrains from political conclusions, but I would say that his find-ings indicate the importance of taking into account societal conditions of West German workers in the 1960s and 1970s. In mentioning the historical and local context, I call attention to the fact that consciousness does not develop out of education per se, but out of a certain kind of education that allows for ques-tions, inquiry, discussions, and access to material and critical perspectives.

   While Brose was mainly interested in workers' experiences and perceptions of their work, studies in this stream of professional and biographical research shifted toward the individuation of workers. Since this interest departs from my study, I will mention it only briefly, highlighting a research question con-cerning social inequality and subjective perceptions. Hans-Joachim Giegel, Gerhard Frank, and Ulrich Billerbeck (1988) analyzed 80 interviews con-ducted in West Germany from 1980 to 1982 with male workers in the metal industry. The authors follow a Marxist perspective for analyzing the relation of work and capital and pursue research questions concerning appropriation and individuation among industrial workers and how they contribute to the consol-idation of social inequality. The authors focus on health behaviors as moments of self-assertion. Starting with single case descriptions, followed by creating types, they investigate the relations of the types and examine whether all cases constituting a type show a similar health (or sickness) behavior. Without going into details about their methods and leaving out most findings of their professional-biographical patterns of orientation, I want to mention only that the authors offer an explanation for a certain paradox: that industrial workers are subject to extraordinary health risks but do not compensate with healthy behavior. In fact, quite the contrary: industrial workers add to workplace health risks with their own risky and damaging practices. The reason for this is that their work coerces them into professional-biographical patterns that impede other patterns that would diminish health risks. In contrast to employees who work in less hazardous workplaces, industrial workers receive more restrictive forms of professional-biographical orientations. Thus, the disadvantages industrial workers face in objective conditions combine with action-oriented patterns and practices at their own expense. A year later, in 1989, Giegel elaborated the specific contribution of biographical research for understanding workers' consciousness and especially the widespread adherence among workers to unfavorable societal structures: "Even if his interests are frustrated, the subject must follow the interest to secure his identity, namely within the societal structures in which the interests were built up. In developing his own biographical orientation without understanding structures of the system, subjects become dependent on the system's structures. The defense of their biographical orientation requires these structures to be in effect" (Giegel 1989: 125). This finding resonates with what we found among supermarket clerks in Germany: in alluding to the importance of selling goods, they contribute to an argument for the importance of their work, despite their low pay and lack of recognition (Kupfer et al. 2019).

To sum up: research on subjective perceptions of work in relation to professions started out taking a rather critical distance from Marxist perspectives, which were seen as conceiving of individuals as mere reflections of objective structures. But this research stream developed an interest in the ways in which structures of personality and action are created through professional work and labor. This development accompanied a focus on abilities (Fähigkeiten) instead of activities (Tätigkeiten). Abilities are tied to human beings and emphasize their interest in subjects, in contrast to structures, which come to light if we focus on human activities. However, later, when sociology of work research shifted to a focus on biographies, it became clear that reconstructing biographies requires analysis of objective structures as constituent parts of people's lives. Since the 1990s, this research has dealt with the question of whether professions were coming to an end because of increasingly flexibilized working conditions. In their study of supermarket clerks, Heike Jacobsen and Ellen Hilf (2019) conclude in their secondary analysis of primary studies that professional qualifications are only valid for higher-level and leadership positions, but no longer for clerks working on the shop floor. While supermarket clerks still identify with their vocational training and professional status, they are unable to have their demands and expectations met such as having careers that provide a living wage. According to Alma Demszky and

Günter Voß (2018), recent research on professions took up the perspective of subjectivity. In late modern flexible conditions, workers and employees are forced to control, commodify, and rationalize their work force professionally. While my reading of the Marxist account of the worker as a subject differs from that of the researchers of the Munich SFB, their account and establishment of a subject-oriented sociology of work is important here as I share their interest in the consequences of societal-structural elements for workers and employees. Nevertheless, my own study is closer to another research tradition to which I will turn now: feminist critical theory in the sociology of work.

## FEMINIST CRITICAL THEORY IN THE SOCIOLOGY OF WORK

The work of Regina Becker-Schmidt is central to this area of research. In the early 1980s she conducted a research project on female factory workers with children. It was the first time that female workers were asked about their work perceptions. While the previous research on workers' consciousness focused on attitudes toward work, Becker-Schmidt and her colleagues were eager to find out about female workers' subjectivity. Therefore, they explicitly included the reproductive work comprising childcare, care for sick and elderly family members, household work, and the emotional work within the family that women carry out in addition to their paid work. Thus, they took into consideration both work spheres. While subjectivity in research on male workers and employees was included by taking life histories into account, subjectivity in the case of women was seen as a product of the interrelation of the two social domains of productive and reproductive labor. The results demonstrated that female textile workers were far from having an instrumentalist work attitude but instead formulated work content expectations going beyond earning a wage. Female textile workers insisted on descriptions of their work tasks as being complex and requiring certain skills and proficiencies, as Becker-Schmidt (1980) asserts. These workers articulated an interest in being good workers for the sake of their own self-respect. At the same time, they suffered from working conditions that impeded their ability to do good work. Additionally, requirements in both work spheres were very different and even contradictory. While they had to work quickly in piecework, they had to "take their time" while educating their children. Becker-Schmidt et al. (1983) sum up their findings in terms of "ambivalences" relating to both their paid and unpaid work. While piecework put them into strict time corsets, it also required focus and individually manageable activity that formed some of the emotional parts of subjectivity (Becker-Schmidt et al. 1983). Becker-Schmidt (1983) outlines three different dimensions of needs that drive these workers' actions: being active, achieving recognition, and affecting appropriation. All three dimensions are interdependent (Becker-Schmidt 1983) and shaped differently, depending on social relations and working conditions. Becker-Schmidt's concepts of dimensions as activity and appropriation are central to my concept as well, although they function in a slightly different way. Female workers related their ambivalent feelings about both paid and unpaid work. They enjoyed their families but at the same time experienced isolation (Becker-Schmidt 1983). Work experiences always affected home and the workplace alike, and female workers felt pressured to apply themselves fully to both spheres. Becker-Schmidt called these workers' ambivalences about level of activity "ambitendencies" ("Ambitendenzen"), referring to their coexisting contradictory orientations and directions (Becker-Schmidt 1980: 716). While female textile workers talked about good and bad work experiences, they gave unambiguously negative evaluations to work tasks they found unacceptable, such as increasing the work tempo, and they objected to their unequal treatment compared to their male coworkers. Becker-Schmidt's work is important for research on subjective perceptions of work as she called attention to the importance of the domain of reproductive labor for informing work perceptions in the domain of productive labor and vice versa. It was necessary to include female workers in the analysis to reach this insight.

## SOCIOLOGY OF WORK IN THE TRADITION OF CRITICAL THEORY

Many years later, Michael Frey (2009) picked up on one of Becker-Schmidt's three dimensions of subjective work perceptions: appropriation. He was especially interested in relating appropriation to autonomy in times of increased marketization and subjectivization of paid work. Frey defines appropriation as "the subjective expression of a demand for control in work" (Frey 2009: 13, without italics). According to Frey, autonomy is "control of essential operational parameters of work" (Frey 2009: 12, without italics). Against the background of operational potential and restrictions on autonomy in work, Frey is interested in subjective means of appropriation. He selected Deutsche Bahn AG as a former state company that was privatized in 1994. His research findings result from an analysis of ten interviews with DB agents working in the operational area. Using thematic codes, these interviews were compared along similarities, differences, regularities, and disruptions. The core of the analysis comprised interpretative reconstruction of subjective logics of practices and interpretative schemes. All interviewees, independent of their qualifications, salaries, and gender, expressed the view that their work was highly relevant. However, among younger employees and those with more formal education, he found higher career expectations and a work orientation emphasizing work content. For employees with university degrees, the loss of employment was partly perceived as a massive biographical disruption, while employees with vocational training only were more likely to perceive job losses as a random occurrence. All interviewees expressed expectations relating to the meaning of their work. Cost-saving measures at the workplace and changes in workplace organization led them to feel resigned and distanced from their work. However, despite oppressive working conditions, employees maintained a sense of exercising some degree of control over their actions. Possible forms of resistance included collective action strategies and independent actions based on employees' own understanding of work and individual work ethics. Fear of losing their jobs did not decrease, but the employees shed their feelings of paralysis, performing what Frey interpreted as a form of appropriation under oppressive working conditions. Although Frey's sample differs from the one used in my study, the respondents formulated similar kinds of resistance to workplace rationalization. However, Frey's definition of appropriation as the attempt to gain control over work differs from mine. Frey focuses on the aspect of empowerment, while my focus is on internalization as an important aspect of appropriation, as I will explain in the next chapter.

Years later, Stephan Voswinkel (2019) picks up the notion of appropriation and defines it as a process that overcomes feelings of strangeness (Fremdheit). His aim is to revive the debate on alienation, which is mainly linked to Taylorism, and he points out aspects of alienation under current working conditions of indirect governance, dissolution of the boundaries between the workforce and individual, individualization, and bureaucratization of work. He follows Rahel Jaeggi (2005) in presupposing a basic difference between the self and work or the world such that work needs to be appropriated. Appropriation is not easy due to the instrumentalization and hierarchical structure of work. His account of appropriation is relevant for my study in that he sees appropriation as a series of activities. He follows Jaeggi (2016), who emphasized that appropriation changes both the object and the subject of appropriation. But mainly he tries to understand where and why alienation takes place in our current world of work, and he even formulates an emancipatory account of alienation in which people no longer identify with an environment that silences their voices.

Recently, Friedericke Hardering and Mascha Will-Zocholl (2020) distinguished different kinds of appropriation among highly qualified employees. According to Hardering and Will-Zocholl, appropriation is the perception and implementation of one's own possibilities, or designing work according to one's own ideas and expectations. According to their definition, the positive connotation of appropriation prevails. Interpreting 40 interviews with physicians and social workers in leadership positions, they construct three ideal types of appropriation as different ways of making meaning. Self-critically, the authors mention that they primarily capture subjective aspects of appropriation rather than objective conditions for appropriation. For my study it is useful to keep in mind that appropriation is linked to workers' and employees' interpretations of their work.

Stephan Voswinkel (2005) discusses another of the dimensions outlined by Becker-Schmidt (1983) of subjective needs employees seek to satisfy through paid work: recognition. Like Frey, Voswinkel analyzes the service sector. His interviews focus on employees in leading positions and the chairs of retail and restaurant work councils. Voswinkel explains why these two branches are overrepresented by female workers and employees: the high demand for part-time work, similarities of the tasks to household work, the close orientation toward others in the workplace setting, the position's classification as nonproductive work, and connotations of servility in service work in general. Voswinkel emphasizes the low prestige of service work for two reasons: the impression that this work could be carried out by anyone, especially in the face of more widespread self-service, and diminishing use of specific competencies at work. Voswinkel detected six framings of work among his interviewees that "also serves to give value to work, to secure workers' self-esteem and enable them to achieve self-confidence and recognition" (Voswinkel 2005: 298). The six framings are as follows: control, which offered employees a position of dominance relative to their customers; help, which also served the purpose of dominance; selling, intended to exploit the customer; advice, which emphasized the professional competencies of the employees; animation, aimed at gaining self-confidence by acting on a stage and invoking a good mood for the customers; and normalization and transfer, which offered recognition by helping workers to deal with difficult and disturbing customers and creating an undisturbed workplace. Voswinkel's study is important for its insights into devalued work areas, which include supermarkets. Later, Voswinkel and Wagner (2013) argued that recognition becomes increasingly uncertain because institutions of recognition such as collective agreements lose validity. Thus, performance receives recognition if it demonstrates output but is less recognized in investing input. Since corporations are increasingly investing in capital, performance relating to production loses recognition. They assert a change in relations of recognition from appreciation to admiration. Increasingly special performances for market success are recognized, whereas recognition for affiliation and social reciprocity with social insurance and rules of seniority lose recognition. As I will show later, supermarket clerks who are largely busy with maintaining the status quo do not expect very much recognition from customers, but they appreciate the performance of their coworkers as they can appreciate the invisible effort behind it.

At a time of increasing precarity of employment in the wake of the economic crisis of 2007 and 2008, sociology of work research increased its focus on employees' demands and expectations of work. This accompanied a period in which workers were called on to be flexible and act as entrepreneurs of themselves. The middle classes were seen as being under threat, and social scientists became increasingly interested in learning about their views and perceptions of work. Thus, Stefanie Hürtgen and Stephan Voswinkel (2014) asked "normal" employees, the ones with regular jobs and with salaries in the middle ranges, about their work-related demands and expectations. The answers were used to indicate the range of precarization and uncertainty in the workplace. Hürtgen and Voswinkel conducted biographical interviews that included the whole life context and generalized their assertions on the basis of their own interpretations. The interviews touched on themes such as work hours, working conditions, wages, the behavior of supervisors and bosses, and collegiality in the workplace. The results demonstrated that the "normally" employed are not insecure about voicing their demands. They expect good wages, adequate working conditions (e.g., enough time to complete tasks without stress), respectful supervisors, and clear demarcations between work and life. They also expect these conditions to prevail in the future. However, a second finding indicates some uncertainty among middle-class employees as to whether the values and norms upon which their demands are based are still considered valid in the society at large. Hürtgen and Voswinkel (2014) detected uncertainty over societal validation of their demands. The authors report that these demands were specifically oriented toward work and not to be confused with assertions of societal changes.

The concept of usefulness as a core aspect of employees' demands concerning work content has been studied by Sarah Nies (2015). Nies critically asserts that employees expect work to be a form of self-fulfillment, as has been emphasized in recent years in the management literature and extensively studied in the field of sociology of work. Following Nies, employees raise demands concerning the content of work that reference the utility to others of the product of their labor. Demands relating to the content of work are "work-related demands that refer to the effect of work and refer to ideas of what the meaning and purpose of the occupation is or should be" (Nies 2015: 118, without italics). Of course, employees also seek recognition, self-fulfillment, autonomy, and so forth, but use value is very important among the demands of the content of work (Nies 2015: 118). Therefore, her study is crucial for mine, especially since she explains that demands about work content related to their utility are independent from professional backgrounds but arise in work contexts. Nies's study does relate to research on subjective perceptions of work, but she also includes societal dimensions in her work by asking about the principal connections between demands relating to work content and corporate expectations in the current conditions of increasing marketization. The answer she finds is that conflicts exist between company objectives and employee expectations. Her sample consists of 20 customer consultants of a bank (of which six are in leading positions and two are members of the work council) and 29 engineers, along with three participants in a group discussion from two different international companies. The interviews evoked a mix of narrative and problem-focused responses that were coded and analyzed in several steps. Customer consultants in the bank faced the highest number of conflicts with regard to social responsibility that could not be reconciled with the companies' rules. Customer consultants sometimes found themselves ignoring the companies' regulations to avoid hurting customers and to establish long-term customer relations, which are beneficial for the bank too, as they argued. In contrast, engineers faced overall fewer conflicts. The red line they were not willing to cross was the work content demand that fundamental criteria of functionality must be met. The main conflict with companies had to do with the use of resources. Engineers felt that they were able to weigh economic requirements rationally and reconcile them with their own professional ideas of quality. Conflicts arose mainly along deadlines and key performance metrics. In these areas, the engineers stood by their demands concerning work content. In conclusion, Nies (2015) points to tensions between demands of work content and market-oriented management. These conflicts are indicative of fundamental contradictions of the capitalist mode of production, in which use and exchange value are in conflict. Nies calls on unions to follow through on workers' demands concerning work content and to recognize these as relevant interests.

Stefanie Hürtgen (2017, 2018) goes a step further in arguing that workers and employees – on the basis of the value they create – could (and should) lay claim to their rights of participation in societal design and development. Instead of dealing on an individual-subjective level with flexible and market-oriented economic and working conditions, work should be viewed apart from its competitive orientation. Here demands concerning work content do not relate to concrete customers or clients but rather take on a social dimension. This perspective especially emerged during the COVID-19 pandemic, when societies' dependence on certain groups of workers and employees, among them supermarket clerks, became visible. However, so far, groups of so-called system-relevant workers and employees are no more politically involved, and their undervaluation continues.

## MEANING OF WORK

While sociology of work research in Germany has focused on workers' and employees' expectations and demands concerning work content, the Anglophone discussion has dealt more with the meaning of work. Several disciplines have participated, including management studies, psychology, philosophy, and sociology. And accordingly, different accounts have emerged around what "the meaning of work" entails (Yeoman et al. 2019). According to Randy Hodson (2001), meaningful work is essential for dignity, which is necessary for self-worth and respect for others. While he reports on how workers find ways to create meaningful work by focusing on peripheral tasks and strong camaraderie and solidarity with coworkers, I will later show another way of maintaining self-worth: by maintaining a strong work ethos. Meaningfulness is generally considered an important element of high-quality work, and some have viewed meaningful work as necessary for human flourishing (Veltman 2016). Thus, occupations lacking opportunities for deriving meaning from work are sometimes changed or redefined to create a positive self-image, according to Wrzesniewski and Dutton (2001). One way of "crafting a job" is to change the nature of the tasks performed. Among my interviewees, I met one such job crafter: a supermarket clerk in charge of produce spoke about how he takes care of elderly shoppers who lack social contacts and opportunities for conversations. As part of his work, he spent time talking to particular customers. This gave him a purpose and a good feeling about his job. Recently, the topic of meaningful work has been related to questions of social stratification, and one study (Williams et al. 2022) analyzing survey data of 14,000 working adults in the UK reported a gap in perceptions of work's meaningfulness between professional and managerial occupations on the one hand and routine and manual occupations on the other. Workers in manual occupations reported experiencing work as less meaningful, mainly due to the lower levels of complexity in their jobs, but also because of the lack of development opportunities. The former reason resonates with Hegel's call for professional associations to take care of and defend the complexity of their members' work tasks and degree of abilities and competencies to allow workers to be recognized for their contributions. I will not go into depth about meaningfulness as a feature of work since this issue was not discussed a great deal among the supermarket clerks I interviewed: the meaning of their work is obvious and not questioned because providing people with food is an essential task. More central issues for my interviewees were their demands and expectations concerning work content and the difficulty of realizing them because of work conditions. Following Voswinkel (2015), people who are impeded in carrying out their work meaningfully lose their sense of performing meaningful work.

## STUDIES ON SUPERMARKET CLERKS AND OTHER EMPLOYEES IN THE LOW-WAGE SECTOR

The last section of the literature overview is dedicated to studies on supermarket clerks. This section uncovers previous insights into the working conditions of supermarket clerks and research findings to date on their subjective perceptions of work. Apart from one study on supermarket clerks in the former

German Democratic Republic (GDR), the others could be classified in terms of three groups: comparative studies, studies conducted in Germany and focusing on changes in working conditions there, and studies on the working poor that deal with larger life contexts beyond mere employment.

The study on retail clerks in the GDR draws a very different picture from corresponding studies on West Germany, Germany after reunification, and the U.S. Following Michael Hofmann and Dieter Rink (1999), sales clerks in the GDR obtained privileged positions due to a general scarcity of goods. Sales personnel in the GDR were involved in procurement and supply chains, creating a consciousness of relative power by virtue of their involvement in important public processes that translated into high social status. Working in the service sector in a sales position was not considered a "bad job." More than 90% of sales personnel obtained a vocational education, and more than two thirds worked full time. Their work schedules required that their partners take care of commitments at home, which in the case of women enabled them to rise to better social positions. Nevertheless, the strains of the job were high because of shortages of goods and ongoing demands and expectations from customers. Asked whether they felt responsible for the sustenance of the population, 94% answered in the affirmative. Still, a high percentage of the interviewees said they were very satisfied with the collegiality at their workplace. During the 1980s, when shortages worsened and the discrepancy increased between customers' expectations and stores' offerings, salespeople felt less responsible for the overall situation, but their professional ethos as providers of food crumbled. Hofmann and Rink report on hierarchies based on shop size and sector. After Germany's reunification, the salespeople reported a lost sense of collectivity, solicitude, being needed, and informal power and authority in relation to customers. On the other hand, the interviewees cited the importance of retaining their jobs, and they also reported that selling things was more fun as more products were available.

Later research on supermarket clerks, such as Gerhard Bosch and Steffen Lehndorff's (2005) study and the one by Dorothea Voss-Dahm (2008), compared countries' low-wage sectors. The comparative perspective referred to specific institutions and factors such as collective agreements in Germany. Bosch and Lehndorff resonate with Esping-Andersen's welfare regime typology, outlined above, in seeing country differences as primarily consequences of different welfare regimes and institutions. They also assign states a significant role in shaping working conditions. After 2000, these agreements ended in the retail sector, and wages became a central factor in competition. Part-time work was implemented as a cost reduction strategy, enabling increasing flexibility in times of increasing work hours. Employees could no longer live on their wages, but this aligned with Germany's conservative welfare regime in supporting male heads of households. Unequal distribution of managerial positions among men and women contributed to the gender pay gap in retail. Following Voss-Dahm, the introduction of new technologies such as automated ordering systems leads to de-skilling and devaluing of work. Overall, rationalization of goods management and branch organization seems strongly influenced by Taylorist models (Bosch & Lehndorff 2005). This resonates with findings grouped in an edited volume by Irena Grugulis and Ödül Bozkurt (2011), who observe that rationalization of retail operations leads to precarious work and "also suppresses the potential for collective action" (Bozkurt & Grugulis 2011: 10).

German retail jobs are rated higher in many respects than jobs in the retail industry in the U.S. (Carré & Tilly 2017), where globalization, changes in information and communication technologies, financialization, neoliberalism, and a shift in business norms regarding treatment of workers have further eroded the quality of these already low-end jobs. According to the authors, in the U.S. the real value of hourly wages declined by 25% from 1975 to 1991, and the real value of the federal minimum wage declined by as much as 32% in 2015 compared to 1968. In addition, few benefits and little formal training are offered. This affects many people, as retail is the largest employment sector in the U.S., with millions more workers than there are in manufacturing. In order to improve working conditions in the U.S., they recommend a higher minimum wage, stronger unions, the establishment of works councils, greater regulation of work schedules, and a more subsidized childcare system.

Studies focusing on changes in retail working conditions in Germany seem to conclude that they are increasingly becoming aligned with conditions in the U.S. According to Dorothea Voss-Dahm and Steffen Lehndorff (2003), tasks have changed along with increasing reliance on part-time staff. Whereas before, qualified staff were fit for use in all areas, tasks have become more specific and less complex. New ordering systems and cash registers require less knowledge and fewer competencies and can be operated by staff with no vocational education. A new customer orientation is emerging that aims at creating a pleasant sales atmosphere instead of offering specific advice to customers. In a case study of one corporation of more than 4,000 shops in Germany and over 60,000 employees, Philipp Staab (2014) reports on aggressive strategies of takeovers by competitors and a general deterioration of working conditions. In this context, work contracts do not take collective agreements into consideration and are principally limited; often workers such as supermarket clerks are contract workers with two years of vocational education rather than graduates of three-year programs. A general shift from a core workforce to peripheral workers is taking place. Staab calls this the "proletarization" of work. Supermarket clerks in Germany belong less to the lower middle classes and have increasingly come to resemble the working poor in the U.S.

Several studies have offered insights into working conditions and subjective perceptions of work as well as structures that keep large parts of populations within the low-wage sector. For example, David Shipler (2005) illustrates how living on the edge magnifies problems by pushing people into increasingly hopeless situations. Katherine Newman and Victor Tan Chen (2007) tie into this insight by pointing to the high vulnerability of people with no savings, for whom even small incidents can come with high costs. Research by Barbara Ehrenreich (2011 [2001]), based on her own experiences going "undercover" as a minimum-wage worker between 1998 and 2000, confirms the near impossibility of surviving at this wage level without working multiple jobs. Demeaning practices such as drug and personality tests as well as searches through personal effects by management contribute to the feeling reported by Ehrenreich and confirmed several of my interviewees that they were being asked "to surrender one's basic civil rights and – what boils down to the same thing – self-respect" (Ehrenreich (2011 [2001]: 208). Katherine Newman (2008) points to the personal toll such jobs take on the individual: "Especially in the low-wage sector, workers need to have a high degree of patience to survive on the job, patience that to some workers might seem suspiciously like acquiescence. They must learn to endure – with a smile – heavy-handed supervision, disrespect, and, at the very bottom of the labor market, the indignity of exploitation" (180). The findings of all these studies are important as they show how societal structures such as industrial relations and welfare regimes as well as changes on the organizational level in companies influence working conditions and life contexts, affecting subjective work perceptions.

To conclude this literature review, I call attention to two broadly defined research streams: a German tradition starting with Marx and focusing on materialism, and a U.S. tradition that is more interested in behavior. While materialist research centers on structures, research on behavior focuses on humans. In the German research tradition, issues of social status and position are central, whereas in the U.S. tradition, issues of identity are prioritized. Accordingly, German research on workers' and employees' perceptions inquired about their views regarding social positioning relative to social class and other professional groups, while Anglophone research was more interested in questions of individual well-being. The focus on identity in English-speaking countries led to the investigation of the meaning of work for individual workers and employees. In Germany, professional socialization is considered an important part of the formation of subjectivity, and research underlined the importance of expectations and demands concerning the content of work. The fundamental insight that structures do not determine consciousness led to the development of the research area of subjective perspectives in sociology. By listening to workers and employees talk about their perceptions of work, it became clear that their work attitudes are not purely functions of their employment positions and job tasks. Among the main research findings is the insight that some of their attitudes even work against their interests and potentially do them harm. With the help of reconstructive analysis, these contradictions are detectable. Social context is an important factor in employees' perceptions of their work. The U.S. and German contexts differ in terms of welfare regimes, educational systems, and industrial relations. However, during the last decades these contexts became more similar, and the working conditions of supermarket clerks aligned more due to neoliberal policies and political trends. Nevertheless, this study on supermarket clerks' perceptions of their work in the U.S. and in Germany fills a gap in comparative studies in the sociology of work with a focus on subjective perspectives. For the analysis of the collected interviews, I next introduce the notion of work appropriation, a theoretical concept enabling the explanation of how subjective perspectives are embedded in their respective social contexts.

## NOTES

1.  Mikl-Horke (2011) contends that recently a couple of studies on the origin and development of the discipline of sociology in relation to the social sciences and socio-political history emerged and points to Dorothy Ross, *The Origin of American Social Sciences*, Stephen P. Turner and Johnathan H. Turner, *The Impossible Science: An Institutional Analysis of American Sociology*, and the controversial contribution by R. W. Connell, *Why is Classical Theory Classical?*
2.  This resonates with Hegel's demand that professional organizations such as craft guilds ("Handwerksverbände," today referred to as "Industrie- und Handelskammer") must defend the interests of their members in preventing de-skilling through division of labor, as Honneth (2010) reports.
3.  Translations are mine unless otherwise indicated.
4.  In July 1968, Cambridge University Press published the first volume, titled *The Affluent Worker: Industrial Attitudes and Behaviour*, followed by the second volume in December 1968, *The Affluent Worker: Political Attitudes and Behaviour*. Empirical data was collected in Luton, a British town that benefitted extraordinarily from economic growth and wealth in the 1950s and 1960s. Interviews and other data were collected at three corporations that were among the best-paying and advanced in terms of their personnel and labor relations policies. Since the empirical data relate to the UK, it remains relegated to my literature and research overview. Of more interest to my study is Gudrun-Axeli Knapp's (1981) critique, in which she discloses Goldthorpe et al.'s reversal of the worker (the active subject) into an object of instrumental valorization leading to the "fatal suggestion of a congruence of subjective and objective, of motives and coercions" (Knapp 1981: 17). Knapp was part of a working group led by Regina Becker-Schmidt that tied in with the tradition of critical theory and funded a feminist approach to the sociology of work, to which I return later in much more detail when developing my concept of work appropriation.
5.  For reasons I cannot explain, the upper classes are not mentioned and are made invisible in studies of that time.

6.   Additionally, three further sets of empirical data have been collected: (1) a standardized survey in one iron foundry in Thuringia (220 evaluable cases), (2) a national telephone survey on perceptions of elites (with 1,114 cases in East Germany and 1,076 cases in West Germany, including data on gender and age), (3) a regional study on social welfare divided into four investigated regions (two in East Germany and two in West Germany) in which employees in the public administration of social welfare (95 or 96 cases) and recipients of social welfare (179 evaluated cases) were interviewed in two waves. A dozen interviews in other regions were conducted as well for reasons of comparison. Secondary statistical analyses also contributed to this regional study.

7.   Here I use quotation marks for the term "Unterschicht," referring to lower social strata, because it carries a devaluing connotation.

8.   Migration background ("Migrationshintergrund") is a German technical term used by the office of statistics (Statistisches Bundesamt) to denote people who were themselves born without German citizenship or who have at least one parent who was. Displaced people from World War II and their descendants are denoted differently and thus are not included.

9.   I am using the term *profession* as a translation of the German "Beruf," which has a field of meanings that include the more nuts-and-bolts concepts of trade, line of work, and occupation – but also the "higher" concepts of profession, vocation, and career.

10.  For this reason, I will leave out many important studies in the area of sociology of professions, such as Kurtz (2002).

11.  From 1986 to 1996, SFB 333, "Entwicklungsperspektiven von Arbeit," built on and secured continuity for a research stream of 26 years. From 1999 to 2009, SFB 536, "Reflexive Modernisierung – Analysen zur Transformation der industriellen Moderne," largely associated with Ulrich Beck's research, also took place at Ludwig-Maximilians-Universität München (LMU Munich). References to research at LMU often denote the location as simply "Munich."

12.  The paper is titled "Grenzen abstrakter Arbeit. Subjektbezogene Bedingungen der Gebrauchswertproduktion und ihre Bedeutung für kritische Berufspraxis" (Limits of abstract labor: Subject-related conditions of use value production and its significance for critical vocational practice). In this study, I refer to the original paper in the journal *Leviathan* and not to the book chapter.

13.  In hindsight, their description of data evaluation and interpretation seems too vague, but during their time qualitative methods were not yet developed to the extent they are today.

14.  Of the 170 analyzed interviews, 65 were conducted with workers in construction and 105 with workers in the electrical industry.

# 3. Conceptualizing work appropriation

This theoretical chapter creates a framework for understanding employees' subjective experiences of the work they perform. However, the framework goes beyond the subjective to include the societal level (Kupfer 2021) by taking into account the social contexts in which work appropriation takes place. These social contexts are dynamic: they change over time and differ from place to place. Thus, my notion of work appropriation could be classified as a process of socialization that makes social analysis possible. While the notion of work encompasses both paid and unpaid activities, I focus on paid work. Still, unpaid work such as reproductive and care work impacts ways of perceiving and performing paid work too; it therefore also constitutes socialization through work. Including social contexts into the analysis of work appropriation means taking into account changes in work due to automatization and changes in rationalized work processes and conditions. From this perspective, as Paul Thompson (2021) has pointed out, the workplace is understood as contested terrain. Another important consideration here is the discrepancy between the essential significance of the work of providing food for the vast majority of the population and the low levels of recognition and remuneration accorded to supermarket workers. The theoretical concept of work appropriation enables an understanding of the "paradox that while work is objectively becoming more pressurized and precarious, it is still a source of meaning and attachment for many employees" (Thompson 2021: ix). One manifestation of work appropriation in particular – work ethos – illustrates the ambivalence of workers' and employees' socialization, which can be both integrative and exploitative. The concept of work appropriation is broader than that of meaningful work because it includes analysis that goes beyond mere descriptions of attitudes toward work (see Kupfer 2021).

While the concept of work appropriation contributes to societal analysis by making sense of the interrelations of subjective and structural levels, it originates with the subjective perspective of workers and employees. Work appropriation refers to their practices. The notion of work appropriation comprehends workers' and employees' perceptions of paid and unpaid work within the social contexts in which they live. Perceptions of work are crucial for forming attitudes and positions as well as ideas and decisions around work practices. These practices in turn lead to experiences that are cognitively and mentally processed to form evaluations of work and labor. Work appropriation is a dynamic process stretching over life courses in changing social contexts. My notion of work appropriation differs from the idea of appropriation as exploitation of the work force by capitalists. Of course, a workforce that is not self-employed adds value that is appropriated by owners, buyers, or contractors. The employers' appropriation is part of the way workers and employees perceive and design their work. But by focusing on the workers' and employees' perspectives, I take into account their perceptions, descriptions, and evaluations of socialization as a constitutive social dimension. These employees constitute a large part of society, and thus gaining insights into their modes of thought and practice allows for societal analysis.

As outlined in the literature review, my new usage of appropriation differs also from other standard conceptions of this term in several respects. Frey (2009) defines appropriation as claiming control of work. This perspective resembles the Anglophone tradition of Labor Process Theory (LPT), which is interested in control of workers and employees by their bosses and employers. As briefly touched upon in the former chapter, LPT has generated studies on workers' and employees' strategies for gaining autonomy in working conditions characterized by changing forms of control. Since Frey mainly focuses on autonomy, this is understandable. But my interest in broader perspectives on workers' and employees' perceptions leads to a wider notion of appropriation. Voswinkel (2019) focuses on alienation in today's world of work and defines appropriation as overcoming alienation. However, my concept of work appropriation is more comprehensive. Instead of taking a single focus, it relies on collecting various empirical forms of work appropriation as examples of what happens. I assume that a lot of work occurs while workers and employees experience alienation, and I assume it is possible to come to terms with various aspects of work despite those feelings; my understanding of appropriation therefore does not necessarily imply a positive emotional state. This will become evident in my discussion of activity as one of the core three dimensions of work appropriation. Workers and employees act, regardless of whether or not the processes and outcomes of their workplace actions and practices are productive. Their actions may even fail to coincide with the meaning of their work. Nevertheless, what they do, even if it is nothing, constitutes their activity. Another conception of appropriation is that of Hardering and Will-Zocholl (2020), who create three ideal types of appropriation: perception of one's own possibilities, implementation of those possibilities, and carrying out work according to one's own ideas and expectations. All of these types assume a very positive understanding of appropriation as something that is not ubiquitous in the social reality around us, ignoring the fact that even those who are unable to realize their own ideas fully are nevertheless appropriating work. Thus, I attempt to look beyond a narrow definition of appropriation that is focused on the subjects' feelings of satisfaction with their work and grasp instead worker practices in social contexts that constitute their socialization and thus contribute to forming society.

A study of employees' perceptions around their paid work would appear to call for analysis of subjective experience as portrayed in the responses of interviewees, but in the case of this research, I am interested not only in workers' views on their paid work but also in how their views are embedded in social contexts and have emerged and developed over time. This will be realized by a reconstructive method outlined in the next chapter. Understanding the context and development of their perceptions means going beyond the interviewees' perspectives in offering their own interpretations.

Regina Becker-Schmidt (1983) offers an approach to understanding work from a fundamentally subjective perspective, taking as a starting point workers' human needs in relation to work. According to her, work meets fundamental human needs for three things: activity, recognition, and appropriation. My study takes Becker-Schmidt (1983) into account in that it incorporates the subjective perspectives expressed by employees in interviews about their work; I analyze these narratives using an expanded concept of work appropriation as a comprehensive framework for understanding how the interview responses are embedded in social contexts. As mentioned above, appropriation is not necessarily restricted to the idea of successfully modifying work to make it satisfying. Picking up on Becker-Schmidt's notions of workers' need for recognition and activity, I add another area to understand workers' subjective experience of their labor – namely, use value – and place the analysis of these subjective experiences within a reordered framework using an expanded concept of appropriation with three dimensions: recognition, use value, and activity. In my view, the use value orientation of workers and employees is not the same as their need for recognition, even though some of their recognition originates from customers whose needs have been met. Nevertheless, of the interviewees in this study, some expressed both use value orientation and perceptions of being overlooked or even despised by customers and society at large. Some of the interviewees expressed a strong use value orientation as feelings of self-worth resulting from the knowledge that their work was important – whether or not their customers knew it.

To explain the three dimensions of work appropriation, I will start with *recognition*. Recognition is fundamental for understanding workers' subjectivity because working is a social activity involving interaction with and evaluation by other people. As such, work is fundamental for social integration, and its division connects people and creates mutual dependency (Durkheim 1977 [1930]). Modern societies obtain a higher level of work distribution than do traditional societies because the spectrum and complexity of products and services require specialized production and delivery. The higher the level of labor distribution, the higher the level of mutual dependence. According to

Popitz (2010 [1957]), the division of labor so that tasks are distributed to meet a variety of needs is a necessity for survival.[1] Still, societal integration does not imply equal recognition among industries and professions. Most societies consist of a variety of social positions whose workers and employees receive differing levels of recognition, and those levels, subject to social struggles and debates, are not fixed, but dynamic. Axel Honneth (2010) made reference to Hegel and Durkheim, citing Hegel's two criteria that make workers feel recognized. The first is adequate remuneration, in the form of salaries sufficient for maintaining themselves and their families. The second criterion is enough complexity in their work for employees to feel that the performance of their duties contributes to the general welfare.[2] With this in mind, Hegel points to the need for professional organizations to ensure that high-performing members receive care, public recognition, and respect now and in the future. If these conditions are met, workers are, in Hegel's terms, able to affirm the economic system. Honneth criticizes Hegel's normative presuppositions as disconnected from real economic development and argues that the majority of employees experience working conditions that are more characterized by emptiness than complexity. Hegel's normative claims about the meaningful nature of work are part of his immanent critique of the economic system. However, Hegel points to two important aspects of recognition in relation to work: the monetary aspect and the concept of citizenship. According to Honneth, Durkheim proceeds a step further in offering a criterion for the design of individual activity: individual workers must understand the extent to which their own activity relates cooperatively to the activity of all other workers. Durkheim and Hegel both see this as possible only when workers' own activities and tasks are sufficiently complex and demanding to relate to the rest of society's necessary work in a meaningful way. In the case of Durkheim, then, demands for meaningful work apply to the performance of tasks, not aspects beyond the work itself. In his book *Der arbeitende Souverän*, Honneth (2023) goes a step further by suggesting that tasks and working conditions should be complex to maintain workers' and employees' ability to participate in their societies' endangered democratic processes. While Honneth focuses on the needs of a democracy, my focus remains on work as a social area of distribution of material and symbolic goods such as wages and salaries as well as reputation and prestige. All of these are critical for the social structures created by workers' and employees' ways of perceiving, relating to, and practicing their work.

My understanding of work appropriation ties in with Hegel's and Durkheim's concepts of recognition in that it relates to both remuneration and the design of work's content. In other words, how people perceive and relate to their work is influenced by the recognition they receive for that work. Later I will transfer the dimension of recognition to a more concrete and institutional level of social status as it relates to occupations. But first, I will touch upon the second of the three dimensions of work appropriation: use value.

*Use value* is a relational concept in that it is contained in every product or service that satisfies a human need. One could say that use values are the motor of work since the satisfaction of human needs, whether by interacting with nature or producing things for the purpose of survival or forming social relations, goes to the heart of human activity. Use values relate to recognition in that recognition for complex work is based on the idea of contributing to the welfare of society, as I outlined above. As Hegel and Durkheim would see it, work that does not visibly contribute to societal wealth and well-being does not earn recognition by fellow citizens. However, some kinds of work satisfy needs but earn very little recognition in terms of remuneration and social prestige – for example, running supermarkets. One criterion for recognizing work's contribution to societal wealth or people's well-being is the presence of people who demand it or whose needs are satisfied by the products and services that work produces. It is not necessary for the whole of society to agree about the utility of the product or service. In fact, the utility of individual products and services is socially constructed based on particular interests and contestations along power relations. Nevertheless, some products and services enjoy a broad consensus concerning their utility whereas others do not. Sarah Nies (2015) describes demands concerning work content as an important yet underestimated and underresearched category of the subjective experience of work. She defines demands of the content of work as "work-related demands having to do with the impact of work and ideas about what the meaning and purpose of the occupation are or should be" (Nies 2015: 118). Nies understands the "meaning" of an occupation as a subjective perception of the goal of work. As I pointed out above, this resonates with Anglophone discussions on "the meaning of work." However, the concept of demands around work content goes beyond the personal dimension and embraces aspects of a social dimension embodied in the notion of use value, which is realized only when others use it. This is an example of the differences in sociological approaches to work and labor in the U.S. and Germany as outlined above. Broadly speaking, the German tradition includes more social structures in the analysis of workers' and employees' perceptions of and approaches to work, while the individual – often creative – interpretation and design of occupations forms a large part of the sociology of work in the U.S. Since my objective is to conceptualize workers' and employees' perceptions, practices, and evaluations of their work as socialization, this study is clearly located within the German approach. Various studies in recent years have focused on other demands such as personal development. However, workers and employees raise demands related to work content because their need to earn an income makes work a means to an end, but these demands are not necessarily linked to enjoying one's work. Those who dislike their work or their current place of work may demand a change in the content of their work, but if those demands are not realizable because of working conditions, tension and conflict can result (Nies 2015). Thus, use value constitutes part of work appropriation as people are not indifferent to the content of the work they carry out daily. In fact, being useful seems to be one fundamental way of relating to other people and forming basic social attachments. People depend on each other for survival, so the usefulness of one's work for another person is essential for society. To be of use to others is also a religious aim. In the Christian tradition, being useful to one's neighbor is a practical expression of belief, as illustrated in a song from Johannes Agricola in 1526, during the Reformation: "The right faith, Lord, I mean, You will give to me, To live unto thee, to be of use to my neighbor, To keep thy word." Here, use value is a moral category. Use value also contains an affective dimension. This is not surprising given the importance it obtains for the existence of society. Not being able to be of use to others is source of great suffering and existential crisis in which the meaning of life and social integration are at stake.

In capitalist societies, use value is the substance carrier of exchange value, as Marx points out (1988 [1890]). Marx emphasizes that the exchange value does not contain use value ("Als Gebrauchswerte sind die Waren vor allem verschiedner Qualität, als Tauschwerte können sie nur verschiedner Quantität sein, enthalten also kein Atom Gebrauchswert"; Marx 1988 [1890]: 52). In other words, use value is used as a means of creating profit. Frigga Haug (1999) examines the historical development of use value and its societal significance. Use value is somewhat paradoxical in capitalist societies: it is central and at the same time marginal. With the goal of affluence, not enjoyment, use value is subject to pressure as it is sought everywhere; new use values are created, and the use value of existing products and services expands with the exploration and invention of new characteristics. Thus, use value becomes at the same time the center of capitalist development and a marginal aspect of it. Compared to exchange value, use value loses importance in capitalist developments. This development is important for work appropriation. Working conditions change and increasingly favor profitability over utility. Many changes in employment and work over recent years such as income insecurity impede the fulfillment of demands concerning work content, leading to the suffering of workers, employees and clients, and customers, as I will show later. This is not restricted to work in supermarkets and currently occurs quite acutely in the care sector. But other sectors are affected too, such as banking, in which clerks face pressure to advise customers against their best interests and needs, as Nies (2015) has shown.

Haug's (1999) outline of the historical development from the dominance of use value to the dominance of exchange value contains a second aspect: the use value of labor power ("Arbeitskraft"), which consists of workers' ability not only to create useful products and services, but also to create more value than is necessary for their production (surplus value). This ability lends labor the characteristics of a commodity. Work appropriation depends greatly on the character of work and labor. Whether subjects are working mainly to create and meet use value or whether their labor becomes primarily a use value unto itself constitutes an important difference. In the latter case, workers are reduced to serving as a means of generating profit. A factor that creates ambivalence about workers and their value is the fact that in capitalist societies, people's labor contains both use value and exchange value, resulting in a dynamic in which the exchange value determines the use value. This means that workers and employees find themselves in constant conflict between different orientations and demands. Nies (2015), in a study on the work content of bank clerks and engineers, traces the question of how the relation between use value orientations unfolds in conditions increasingly shaped by rationalization and new forms of governance. The degree of tension depends on the power of corporations to shape working conditions in a way that advances corporate interests in raising profits. According to Stefanie Hürtgen (2021), workers who insist on the societal meaning of their work defend their status as social subjects and reject being reduced to private citizens. Use value makes up a part of work appropriation in terms of design, understanding, and the attitudes toward work content and tasks. In design in particular, the focus is on the struggle between interests directed at satisfying people's needs and creating profits. The design of work content and tasks influences activity, the third column of work appropriation, as I will explain next.

As I have mentioned above, Becker-Schmidt (1983) refers to *activity* from a subjective perspective, as one of three fundamental human needs satisfied by work. To understand activity from an objective perspective, it is useful to draw on the work of Alexej Leontjew (2012 [1975]). He conceptualizes activity as how human beings (in contrast to animals) grow up, orient themselves, live in a society, and contribute to the perpetuation of society. Activity forms "a system with its own structure, its own internal transitions and conversions ('Übergängen und Umwandlungen'), and its own development" (Leontjew 2012 [1975]: 80). Activity is, like recognition and use value, a relational notion. It can never be analyzed in isolation, independent of social relations and life in society. "Despite its diversity, the activity of human individuals is a system enclosed within the system of legal relations ... It is self-evident that the activity of each single person depends on his/her place in society, on living conditions, and on nonreplicable individual circumstances under which it is shaped" (Leontjew 2012 [1975]: 80). The constitutional characteristic of activity is its objectivity in the sense of materiality ("Gegenständlichkeit"). This materiality is twofold. First, it exists independently, and subjects' activity is subordinate to it. Second, it exists as an image or picture ("Abbild") of the object, as a product of reflections of a subject's activity (2012 [1975]: 81). Activity is distinct from behavior because the objects of activity contain general social meanings to which activity refers. Through activity, people become members of society and perpetuate society. They appropriate the general social meanings of objects and thus are able to take part in society at a certain historical level, as Ute Holzkamp-Osterkamp explains (1981 [1975]). Here Leontjew (2012 [1975]) mentions Lewin's "invitational character of things" ("Aufforderungscharakter der Dinge"; 85). "'Activity' becomes 'work' when the individual human being contributes with his or her activity to production and reproduction of the life of society and thus contributes to the advancement of social-historical processes" (Holzkamp-Osterkamp 1981 [1975]: 235). So far, I have emphasized the social content of the objects of activity. But activity also contains an important sub-jective dimension: through interiorization, activity, like consciousness itself, creates subjectivity (Leontjew 2012 [1975]). Leontjew refers to consciousness as co-knowledge (Mit-Wissen) that requires language and is produced by society. In activity, both parts, the objective and the subjective, are interrelated and connected. Without going deeper into psychology, here it is important to underline the significance of activity for work appropriation in that workers must appropriate to perform labor (Leontjew 1975 [1959]). In this study, work appropriation is not understood as a process resulting from success and leading to satisfaction and well-being, but rather as something that takes place during work. Thus, I do not understand appropriation as a positive antithesis of alien-ation. Activity is closely linked with use value as it refers to the work objects' meaning. The object of activity, work content, is dependent upon societal norms for the weight of use value in relation to exchange value.

From a gender perspective, the three columns of work appropriation are clearly male-biased. In terms of the gender divide, this means that women, who carry out most of the unpaid work, are not only relegated to "invisible" work in the private sphere, they are excluded from social integration and considerations of what constitutes sufficient income. Although reproductive work carried out in the so-called private sphere enables productive work in companies and organizations and contributes to societal reproduction on the whole, it is not recognized as such and is treated as something apart from the rest of necessary work. In addition, reproductive work is devalued and not recognized as a series of complex tasks. Thus, recognition is conceptualized in our societies as priv-ileging men and tasks carried out mainly by men. Use value also has gender significance. Women are traditionally assigned tasks heavily loaded with use value. In capitalist societies, use value is generally devalued and seen as count-ing less than exchange value. This weakens women's social positions. The interrelation of the social content of activity with the interiorization leading to subject formation also includes social positioning, which in turn is important for the way an activity is carried out. It makes a difference whether the object of one's activity conveys a meaning that is closely connected to the world or milieu one lives in or whether it conveys a meaning that is distanced from one's living context. Socially dominant groups are more likely to influence the social meanings of objects according to their perspectives and needs. In turn, these objects might be more difficult to deal with for some than for others. In sum: men and women appropriate work under different social conditions, and it is likely that male and female employees differ in their perceptions of paid work.

So far, I have explained the more abstract dimensions of my notion of work appropriation by referring to recognition, use value, and activity. Next, I relate these general dimensions to a more concrete level in order to be able to apply the theoretical concept of work appropriation to empirical analysis of workers and employees' perceptions of work.

To understand how recognition functions as part of work appropriation, it is useful to refer to the *occupation's social status*. This is institutionalized in two ways: by salary and by the classification and prestige of the profession. One basic institution that assigns at least a certain amount of recognition to an occupation is the minimum wage. Occupations that are remunerated at the minimum wage level are generally seen as belonging to the lower end of recognition. Other institutions for establishing salaries and the accompanying recognition are the market and collective agreements. All three institutions involve power relations and implicit social dynamics. Whether an occupation is classified as a profession or not is already the result of a negotiation process. With regard to the occupation this book focuses on, that of supermarket clerks, there is a crucial difference between the U.S. and Germany in how this occupation is viewed. In the U.S. it does not rise to the status of a profession, whereas in Germany it does. After two or three years of systematic vocational training within the dual education system, involving training in both vocational schools and in companies, German supermarket clerks earn an official professional title. A two-year program qualifies the trainee for work as a salesclerk, and three years is required to become a management assistant in a retail business. Vocational education is a period of socialization that contributes to identity formation. In order to answer the research question of how supermarket clerks perceive their work, one must take into account the social status of the work as a professional occupation. Trained professional standards are likely to serve as reference points for expectations of work content. Acquired knowledge and earned competencies may instill feelings of satisfaction if they are deployed in workplaces, but where qualified employees are replaced through automation, this training may contribute to feelings of frustration. Another dimension of the social status of an occupation is the gender with which it is commonly associated. Many occupations are mostly performed either by men or women, and this association impacts its prestige. Generally, "male" occupations are classified higher than "female" occupations. Historically, merchants were primarily men, but over time, clerks began carrying out the tasks formerly performed by merchants, and the occupation became feminized. Losing autonomy went along with increasingly specialized tasks, lower wages, and precarious employment conditions. Nowadays, the occupation of supermarket clerk belongs to the feminized work sphere. However, apprenticeships in this field are selected by many men in Germany. One reason for this might be the prospect of running one's own shop, one of the options open to those choosing a retail career path.

Not only salary but also the categorization of occupations as professions are the products of different evaluations of the complexity of the tasks involved (see, for example, the International Standard of Classification of Occupations by the International Labour Office [2012]). Despite the differences between the countries under focus in this study, the occupation of supermarket clerk is seen as belonging at the lower ends of prestige and gratification scales in both contexts (Carré & Tilly 2017). It is a mostly female occupation situated in the service sector and directed at providing the population with sustenance.

Since the COVID-19 pandemic, another fundamental categorization of occupations has become socially relevant: the question of whether or not these jobs are essential (i.e., system-relevant). In several countries, people working in so-called essential occupations have received applause, and some also received short-term supplements to their salaries. In Germany, parents in system-relevant occupations were also privileged in that public childcare facilities for their children remained open during the pandemic to allow them to work. The category of system relevance certainly relates to the occupation's contribution to general welfare; in the case of supermarket clerks, that contribution consists in providing food to the population. As a result of the pandemic lockdowns, these system-relevant jobs gained a new-found status and recognition from the public. The discrepancy between the change in supermarket clerks' image despite the low wages they continue to receive could have the effect of influencing their work appropriation. Anyone taking up a new line of work already has an idea of the job's perceived social status. Stephan Voswinkel (2015) argues that processes of appropriation are regulated by social institutions. Social institutions such as professions, salaries, vocational degrees, and job titles offer orientation for appropriation and interpretation of the meaning of work. Thus, these institutions connect objective and subjective interpretations of work. Voswinkel concludes that the appropriation of work is not an individual process, but one regulated through institutions and relations of recognition that define the meaning and worth of any occupation. This is obviously a highly contested process in which different interest groups pursue their intentions, and outcomes are highly dependent on power relations.

Use value, the second dimension of work appropriation, manifests mainly in the form of the *tasks and work content* carried out daily. As Nies (2015) has demonstrated, employees raise work content expectations as important motivations for working. Rationalization, automatization, and digitalization are major developments influencing tasks and work content. Because they aim at cheaper production through the more efficient application of human labor, they come with promises of less routine work and more interesting and demanding tasks and work content. However, these promises are often not realized, and workers and employees end up with less complex tasks, as in the case of supermarket clerks. Digitalized ordering systems, for example, replaced counting; obtaining an overview; making decisions based on experience and knowledge of customers; and ordering through lists that are sent by fax, email, or phone. Rationalization strategies in the use of staff diminishes the amount of time staff are available for offering professional customer advice – an example of direct use value fulfillment. The share of tasks that mainly contribute to running the shop increases relative to the share of tasks that demand knowledge about the company's products and internal course of actions. This shift degrades the value and recognition of workers and employees, who are reduced to becoming small cogs in a big machine. Michael Frey (2009) argues radically that in service work, employees no longer appropriate concrete products, but at most create frames of meaning. In the process of increasing the use value of work, people lose any opportunity of applying themselves as they are forced to function as mechanisms for advancing profit interests. Autonomy diminishes, along with possibilities for creative activity. Such developments impact work-subjects in ways I will now explore.

Activity as part of work appropriation leads to subject formation in *work-subjects* (workers and employees). It presumes that human beings are socially formed, but never determined. This means that people are seen as being embedded in societies while also exerting social influence through their individuality and creativity. Activity includes internal modification or alteration, which Leontjew (2012 [1975]) called "Umbau." By this I refer to employees' changed attitudes resulting from work experiences. How these experiences are received and processed relates to work-subjects' living conditions and situations. They must deal on a daily basis with objectivity in several forms, such as material or nonmaterial tasks at work, the conditions under which these tasks are realized, and coworkers and bosses. As workers or employees, people are thrown into social contexts they must make sense of and act in; their situation is one Leontjew (2012 [1975]) compared to that of a newborn child. Whatever the work content is, it confronts work-subjects with society and forces them to actively appropriate new meanings. Through this process of confrontation and interiorization of meanings, the work-subject changes over time, along with working conditions. Activity forms an important dimension of work appropriation as it means working, carrying out tasks, dealing with colleagues and customers, producing, and reproducing. The ways people work inform the ways in which they perceive their work.

I end this discussion by emphasizing four main reasons for understanding my theoretical concept of work appropriation in terms of use value. *First, appropriation is involved in any kind of work.* According to my working definition, appropriation is not the opposite of alienation.[3] Appropriation is involved no matter the tasks or work environment. Even alienating working conditions and tasks require a subjective approach to work in which tasks are executed and competencies are put to use. Work-subjects facing useless or meaningless tasks must find strategies for performing those tasks, whether by accepting, transforming, or ignoring them. This process entails developing subjective attitudes toward and ways of handling work activities. Thus, appropriation is a necessary aspect of work and a survival tool in any workplace. *Second, appropriation is a human response to being in the world.* This is an anthropological assumption. It follows from the observation that human beings must actively engage with the world to survive and acquire abilities through activity. Through creativity and self-expression, human beings coin and change things through appropriation. Appropriation is therefore a useful tool for analyzing work-subjects because the desire for appropriation leads to unlimited ways of dealing with work, according to the subjects' ideas, needs, life circumstances, and experiences. *Third, work appropriation always includes both social and subjective levels.* Humans are social beings who need interaction. Appropriation is a social and subjective act because activity is carried out by individuals. All three dimensions of work appropriation – recognition, use value, and activity – involve objective and subjective levels. Their analysis, then, should take place at the intersection of the macro and micro levels where the interplay between structures and subjectivity takes place. *Fourth, appropriation is not limited to work that is successful or fulfilling.* Rather than use the concept of appropriation to contrast with alienation in the workplace, appropriation as I use it has a wider meaning. However, this does not exclude the analysis of conditions that enable workers and employees to work in meaningful ways, producing and offering services that meet needs and enjoy recognition.

Finally, I want to point out what does *not* belong to my working definition of work appropriation. First, it is not the same as what some studies have called workers' consciousness. Studies on workers' consciousness focus on perceptions of work situations and social and political positions (e.g., Popitz et al. 1972 [1957]; Kern & Schumann 1977; Dörre et al. 2013). In contrast, the concept of work appropriation focuses more on how actively dealing with work forms workers and employees as subjects. Second, the current debate on the subjectivization of work, in the double sense of extended access to labor power and of internalized expectations of self-realization in work, differs from my concept of work appropriation in that the debate on subjectivization is restricted to a certain discourse on employees' requirements and purposes, while work appropriation is much broader and open to any content. Also, in many studies on subjectivization, employees are conceived as carrying out socially dominant expectations and thus as being mainly receptive and less active in dealing with work. The concept of work appropriation allows the analysis to take into account the self-will of workers and employees. Third, the concept of work appropriation goes far beyond the subjective views of workers and employees because it includes the reconstruction of practices.

To sum up: the concept of work appropriation enables us to systematically conceptualize individual modes of development and ways of becoming a subject in relation to working conditions. A comparative perspective of work appropriation in different societies allows for the normative evaluation of national systems of education and work by offering answers to questions about the design of current conditions for work appropriation.

## NOTES

1.  Popitz explains his point with the classic example of being shipwrecked on an island. Tasks such as building huts, gathering fruit, and taking care of children and the elderly must be distributed in order for all to survive. As a result of this distribution, everyone becomes an expert at a particular task, and this in turn leads to stabilization of the distribution of work.
2.  As I will later explain, general welfare is linked to the use value of products and services.
3.  In this respect my concept of appropriation differs from those that only deal in ideal circumstances, addressing only a utopian, emancipated, just society. My definition also requires a broad approach to human activity as Tätigkeit or Handeln. In this respect I follow critical psychology, which includes social dimensions in the analysis of mental processes. My aim is to link my empirical study on supermarket clerks to social analysis (Gesellschaftsanalyse).

# 4. Methods and sample

In this chapter, I first present the data and methods of analysis and then report the results. For the purposes of collecting and understanding subjective perceptions of work among the study's interviewees, I used a qualitative research design. Qualitative methods allowed for the gathering of open-ended information that was not limited to the researchers' perspectives and therefore could lead to unexpected insights.

I start with a description of how I approached the field and recruited interviewees. After describing the sample, I explain the methods used for data collection. Finally, I explain the methods used to interpret the data.

## APPROACHING THE FIELD AND RECRUITMENT PRACTICES FOR INTERVIEWEES

First, I decided to approach all kinds of supermarkets, ranging from discounters to high-end stores. I was interested in all kinds of work experiences in different kinds of shops belonging to a range of companies. Operating under the assumption that work appropriation is tightly connected to work environment, I was interested in finding out about a variety of different work settings. For that reason, each one of the interviewees I engaged works in a different supermarket. Being unfamiliar with supermarkets in the U.S., I started visiting a wide variety of shops to collect impressions of differences in products, prices, designs, and atmospheres. To recruit interviewees, I employed various strategies. My objective was to interview a wide variety of clerks, so I employed purpose sampling (Bryman 2016). In the U.S., I visited different supermarkets, asking for permission to put postings on blackboards and in break rooms. Many supermarkets did not allow any postings inside. In those cases I placed the postings outside, on lampposts and other objects. Often these postings were removed quickly thereafter. In general, service desk personnel did not welcome my inquiries about the possibility of interviewing staff. In one case, I was even escorted outside by a shop's security employee. I also placed a call for interviewees on Craig's List, an internet platform for various exchanges, including job searches, and I visited an adult learning center to seek interviewees. In Germany, a student aide posted in different supermarkets. This process was rather straightforward and did not meet with opposition. I also approached a labor union official who offered contacts to members of the works councils. In addition, in both countries I employed snowball sampling by asking colleagues and friends if they knew potential interviewees, and I received some contacts through that approach. While it is important to ask for systematic gaps that might go along with this sampling strategy (Kruse 2015), the group of interviewees it yielded was significantly heterogeneous, even though the majority worked in lower-level positions.

## THE SAMPLE

Overall, I conducted 55 interviews with supermarket clerks plus one interview with two vocational educators for supermarket clerks in Germany who provided background information but were not otherwise included in my analysis. Thirty-five of the interviews took place in the U.S. and 20 in Germany. The interviewees consisted of 30 men and 25 women. This meant that men were overrepresented in my sample compared to their percentages among supermarket clerks. Twenty-three of the interviewees were black or people of color, and 31 were white; one person's race was unknown since the interview took place via the phone, and I did not ask. The ages of my interviewees ranged from 20 to 61 years. Apart from American and German nationalities, the interviewees represented nine more, hailing from Cape Verde, Chile, El Salvador, Ethiopia, Guatemala, Haiti, Kenya, Portugal, and Turkey. Their employment positions ranged from shopping cart retriever to shop manager, but the vast majority were cashiers and salesclerks. In the U.S., most interviewees worked part time, and only six were employed full time. In Germany, eight were employed full time. The supermarkets ranged from discounters to high-end grocers. In Germany, the interviewees included an employee of a cooperative, nonprofit, organic supermarket.

## DATA COLLECTION

During my stay in the U.S., I received a research ethics approval for conducting my study. All interviewees signed a consent form. Interviewees were offered compensation of $30 per hour in the U.S. and 20 Euros plus travel expenses in Germany. Apart from one interviewee who did not accept the compensation and declared that she saw the interview as an opportunity for practicing English, all of them accepted the compensation. All were asked whether they consented to be recorded, and almost all agreed. Two interviewees in the U.S. did not want to be recorded, but one of them agreed after seeing how much I had to write. The length of the interviews varied from about half an hour to two-and-a-half hours. Generally, the interviews in Germany took longer, probably due to descriptions of vocational education and longer work experiences. I took notes during all of the interviews and often afterward to remember

*Table 1*        *Overview of all interviews in the U.S.*

| No. | Pseudonym of interviewee, age, gender, color, nationality | Place of work, hours, job title, $ |
|---|---|---|
| 1 | Miguel Hernandez, 32, male, person of color, El Salvador | Shaws, 16h, shop assistant, produce |
| 2 | Oscar López, 36, male, person of color, Guatemala | Market Basket, full time, clerk |
| 3 | Maria Alvarado, 61, female, person of color, Chile | CVS, full time, photo technician |
| 4 | Steven Hill, 30, male, White, U.S. | Trader Joe's, 30h, wine section, $16.30 |
| 5 | Tracey Nigel, 34, female, Black, U.S. | Food samples, $15–18 |
| 6 | Ben Johnson, 32, male, Black, U.S. | Stop & Shop, 16h, grocery clerk, $12.50 |
| 7 | Robert Smith, 23, male, Black, U.S. | Stop & Shop, 20–25h, deli department clerk, $9.55 |
| 8 | Baptiste Laguerre, 32, male, Black, Haiti | Star Market, 42h but officially employed part time, $9 |
| 9 | Debbie Miller, 50, female, Black, U.S. | Market Basket, 25h, cashier |
| 10 | Victor Mejia, 43, male, person of color, El Salvador | Star Market, 12h, bakery clerk, $10.50 |
| 11 | Agwé Jean, 49, female, Black, Haiti | Shaw's, 32 or 34h, cashier, $11.75 |
| 12 | Kokebe Tesfaye, 29, female, Black, Ethiopia | Leverage Market, 28h, cashier, $9 |
| 13 | Carla Silva, 27, female, Black, Cape Verde | Whole Foods, 30h, produce |
| 14 | Catherine Taylor, 57, female, Black, U.S. | Trader Joe's, 37.5h, crew member |
| 15 | Peter Swing, 28, male, White, U.S. | Shaw's Star Market |
| 16 | Nikoleta Papadopoulos, 22, female, White, U.S. | Shaw's, 20–25h, bagging, cashier, service desk position, $8.50/8.75 |
| 17 | Nyala Girma, age not disclosed, female, Black, Ethiopia | Star Market |
| 18 | Robert Clark, 23, male, White, U.S. | Stop & Shop, 22h, self-checkout cashier, $9.30 |
| 19 | Joseph Cadet, 37, male, Black, Haiti | Whole Foods, 20–30h, produce market, $11.50 |
| 20 | John Williams, 52, male, White, U.S. | Roch's Brothers, full-time, grocery associate, $21 |
| 21 | James Larrington, age not disclosed, male, White, Down syndrome, U.S. | Star Market |
| 22 | Vasiliki Papadopoulos, 47, female, White, U.S. | Target, 21-22h, $11 |
| 23 | Charles West, age not disclosed, male, Black, U.S. | Foodies in 2008, $8.50 and Johnnie's Foodmaster in 2010/2011, 30h, $9.00 |
| 24 | Izara Tadesse, 44, female, Black, Ethiopia | Trader Joe's, 39h, crew member: cashier |
| 25 | Anthony Miller, 27, male, White, U.S. | Thomas supermarket, Weis supermarket, Deluca's, Walgreens |
| 26 | Ava Smith, 50, female, person of color, U.S. | Stop & Shop 2010–12, 30h, cashier, $9 |

| No. | Pseudonym of interviewee, age, gender, color, nationality | Place of work, hours, job title, $ |
|---|---|---|
| 27 | Salee Perodin, 37, female, Black, Haiti | Whole Foods, deli department, then cook, full time, $12.10 |
| 28 | Pedro Sousa, 48, male, White, Portugal | 7-Eleven, two shops, one: 25h and the other 21h, clerk/sales associate, $11 in one shop and $10 in the other |
| 29 | Brian Mwangi, 44, male, Black, Kenya | Whole Foods, cashier/customer service in 2008, $15 |
| 30 | Thomas Berry, 37, male, Black, U.S. | Stop & Shop, merchandiser, load and dock, $13 |
| 31 | Andrew Harris, 49, male, White, U.S. | Trader Joe's, almost 40h, crew member |
| 32 | Khalan Wilson, 29, male, Black, U.S. | Stop & Shop, 15h, cart retriever, $11.50 |
| 33 | Jane Wood, 60, female, White, U.S. | Whole Foods: cashier, $6.00 Deluca's: cashier, $9.00 |
| 34 | Rose Kerrington, 42, female, Black, U.S. | Wegman's, 20–29h, $11.45 |
| 35 | Alexander Jones, 46, male, U.S. | Star Market, 36h, $9.25 |

special incidents, observations, questions, and ideas. The interviewees were explicitly offered the chance to skip certain questions without giving responses and also to retreat from the interviews if at any point they felt uncomfortable. Several of the interviewees did not want to say how much they earned. None of the interviewees asked me to delete the interview. Since I was interested in specific aspects of their work, such as their training and vocational education, work atmosphere, their perceptions of their job's social status, and so forth, I decided to conduct the interviews using a guideline. This also enabled me to compare interviewees' answers. At the same time, I wanted to leave room for them to bring up topics I might not have considered. Also, to better understand their answers, I needed to know something about their biographies. Therefore, the guidelines included open-ended questions. I began with an open question about their life histories and ended with an open question about whether they thought any information was missing or needed to be added. Questions on specific topics such as training and vocational education were also posed in an open-ended way. During the whole interview, interviewees were invited to explain their subjective views. The guidelines were structured in a (chrono) logical order, in which, for example, questions related to training and voca-tional education were placed near the beginning and were followed by ques-tions on working conditions, work experiences, and reflections and evaluations concerning work. The interviewees were encouraged to offer examples or relate incidents to illustrate or provide concrete explanations. In general, I used the guidelines as a memory aid (Menz & Nies 2018). Often, interviewees had

*Table 2*      *Overview of all interviews in Germany*

| No. | Pseudonym of interviewee, age, gender* | Vocational education | Employment position and company where longest employed |
|---|---|---|---|
| 1 | Simone Koch, 38, female | Trained retail saleswoman (3 years) Tengelmann | Trained retail saleswoman at Netto |
| 2 | Thomas Schmidt, 26, male | Trained retail salesman (3 years) Rewe | Trained retail salesman at Rewe |
| 3 | Angelika Nemitz, 22, female | None | Temporary aide at Edeka |
| 4 | Tobias Emons, 28, male | Trained retail salesman (3 years) Lidl | Trained retail salesman at Lidl |
| 5 | Nils Hasel, 31, male | Trained retail salesman (3 years) Netto | Trained retail salesman at Edeka (Simmel) |
| 6 | Andreas Meiners, 26, male | Trained retail salesman (3 years) Netto | Branch manager at Aldi |
| 7 | Kerstin Keller, 47, female | Originally furniture salesperson (2 years), later organic food salesperson | Branch manager at Verbrauchergemeinschaft (a cooperative) |
| 8 | Nicole Binz, 20, female | Trained retail saleswoman (3 years) Lidl | Trained retail saleswoman at Rewe |
| 9 | Max Heinemann, 23, male | None | Fixed-term skilled retail salesman at Verbrauchergemeinschaft (cooperative) |
| 10 | Stefan Häuser, 24, male | None | Minijobber (450 Euros) temporary aide at Verbrauchergemeinschaft (cooperative) |
| 11 | Sabine von Busch, 25, female | None | Temporary aide at Kaufland |
| 12 | Christine Wagner, 32, female | Trained retail saleswoman (3 years) | Trained retail saleswomen at Verbrauchergemeinschaft (cooperative) |
| 13 | Asiye Kaya, 28, female | Social assistant (2 years) | Skilled retail saleswomen at Pfennigland |
| 14 | Jochen Hilmer, 25, male | Master in wood technology | Biomarkt |
| 15 | Axel Conradi, 56, male | Skilled tradesman in telecommunication (2.5 years) | Allkauf, later Real, workers' council member |
| 16 | Stefanie Moser, 50, female | Skilled tradeswoman in postal system (2 years) | Rewe, deputy member of the workers' council |

| No. | Pseudonym of interviewee, age, gender* | Vocational education | Employment position and company where longest employed |
|---|---|---|---|
| 17 | Kerstin Jansen, 49, female | Skilled saleswoman (2 years), after reunification, further education to become floor manager at Reichelt, later further education to sell Lotto | Part time at Edeka, member of the workers' council since 2010 |
| 18 | Markus Willert, 45, male | Trained retail salesman in electronic shop (3 years) | Exempted member of the workers' council; otherwise branch manager at Netto |
| 19 | Wolfgang Gerke, 33, male | Skilled electronic technician for devices and systems (3.5 years), early retiree, depression and social phobia | Early retiree, working poor receiving top-up benefit with 60 hours/month at Edeka |
| 20 | Gabriele Sibelius, 48, female | Skilled tree nurse (two years) | Skilled retail saleswoman at Lidl |

*Note:* * All interviewees were White and held German citizenship; one had Turkish parents.

already answered questions from the guidelines that I had not yet asked. The interviewees were thus able to emphasize aspects according to their own priorities and interpretations of what was most relevant. In turn, this enabled deeper insights into their perceptions. The course of the interviews was characterized by a listening-oriented attitude, in which interviewees could speak without interruption. Follow-up questions were posed to clarify what had been said and/or to follow up on topics that interviewees emphasized either implicitly or explicitly. This allowed for an acknowledgment of the relative importance they gave to different topics ("Relevanzsetzungen," Kruse 2015: 212).

The locations of the interviews varied according to interviewees' preferences, ranging from cafés and parks to their homes or my office. Three took place on the phone. The period of data collection started in 2011 and ended in 2019. All interviews have been transcribed by professional services. The transcriptions indicated breaks, laughs, sighs, and other nonverbal utterances.

## DATA PROCESSING AND INTERPRETATION

The mixed character of the collected material, consisting of answers to guided questions and the respondents' open narrations, required a mix of data processing and interpretation. First, I started by compiling information on the interviewees' life courses and arranging it in chronological order (Rosenthal 2008). As a result, I created a CV for each interviewee. I used the CVs for later interpretations of assertions by relating the statements to aspects of the respondents' life courses, individual life circumstances, and biographies as a whole. The information on life courses was generated by an open initial question and depended almost completely on the interviewee's (un)conscious decisions about what to tell me. In a second step, I collected sections and assertions according to topics I was interested in. I did not use software as I wanted to be able to sort out the narrations without the use of a search of codes or rigidly applied categories. This led to several readings of all of the interviews, which in turn led to a familiarity with and deeper understanding of the data. Some sections and assertions were categorized according to more than one topic as they overlapped. For example, when interviewees talked about their training devaluing its quality, the remark pertained to both vocational education and social status. During this categorization, I marked and extracted important sections in which interviewees had given a vehement statement or evaluation, an emotional account, or another form of key content. These were later used for detailed analysis (Lucius-Hoene & Deppermann 2004). Single words, ways of speaking, omissions, and the like were analyzed and then referred to the general analysis of the whole interview, which was structured in themes and sequences. In some cases, I listened again to the recordings of these sections for a deeper impression of what the respondent wanted to express. Finally, I condensed the interviewees' themes. By this, I refer to a kind of individual "melody" of each interviewee, consisting in a dominant evaluation of his or her work, in most cases not even consciously or explicitly spelled out, which I sifted out from the empirical material. These themes are often emotional, containing in some cases a sense of deep disillusionment or resignation – or expressing satisfaction with the arrangement of work in their lives. While these formulations of interviewees' themes are a product of interpretation, they also served as a basis for interpreting selected assertions in relation to a personalized background. Other reference points used for a deeper understanding of the interviewees' narrations and answers were information on their gender, ethnicity, and nationalities, and social contexts as well as biographies and life circumstances. This information was used for a reconstruction of the interviewees' narratives. As mentioned in the introduction, gender inequality is still prevalent in both the U.S. and in Germany, and in both contexts women take on more unpaid labor in the home than men. Consequently, women are often employed part time and have fewer career opportunities than men. In the retail sector, which is characterized by low wages, women are overrepresented, and the share of workers who are migrants is higher than in other sectors that offer better pay. In the U.S., where individuals and their families by and large pay for studies beyond high school, chances for obtaining college degrees are lower for migrants than for natives, whose families are better positioned to save money for their children's higher education. Additionally, as some of the responses quoted in this study attest, migrants without legal residency are a vulnerable group exposed to discrimination that takes forms such as unfavorable work hours. Reconstruction asks for the foundations, the structures that contribute to the creation of a phenomenon. Rosenthal (2008) describes reconstruction as the "rule" of materialization of life history. According to Kruse (2015), reconstruction refers to the "how," while content analysis refers to the "what." For my purpose of understanding how supermarket clerks perceive their work, I needed both the "what" and the "how." The overall aim of this study was to find out *what* supermarket clerks say about their work, but at the same time, I am always interested in *how* their assertions are presented. Both content and the process of creating that content are explained in the results, and the supermarket clerks' perceptions of their work are coupled with information on their biographies. My inquiries concerning social status, use value, and activity evoked responses that I grouped according to emerging patterns of similarities and differences. These groups are presented in the following chapters.

Finally, I want to mention that several of these interviews were discussed by a small group of social scientists to share and discuss impressions.

# 5.   How the social status of the occupation impacts work appropriation

Work appropriation with regard to recognition and the social status of the occupation varies largely between the U.S. and Germany. While it seems that in the U.S. supermarket jobs are largely perceived as being for those who are located at the social margins or performing entry-level or temporary jobs, in Germany the position of supermarket clerk is one that many workers find satisfactory. People do have images and ideas they associate with their jobs. An occupation or job has a "name," an image. Societies evaluate jobs explicitly, through professional training or vocational education curricula, or through regulations related to compensation. Jobs are discussed in the media, particularly when issues arise such as scandals involving work conditions, as occurred in recent times (Glaubitz 2019; Oxfam 2019; Bosse 2022). During the COVID-19 pandemic, supermarket occupations were deemed "essential," and clerks received praise for their work – although mainly symbolically, not materially (e.g., through increased wages and salaries). Workers and employees are aware of public discourse on occupations and jobs, and they relate it to their own experience in forming perceptions of their work.

Generally, in both countries, the occupation of supermarket clerk is regarded as a lower-end job. It belongs to the service industry and generally entails, as Vallas et al. (2009) have pointed out (see Chapter 2), "doing deference." In service work such as supermarket jobs, women are overrepresented, a sign of the low social status and modest wages associated with such positions. This has not always been the case. From a historical perspective, sales work has been degraded, in large part because of automation and rationalization. Consequently, this kind of work now receives less recognition because it has become less secure and more output-oriented, as Voswinkel and Wagner (2013) have pointed out. Features of subordination, such as nametags, are common (Ehrenreich 2011 [2001]). However, unlike in Germany, in the U.S. work in a supermarket is not categorized as a profession that requires vocational training. Its status therefore differs widely in the two countries, even though in Germany supermarket professionals are positioned at the lower end of the occupational scale. This difference leads to significant disparities in the subject formation of supermarket clerks in the two countries.

At the one end of the spectrum, supermarket clerks feel they are looked down upon. "That you didn't go to school to get an education to get a better job that paid more or that you didn't aspire for anything more in life; it's just really looked [down] upon ... And the thing is where I work strangely enough it's a lot of non-English speaking, they barely speak any English so it's kind of ...," states Vasiliki Papadopoulos, 47 years old, a daughter of Greek immigrants who has been working for Target for six years. In her quote, a common topic is raised: not only are those with little formal education referred to dismissively, but they are also blamed for their difficulties. Blaming people, often immigrants, with low social status for their situation is a coping strategy in which observers free themselves from acting against a social system that denies people opportunities. The fact that many non-English-speaking people work as supermarket clerks and that this occupation forms a typical area for migrants' jobs is shared by Miguel Hernández, a 32-year-old man from El Salvador, working in Shaws and living in the U.S. for the last ten years. In his view this fact is not related to working in a low-wage sector, but he still points to the circumstance that many migrants – upon obtaining high school and academic qualifications – still end up in low-wage jobs in the U.S.: "Like I said, people in the store keep a low profile and the people from here, from this country, people work in this market and they don't have a lot of education, they don't even have ... high school and when they look at you, you come from [another] country, probably with a little more education and they can't understand, probably you don't speak English very well, but you have a little more ... ."

This resonates with the account of Maria Alvarado, an immigrant from Chile. She is 61 years old and studied administration in Santiago de Chile, where she worked in a leading position. Over the last 16 years she has lived in the U.S. and has worked for seven years in CVS. She complains about her coworkers:

> I don't like the work team, the people. No I don't like it. No. And I find that people have a low level of education, so that's why they're like that, right? So, people do not have, eh, interest in anything, the only thing they are interested in is working, working, going shopping, go shopping, and what else? And that's their life. Ah, go to a restaurant, a good restaurant, but no ... People do not have another interest. I am unable to talk about a book ... And this frustrates me, because, no ... no ... no ... I can't. Because if I would be in another company where people are much more educated, obtain more knowledge, I could learn. This makes me happy. But here I can't, because I think people are vapid, no ... they don't have ... very little culture, not a lot of culture.[1]

"It is an entry job. It's not like considered like a high-end job," states Brian Mwangi, a 44-year-old black man from Kenya working in Whole Foods. Most interviewees in the U.S. refer to the job as one that is for people without education, resonating with the comments made by Maria Alvarado.

Some interviewees point out that not only is the occupation considered an entry-level job, it also offers no opportunities to develop. As Ava Smith, a 50-year-old woman of color working at Stop & Shop, puts it, referring to people's views on supermarket clerks:

> Yes and they just probably feel like they are not educated. They don't have many choices so they just work there for those reasons ... You just feel like you're a cashier and that's what you're going to be unless you get an education and move on to something different but I feel like if you're a cashier, like that's what you're going to be doing, there's no opportunity. Very few may move up and go into corporate or something like that but the majority ... that's what you're going to be at. You're going to be a cashier; there's not a lot of room for growth.

In other words, it is perceived as a dead-end job, and people working there are written off. This is a heavy load for supermarket clerks in the U.S. to bear.

While some interviewees explain the low status of supermarket work by pointing to the lack of an education requirement in the U.S., others point to the content of the work itself. Jane Wood, a white, 60-year-old psychologist who worked in her late twenties and early thirties in Whole Foods and Deluca's, remembers: "I think that when you work in a store like Whole Foods or Deluca's there's nothing really to say about [your job] because all you're doing is scanning food. And then you give the money and give the receipts. So what is there to say? There's nothing to say. I mean you're not going to go to a party and say to somebody, 'Oh I sold a really beautiful apple.' You're just not going to say that."

As these quotes from the U.S. reflect, an occupation's prestige is tied to both the education it requires and the possibility of learning and growing on the job. When an occupation entails the performance of few tasks, or only simple and repetitive ones, little value is attached to it. One could argue with Hegel that professional associations are needed to ensure that jobs have a certain level of complexity to them. Moreover, the essential nature of this work in relation to feeding the population does not appear to enhance its recognition among the public. At the other end of the spectrum of responses about recognition for supermarket clerks, German interviewees reflect the fact that work in a supermarket is an accepted profession. But even so, it is not a prestigious one.

In this chapter, I present very different pictures of subjectivity formation among supermarket clerks. These pictures are informed by perceptions of the occupation's social status. As the occupation's social status differs between the U.S. and Germany, patterns of perceptions differ along the countries too.

In the U.S. one pattern I discerned in the interview responses was that of the "unsettled clerk," unable to settle into a job conferring low social status and perceived as temporary and unsuitable for a permanent career. While working at this job, many of these employees find themselves constantly rejecting it and imagining themselves in the position for the short term only. In another pattern, some supermarket clerks deal with the low recognition of their work by pointing to its instrumental nature in serving an important purpose or function. A third identified pattern in the U.S. that functioned as a strategy for dealing with the low recognition associated with the job is a personal story centered on a lack of opportunity. These three patterns are embedded in the social context of the U.S., where the absence of vocational education for retail jobs means that work in this sector is devoid of any professional status. In Germany, where supermarket clerk is an accepted profession, people are able to settle into their jobs and work for years with satisfaction. They are conscious of the generally low prestige of their work, but this does not lead to rejection of their occupation because they can still feel that their profession is socially accepted and can serve as a path to meaningful work.

## PATTERNS OF SUBJECT FORMATION IN RELATION TO LOW RECOGNITION

### The Unsettled Clerk

The unsettled clerk has been working for many years in supermarkets while emphasizing that his[2] work is transitional. Because this is a "bad job," a low-wage, low-status position, he does not identify with his occupation and aspires to leave. Nevertheless, he remains. This causes a sense of tension and unrest that prevents him from feeling settled in his career. Here are two life histories of unsettled supermarket clerks.

### Ben Johnson

I meet Ben Johnson at a metro station in a Boston suburb. He is a 32-year-old black man. Johnson was born in 1983 in what is now considered a safe and diverse neighborhood in Boston. He grew up with his sister and parents and has never left the U.S. "My whole passion is I want to be a writer," he says at the beginning of the interview. He started writing at the age of nine. "So I went to school with that in mind and that's why I took liberal arts," he continues. He initially wanted to move out of the state and go to college, but he decided to stay and study online to save money. He obtained a BA in Liberal Arts from a private college. Johnson has worked for 14 years at the Stop & Shop. "I went over to Stop & Shop and it looked very interesting. I said, 'Okay, maybe I should just walk in and apply for a job.' And so I went in, applied for a job, I went for the interview and that's it and I was offered a job. And that's how I started. I just walked in, applied and, you know, got a job." Johnson has always worked part time, but he started with 30 hours a week and was cut down to 16 hours after the financial crisis hit the company in 2009. He was hired

> right before Christmas, it was, like Christmas Eve. The supermarket was packed to the brim. I didn't know what I was doing and, like I said, I was hired on the spot and then I was put out on the floor to start working as a bagger and I got confused about what I was doing. It was extremely complex, like it was crazy. But as soon as I got the hang of it, I started bagging, when I got the hang of how the job is and what my duties were, then it just came naturally to me. I basically knew how to bag, which is easy to do. It started off intense but I got the hang of it throughout the day.

Later, he was transferred to the file maintenance department, "which is all the technical responsibilities of the store, like file work, like filing, scanning prices, putting up price tags, making signs." He didn't stay there either but went to stocking general merchandise. For a brief time, Johnson worked as a "CEO clerk," "which is I was seeing the whole store and order products and check products to see if they're damaged or just doing inventories." The company kept assigning him different workplaces. So he got transferred again, this time to the natural foods department. "So that's where I work now. And then my hours have just steadily been cut down from there." Johnson faces existential problems: "I only work 16 hours a week which is not enough to get by. It's like my pay check goes to my landlord, so I'm really hoping ... I mean, if I could get more hours, I would really love to do so. I mean, 35 hours is enough for me." What was originally meant to be a job for getting through college is now a job he needs to survive.

> I went to school and I needed a job to pay my way through school, and this was the only job that was really convenient for me. And it was, kind of, like a safety-net almost, it was a backup, so I decided to just stay and just deal with it until I get out of college and find something better. But I got out of college and I'm still here, only because I have a lot of school loans to pay off.

Generally, obtaining a college degree is seen as a way of getting away from low-paid and low-prestige jobs, but for many Americans this ends up being a trap. Many stay in low-paid jobs to pay off their student loans.

> I got my degree for myself because I wanted it, it was for my benefit. It wasn't because I wanted it for Stop & Shop. Before I got my degree I was already working for Stop & Shop, my degree is more like an attribute so that when I quit Stop & Shop and I find another job I can have something that employers will look at and say 'Oh, you went to college, you have more skills other than working in retail.' So that's why I wanted my degree, so I can venture out and find other jobs.

Strikingly, Johnson is not seeking another job. We talked about the possibility of working elsewhere, where he might get more weekly hours and a higher salary than $12.50 an hour. "I'm conflicted when it come[s] to the money and things like that. I feel like even though I would probably get paid more money, I feel like I just don't want to work at another supermarket right now because I just don't want to work for another retail chain. I want to broaden my horizons. I want to pursue other career choices." It seems Johnson feared he might feel more pulled into the world of retail if he switched stores and earned a higher wage. Staying at his inadequate job may have struck him as safer in terms of getting away someday, getting out of retail work altogether. From the outside, this appeared to be an irrational decision.

> My parents are really urging me to do something else. They're always asking me, when are you going to quit Stop & Shop? You've been there for years and they're not giving you any promotions. I've been here for 14 years now and I've been in this stagnant state where I'm not getting any promotions, my benefits are being taken away and my parents are kind of wondering, when are you going to leave and what are you going to be doing? I agree with them, because I don't plan to stay at Stop & Shop. I've never planned to stay there. I just only stayed there to support my way through college.

His childhood dream of becoming a writer is still very present. "I'm working on a novel right now and that takes up the majority of my time, and my whole … I'm trying to venture into the field of writing. That's my prospect, that's my goal, is to be a writer and to live as a writer. That way I can quit Stop & Shop. I don't have to work all these odd jobs and I can start my career doing what I love still. So that's my purpose, you know?" Johnson's interview resonates with Brose's (1983) findings (see Chapter 2) on workers with biographies characterized by continuity and by precarious and threatened stability, tending to focus on the consequences of strains rather than the reasons for them. Johnson cannot settle into his job as a supermarket clerk. It is an occupation he has always excluded from his life as one not meeting his middle-class expectations given his liberal arts degree. When I asked him how likely it was that he would leave Stop & Shop, his face fell. I could see his shock at the thought that he might be there for a very long time still.

## Victor Mejia

Victor Mejia is an immigrant from El Salvador. He immigrated to the U.S. when he was 15 years old. He lived for three years in a town in Massachusetts and later moved to Cambridge, Massachusetts. He says about El Salvador, "we had a civil war going on over there," and for his schooling, this meant "I lost three years without going to school over there, so when I came here I came to a lower grade because of the time that I lost. So until … Sorry sort of … Long story shorter, I ended up finishing high school at 20 years old." Back then, he already worked full time at a hospital cafeteria while attending high school. For Mejia, it is essential to support himself and live separately from his family, parts of which are still living in the town where he lived when he first arrived in the country. His family members do not accept his homosexuality, so he lives independently from them.

> Reason for it … One of the main reasons for it maybe is none of their concerns. Because I'm okay and they don't agree with me and I say they don't want part of me and I just needed to be a man. I mean because I … Well they love me. I can sense that but they don't … There's a part of me that they don't accept. They don't like me and therefore I have to … I don't want to bother them for favors like that. So I have to go on my own and try to do better for my own. And be strong about it and don't let that … So (inaudible) I'm alone is something is a sensitive issue. I don't want to bother them. I don't (background noise). And I don't want it thrown in my face the aggravation, the rejection that I will get from them. So that's why I decided to do everything on my own. And I've (inaudible) as much as I've been able to.

He seldom visits his family, but he has gotten airfares for two family members on two occasions since living in the U.S., and sometimes he pays their utility bills to help them out. Hurt feelings and distance have affected his relationship with family members. After leaving high school, he got another job in the hospital, in the billing department. Since then he has worked two jobs. He switched from the cafeteria to working in Star Market. In the interview he recalls that having dealt with food previously seemed to qualify him for becoming a supermarket clerk. Upon being hired, he was shown a video with a group of four or five other new hires.

> The orientation took place about, maybe two hours because we needed to watch a video of the regulations of the company … of their regulations, of their policies when it comes to … You know whether you see somebody stealing. What would you do? And what are the procedures to take and things like that in general. Safety you know of the equipment. How to greet the people. What else is there? Mainly that was as far as I remember, to tell you the truth.

It is mainly the way customers greet him, or rather do not greet him, that allows Mejia to experience the general disregard the public has for his job.

> I mean I've been ignored so many times when I say hello I mean which is fine. I mean that's (overspeaking). Customers, I mean in this country, seems like people don't have time to say hello and … You know … Which is fine I mean you know. It's something that they ask us to do. And in most cases we forget because we feel like fools saying hello to people … Or pretend they didn't even quite see you (overspeaking) wasn't there.

At the time of the interview, Mejia is 43 years old. He hasn't gone to college yet, but this is what he wants to do. "So I'm kind of leaving that place. Not yet. But that's my goal. To leave. I mean I like it yes. But it's not something that I want to do for the rest of my days." Mejia wants to go to college part time. "I can't do a full-time. It's not possible." He wants to study to become an accountant. For Mejia, leaving seems like a distant prospect. The main reason for this might be that he is very tired. Since he was a teenager, he has worked two jobs. Over the years, he has already reduced the number of hours from seventy to over fifty a week. Still, he leaves at about 5:30 in the mornings and returns home at about 11 o'clock in the evenings. Apart from working, there is not a lot left in his life. Asked about any activities apart from work, he answers:

> My personal life? You see to tell you the truth ... I hate to tell you the truth but right now I think I got very burned out from working way too much because ... I hardly do that much ... I just ... On the weekends I kind of rest a lot. I watch TV, which I shouldn't do. Sometimes I go visit my family but that's once in a million. You know I do my personal stuff like cleaning the house, my laundry, do my personal errands, you know, my groceries and ... .

Mejia's tiredness resonates with Marx's alienation of the human species in working conditions that allow only the reproduction of the work force. However, Mejia is unable to settle into his job: "I need to change. I need to move on. I've been there too long, that's it." Working as a supermarket clerk is not an occupation one can stick to for a lifetime. It is not a recognized job. In the U.S. discourse, this is a transitory job enabling one to study, to move on, to become someone better than just a supermarket clerk.

**The Instrumentalist Clerk**

The instrumentalist clerk is someone who relates very differently than the unsettled clerk to the low social status of the occupation. For the instrumentalist clerk, the social status of the occupation is of less relevance and so she suffers less than the unsettled clerk as she uses the job for an aim beyond the job. She shares the unsettled clerk's reluctance to identify with her occupation, but she does not struggle with the fact that she is working as a supermarket clerk. There is no need to get away from the job as the job fulfills another aim in life, beyond the job itself. In contrast to Goldthorpe et al.'s (1971) understanding of instrumentalist workers as those who are only interested in their wages as a means to afford a middle-class lifestyle, the instrumentalist clerk I met among my interviewees is overqualified for this work in terms of education. Thus, she needs to legitimize her work there. This means that working in socially low-ranked jobs evokes attitudes of legitimation and efforts to avoid being categorized in terms of the job's low social status. Here are the portraits of two instrumentalist clerks.

## Kokebe Tesfaye

At the time of the interview, Kokebe Tesfaye had lived in the U.S. for one year and seven months. She is still not fluent in English and works as a cashier in a supermarket where all other cashiers are also from Ethiopia, her home country, so she does not practice English very much. The manager who recruited her asked her: "From Ethiopia? Oh, Ethiopia lady; silent, hard worker." She did not accept compensation for the interview, unlike all the other interviewees, because she said she viewed the interview as an opportunity to practice her English. Tesfaye is 28 years old at the time of the interview. A green card lottery winner from a "poor country" whose father died when she was ten, she went to the U.S. to earn money and support her family. Tesfaye has a bachelor's degree in management and has worked in a bank, but upon arriving in the U.S. she first had to learn English and worked as a babysitter for her cousin, taking care of two children and then working the register in a Dunkin' Donuts overnight. She didn't like working nights, so she switched to Leverage Market, where she works 28 hours a week and earns $9 per hour. She has no health insurance and does not receive any benefits, just a discount of 20% when buying products from the supermarket. She would like to work full time. Before starting to work, she had to pass a test proving she is able to read and write. Tesfaye does not complain. She has sent her brother $500 to obtain a driver's license, and she sends her sister money for her education so that she can become a teacher. "He: driver's license; and my sister learning teaching in the school, I responsible." Tesfaye accepts her responsibility to support her family. She problematizes that she is not fluent in English and argues that it's partly because in her country it is common not to talk a lot.

> The customer English, the customer: 'Hi, how are you? Having a good day? Having a nice day? Goodnight; morning' because the line is a big line so more talk, it's fast, fast, fast. It's my problem. In my country: shy, no more talk in my country; more talk: crazy. Natural shy we. It's my difficult. No more talk. Some understand I am silent, no talk.

On the other hand, she argues that her brother, who is seven years older, always told her to shut up when they were young: "My brother: 'No more talk, keep silent. No more talk, you silent.'" In classes she suffers: "Sometimes I feel bad because some students more talk. I don't like." At work, Tesfaye receives much praise. Her manager often says "'She is nice, she is intelligent, she is good, everything is clean, a hard worker.'" She likes her work, especially the silent mornings, but also when it is busy. Tesfaye keeps pressing ahead. Next week, she is starting to work at a bank in Chinatown, where she will have more opportunities to practice English. Her objective is to get a "good job" after studying. "Now I need to work because I help my family. My family are just everything. I go to learn. I start to learn." Tesfaye is focused on one aim: supporting her family financially. With a bachelor's degree in management, she is overqualified for the occupation of supermarket clerk. However, she does not seem bothered by this. It seems that she accepts that her university degree from Ethiopia is not recognized in the U.S. She performs good work in a low-status occupation, not caring about the social status other than the fact that the pay is too low. But because of the low pay, she quits. In addition, she works on improving her English so that she can one day study. Tesfaye does not seem to suffer from the low social status of her job as long as it enables her to fulfill her duty to be a good daughter and sister, supporting her family economically.

### Catherine Taylor

"I'm too well educated to be working in the job that I have, but that's okay," says Catherine Taylor, a 57-year-old black woman and crew member at Trader Joe's (called "TJ's" for short). Taylor holds a degree from Harvard Business School and had worked for three-and-a-half years at TJ's at the time of the interview. Before she joined TJ's, she worked as a management consultant. There she had to travel a lot, and she "got burned out." Also, she adds, "I don't know how else to say it but this idea was tugging at me." What tugged at her was an idea she developed several years ago. It is an online game she is constantly developing further and offering to others. The game aims to reduce aggression and is what she calls her "life's work." Taylor quit her management consultant job and joined TJ's full time because "It is the first time I've felt like, oh, I can have a little bit of rest, so I do not have to drive the ship, I can just be part of the crew." Throughout the interview, Taylor repeats that she is not typical supermarket clerk "material," but belongs to the middle class. Born in London, where she grew up until she was 11 years old, her mother married an American GI, and she moved with them to the U.S. for three years and then to Ramstein, Germany, for five years. As an adult, she relocated to the U.S., where she has lived ever since. However, it is fully clear why she works at TJ's: to realize her project. It also helps that "Trader Joe's has such a positive reputation and response that people immediately gush, 'Oh, Trader Joe's, I just love …,' you know, they immediately start talking about everything they love about Trader Joe's and the food they like, oh everyone's so friendly, so it's positive." It would probably be harder to work in a supermarket with low prestige. The instrumentalist clerk uses the job at the supermarket strategically;

it has to serve her purpose outside of the job. Taylor talks about her decision to look for work at TJ's:

> I was hunting for a job but I was more focused on my project ... Yeah, and so normally I would take a job that would have taken this part of my brain and paid a lot more money, you know, much more like a corporate job, but I made a decision to follow this, and so it's like well, at my Trader Joe's job I use my social side, I call it. This is my social side, and all of my creative and mental energy is going towards my project because it's not needed.

From an instrumentalist perspective, the job allows her to emphasize one part of her personality. Instead of suffering from the need to suppress other parts of her personality and life so that she can devote herself fully to a corporate job, she is able to work a less demanding job that allows her to focus on her passion: creating a challenging game. Enthusiastically, she discusses her ideas for the game during the interview, which takes place at her home. She shows it to me online, and I have to remind her several times to come back to her work in the supermarket. She explains that her game is constantly on her mind and that

> Trader Joe's is not tasking me in that way, now of course they might think, well, we would like some of your good ideas, you know, it looks like it was working to me so it doesn't seem like they need anything from me, you know, that's innovative or new or different. It's like, I don't know, just regular things that, I don't think they need my help in that way. Maybe that's something that's, you know missing or I don't know, maybe I feel a little guilty for that, but I don't really have ideas.

Normally she would bring her ideas to work, but this job allows her to develop her own ideas outside of work, and she assures herself that TJ's does not really need her ideas: "it feels like if I don't do it they're still successful, you know it doesn't hurt anything." Situating her mental work outside of work is something new to Taylor that does not fully accord with her general views on work. Working in a low-status job required her to make quite an internal change. However, that doesn't mean that she is suffering from this change, even though the job is not mentally challenging. The work offers her more than just an income and time for her project:

> It's a very friendly place, and when I say that I'm not [giving] all of my intense mental energy to it, it isn't that I'm not getting anything, it's that I'm just giving a different part of myself. So if I saw something that could be improved, of course I'm going to say that, but I'm not doing deep management mental analysis. You know, it's more like something that I would see that's wrong that I would mention, so that keeps it interesting and fun, but it's more just the social engagement with the customers, it feels like a very safe place, feels very warm, you know feels very

friendly. I don't ever think 'oh my god I have to go to work today.' I never have that experience.

In contrast to the unsettled clerks, Taylor is at peace with herself while working in a low-social status job. Coming to the end of the interview, she concludes: "Well, this conversation has made me realize that it was a good choice because it is a good fit for who I am. It's not a good fit for how I was educated, that's different, but it's a good fit for who I am and the purpose of my life, I think."

## The Low-End Clerk

My interviewees included supermarket clerks who identified with the low social status of their jobs and thought of themselves as fitting in within the low-wage environment. They demonstrate that for the perception of the social status of the occupation, not only the dominant societal classification of a job is relevant, but also the class and social position of the interviewee. While in the case of the instrumentalist clerks their own social status (partly) surpassed the status of the occupation in that they held higher degrees, in the cases of the low-end clerks, the job's status conformed to their own social status. Their lives were marked by a lack of privileges and possibilities that could help them to achieve better living conditions. Below are portraits of two such clerks.

### Rose Kerrington

Rose Kerrington, who grew up in Boston and has lived there all her life, is a black 42-year-old dishwasher at Wegman's who works 20-hour weeks. Her mother works in a school kitchen. She cannot remember where her brother works. Diagnosed with a mental disability, she took her first job as a teenager, bagging groceries in a supermarket for two years, after which she switched to McDonalds for another year and a half. After this she was unemployed for many years. Kerrington receives social security disability insurance payments for her rent and "light bill and gas bill and stuff." She has had a job coach from an organization supporting mental illness, but it has never worked out. For four years she was searching before finally finding a job as dishwasher at Wegman's. "So I started applying online for different positions like dish-washer, bagger, food prep, anything that was available and I got no response." Finally, she was invited for an interview. "I go for an interview down there. So I'm going for the interview, and the lady interviews me. And she said same thing they ask like what happens if somebody wasn't to work. Would you be able to come in? If somebody was sick are you going to come in? That would happen in this situation. So I said you know I would be able to still work you know whenever you needed me." Offering her complete availability, Kerrington got the job. Now she goes online to look up her schedule, which is always changing according to the company's needs. Kerrington does not complain. Quite the contrary: "I feel proud because I actually accomplished something finally," she says.

> I actually thought I would not be able to do was get a job again. So I'm really happy that even though it's been a long time since I've had a job that [I] kept pushing through it instead of giving up and saying, o well I'll never get a job. And I said to myself, I was like there's something out there for you. Don't give up. And I looked on the internet all the time. I looked in newspapers. I looked everywhere and I finally got a job.

Having been unemployed for a very long time, she is happy about this job. At work she has different tasks, some of which she describes:

> Then the person who is probably rinsing [the dishes] off and going to do the sanitizer would do that for two hours. Then the person who doesn't do that put them away. There was a choice if I wash then I might put them through the sanitizer and put them away. So it's not that I'm doing the same thing repetitively. I'm doing something different. It's ... You know so it won't get boring. So I fluctuate.

Kerrington seems to be happy not only that she has a job but also that the job's tasks and the way they are organized are not completely rote. Asked to compare her time while she was unemployed with today, she relates:

> Well [pause] it's just really ... I was limited to money. I don't know I lived off $450 a month. You know because I had to buy (background noise) I had to buy tissue for the bathroom, towels, soap, personal hygiene things. So that's about $60 right there, $50, $60 if you add it all up so I have whatever's left over. I have to budget. But even though I got a job doesn't mean I don't have to budget. I still have to budget my money (pause). I have to look at it where I have to put something away for savings, you know until I retire or something or ... You know what I'm talking about? So I have to, you know, keep money. And I want ... Oh when I get $100 (background noise) ... Be able to keep it in.

Me: "Yeah right. Apart from having the budget and earning the money is there something else you would describe as important about the job for you, that it has a significance for you?" Kerrington: "Feeling appreciated by others. They will accept me. Sometimes I never felt accepted meaning that my mental illness kind of ... I had a hard time (background noise) mental illness and I felt that people were judging (background noise) because of mental illness. They think it's just I have mental illness that I'm not able to function." Working as a dish-washer in a supermarket means that Kerrington is able to function. Despite her mental illness, she is able to show up at work whenever she is scheduled. She is able to perform various tasks in shifts. This ability means social acceptance for her. She fits in. Completing our interview in a noisy location, Kerrington's final words were: "I'm just happy I actually got a job."

### Khalan Wilson

During the interview with Khalan Wilson, my questions elicit responses in the form of very short sentences. Wilson's life bears some similarities to Rose Kerrington's, but at the time of the interview, he is much younger: 29 years old. He is also black and works part time as a shopping cart retriever at Stop & Shop, collecting shopping carts from two parking lots and lining them up in front of the supermarket. Wilson grew up in Dorchester, a neighborhood of Boston. Like Kerrington, he receives support from a job coach who literally walked with him into Stop & Shop to ask for a job for his client. Wilson got a date for an interview.

> They were asking me if I had a criminal record, if I'd got into any ... it was a quarry check – a quarry check is like a background ... They were asking me if I smoke, drink. And they were asking me what kind of job title I wanted, what job title I was comfortable with when getting a job, and I chose carriage [shopping cart] retriever.

Wilson could choose between becoming a bagger, a cashier, a porter, and a deli seafood cutter, and he chose to become a carriage retriever because he wanted to move around and not just stand in one place. Prior to this job, he was unemployed for about three years. Before that, he attended a kind of vocational education program in which he worked in a hotel as a houseman, collecting laundry from the floors. When school ended, this job stopped as well. Wilson started working 20 hours a week, but he became tired and asked for a reduction in hours. The 15 hours are divided over three days a week in a fixed schedule, from 6 a.m. to 11 a.m. When he was working for 20 hours a week, "They used to change my days around, they used to mix me up." Asked to describe a typical working day, Wilson states: "I arrive before my time. I go there around 5:30; I go in the break room and wait until my shift." I ask why he arrives so early and he answers: "So I can just ... probably sleep a little bit, go on my phone, and then when six comes I prepare for work." He usually collects ten carts at once. Sometimes he has to help customers to load their cars. "I get a tip once in a blue moon, but usually I don't." When he started working at Stop & Shop there were ten cart retrievers, and now there are about five. Now he works alone and thought it was better with people working with him. Asked whether he likes his work, he answers, "It's okay." Sometimes he is asked to collect trash, and once he had to do it without being given gloves. "I tell them, 'You should give me gloves to wear' or something like that. There was a time she asked me to use the store bags instead of gloves but I didn't feel comfortable with it so instead I went to the seafood department and I had to ask them for the seafood gloves." If this were to happen again, he could inform his union. "My job is actually a union, meaning if they ask me to do something that ... like if I was going to need gloves I could talk to the union about it." Working in a unionized job provides him with some security. In contrast, his manager does not protect him from rude customers who yell or swear at him. "He would help the customer." Wilson shares the view that working at supermarkets is an entry-level job. "I don't think it would be something people would appreciate." Jobs being appreciated are "policeman, a fire fighter, EMT, library." I ask him whether he has plans for the future. He answers, "No." But after about five more years he can think of himself as working in delivering food to the elderly in Meals on Wheels. Asked why in five years, Wilson says: "I'm actually comfortable with Stop & Shop as of now."

The clerks who see themselves as fitting in at their low-end jobs are people with few resources and low expectations. Long periods of unemployment helped prepare them to accept jobs with low social status. These "fitting in" clerks settle into their jobs and the low social status that comes with them. Even a low-wage, devalued occupation is better than unemployment. For Kerrington, her job provides a certain degree of social integration. She feels accepted because she functions, and that would not be the case if she didn't have the job. In contrast to the assertion by Durkheim and Hegel, having a complex occupation is not always a prerequisite to feeling like a member of society.

## PATTERNS OF SUBJECT FORMATION IN RELATION TO A PROFESSIONAL JOB ON A LOWER RUNG OF THE JOB HIERARCHY

The German supermarket clerks I interviewed also note the lack of prestige and recognition associated with their occupations but, in contrast to the U.S., Germany accords a certain amount of respect to work in supermarkets because of its categorization as a profession. Some of the interviewees point to a decrease in the respect and recognition accorded to supermarket clerks in Germany, but this change is in the context of a period of decades of employment. Over time, working conditions for supermarket clerks have deteriorated notably: apprentices are taught less and are increasingly used as part of an expanded workforce that enables stores to extend their opening times. The interviewees' descriptions resonate with other studies' findings on changes in retail working conditions such as Voss-Dahm and Lehndorf's (2003) work on increasing part-time schedules for flexibility (mentioned in Chapter 2). This makes the job less attractive. A major topic of the interviews with German supermarket clerks was their vocational education, which typically entailed systematic training in different departments of the supermarket and instruction on completing written reports. In vocational schools, trainees are taught various subjects, from business administration to merchandise studies, English, and psychology, to name just a few. Some interviewees managed a store for a couple of weeks as a training project.

The next section explores how having an occupation that is viewed as a profession leads to identification with the job. When an occupation offers room for development and comes with special expertise, it can gain centrality in the employee's life and replace other orientations. These factors can be seen among some of the German supermarket clerks who have been able to "settle" into their profession.

## Career Aspiration: Supermarket Clerk

In the U.S. context, the idea of anyone aspiring to a career as a supermarket clerk might sound strange. As I have already laid out, in the U.S. this occupation is one in which people normally do not want to remain; it is usually seen as an entry-level or transitional job. Only those without the resources to find a better job, or any other job at all, are likely to be satisfied with this kind of occupation.

This is different in Germany. Since it is a profession, many young people do decide to work in supermarkets. Supermarket clerk is among the top ten most selected apprenticeships in Germany and one in which the numbers of women and men are quite similar in an otherwise relatively gender-segregated job market (Statistisches Bundesamt 2020). While Voswinkel (2005) revealed employees' ways of upgrading the prestige of their work to gain more recognition, as outlined in Chapter 2, my comparative analysis demonstrates how crucial the societal status of the occupation is for employees' work appropriations.

### Kerstin Jansen

Kerstin Jansen, born in 1969 in the former German Democratic Republic (GDR), opted consciously, with her mother's encouragement, to become a supermarket clerk in her teens. From Hofmann and Rink (1999) (see Chapter 2), we know about the attractiveness of the profession of supermarket clerk in the GDR because it provided access to scarce goods. Parts of the following description of her life course are relevant later, when I come back to her in Chapter 7 on activities. This applies mainly to her experiences at kindergarten. Jansen's father was a painter in the GDR before reunification and a truck driver afterward; her mother was a nurse. Her younger brother became a carpenter. She and her brother attended a kindergarten that was open 24 hours, seven days a week. Children could stay overnight. When her mother was on night, evening, or early morning shifts, she and her brother stayed in the kindergarten. Jansen still maintains a relationship with friends she met there. When her mother was off for a couple of days in a row, Jansen would stay at home, where her mother dedicated herself 100% to the children. During summer holidays, she went to union houses where the hospital and her father's firm organized summer camps for the kids. "And there were, as I said, certain things, and, I don't know, some may demonize me for saying this, but not everything was bad in the GDR. I can remember, for example, I had a beautiful childhood. Every year I went with my brother and many other kids to summer camps, organized through my parents' workplaces." Jansen finished school after ten years, obtaining a common degree from a polytechnic secondary school in the GDR. Actually, she wanted to become a nurse like her mother or a care nurse for the elderly; she had already jobbed in her mother's hospital while in school. But her mother intervened and stopped her. "One daft one in the family is enough," her mother told her. "You are becoming a supermarket clerk." As she explained, "Because, in the GDR, supermarket clerks, yes, this was then, they had connections. They got everything with connections, right? Whoever worked in retail was well positioned because they had access to stuff not everybody could get." As noted by Hofmann and Rink (1999), access to scarce goods in the GDR gave retail clerks social clout, a sense of being important and a participant in public challenges. Along these same lines, Jansen narrates vividly how her boss, a master butcher, ran a small smokehouse, and when she informed the hairdresser, she got a nice cut on Fridays after work to go out dancing. "That's why retail clerk was a reputable profession."

**Kerstin Keller**
In another case, Kerstin Keller recalls, "I was born in 1968 in [X], a small town with a hundred thousand inhabitants in Saxony. I am a working-class child in the classical sense. And I went to a completely normal polytechnic secondary school and attained my own career aspiration to become a salesperson." Keller wanted a profession where she could "really assist people and sell things that would accompany them over many years." She completed her apprenticeship and specialized in furniture and arts and crafts. She performed very well, and her training supervisors wanted her to continue and become a store manager. But she wanted to interact with customers rather than ending up in an office. So she resigned and went to work at a theater with which she had been closely connected since childhood to work as a props assistant and technician for pyrotechnics for 16 years. When I asked her how she has developed her career aspiration to become a salesperson, Keller explains:

> I don't like shopping, this is not something I like to do. But I've always liked to browse shops and see what's being offered and to observe salespeople, and I usually found them wanting. I mean, how they dealt with goods and people. And this must

have been what gave me the idea as a teenager to think I could do this differently and better.

Keller admits that she finds it actually quite challenging to continually improve on the job. At the time of the interview she had been working for 11 years in a supermarket that sells only ecological products. This is a specialized supermarket that is not profit oriented but instead works on a cooperative basis. She started with an internship to which she was steered by the unemployment center and was asked whether she would like to stay. She was a consumer of ecologically minded products herself prior to working there and also sympathized a lot with the cooperative model. She decided to stay. A part-time salesperson position was available, and she said: "'Stop, I won't do it without doing another vocational education.' And then we had a little deal with the unemployment office that they would pay for distance learning to become a natural foods salesperson." Keller had a steep career path from salesperson to retail salesperson to floor manager and finally store manager. She has worked for six years. Her identification with her profession was confirmed by the experience of having customers seeking her out for her expertise about products. Sometimes she looks up study materials from her vocational education to support current apprentices or inform family and friends.

> So in my family, it took a long time for the organics fad to catch on. They thought all of this was weird, they lived completely without reflection. Even though my mom grew up with a garden, and me too. But all this was not a topic for her. Only now is my mother starting to think differently and taking her health more seriously. And for her, price was always important. I, on the other hand, am someone who doesn't look at the price. And among my friends and acquaintances, it was really cool: 'Kerstin, you can ask her everything, she knows everything. And you can trust her, if she says something, that's true.' This was the result of the vocational education. It's the same for my colleagues, we all remember what we learned in our training. You can ask me about any of it. It's really kind of nice. And if there's something I don't know, I am luckily in a position to give it some thought. A lot of people can't do that at all. They simply don't trust themselves to be able to do it. But I just simply start thinking, how could it be? Sure, then I can go and look things up and so on. But most of the time things just fall into place pretty quickly. And this is really valuable. So, I really have to say, this is where vocational education can lead you to become someone.

This quote culminates in the speaker's assertion of selfhood as a result of her vocational education. Knowledge leads to recognition and recognition to self-worth. Identifying with an occupation that entails formally acquired knowledge and is socially accepted by institutions enables identification with the job and does not require identification beyond the job.

Additionally, some supermarket clerks in Germany point to another important characteristic of a profession: whether it offers room for growth. Keller gives herself as a good example:

> So, there are just good opportunities for us here. I'm an example of that. I went from intern to store manager. That's always a possibility. If someone is interested and engaged, there are no barriers. All posts are announced internally first. We offer all temporary staff the chance to become salespeople. Or we offer salespeople a job even if the position was advertised with the IHK (chamber of industry and commerce). Or for becoming floor manager, all posts are announced internally first. We look in our pool to see who wants to be where. In any case, everyone has an annual review where one looks at the direction they are moving in and what their potential is. We look at what kind of interests are there. And of course we apply all that information. And then there are always further education courses. These are now obligatory. Of course we make sure we talk to the people and that there is an interest. There is no point in sending someone to additional training if they say, 'I am not interested in it at all.' But since there are so many of us, there is always someone who goes, 'Oh, yes, I am interested. I want to do it.' But the possibilities of career advancement are still really, really good.

### Tobias Emons

Another example of an interviewee who emphasizes career opportunities is Tobias Emons. He was born in 1986 in a village in the GDR. His father worked in rail construction, and his mother is a nurse. He has a younger brother with whom he shares a flat. Their parents separated when he was about 13 years old. Emons repeated the ninth grade and finished with a secondary school certificate. He played the guitar and percussion and wanted to become a clerk in a music shop. But he applied without success and instead received an apprenticeship in Lidl, where he is still very content. On top of his three-year vocational education, he studied to become a commercial economist. He states: "I could apply now to become a branch manager if I wanted, yes, of course the higher ups would have to decide whether I am suitable, but generally Lidl offers everybody a chance to develop as far as possible." It is this room for career growth that he finds attractive.

### Nils Hasel

The same is true for Nils Hasel, born in 1985 in a small village in Saxony, who grew up with his father, a bricklayer, his mother, a homemaker, two older siblings, and many animals in the countryside. After elementary school, he went to secondary school in another village close by and left school after the tenth grade. He was looking for an apprenticeship and sent out about 60 applications to very different firms. He was invited by Edeka to work for one day. He had fun and soon received an offer for an apprenticeship. Most of their applicants were women, and as a man he was preferred. Hasel emphasizes that for a career in retail, vocational education is sufficient, and university studies are not required.

> [Career opportunities] in our firm are very good because all of the personnel come from the stores in our company, independent of the job they do, even district managers – I mean, my current district manager was my training supervisor, she was store manager then – even district managers or even saleswoman – it is important that in our company only those with the relevant experience have the corresponding jobs and have a say. That's why in principle everything is possible. If someone wants it and opportunities arise. With a traditional vocational education, one does not have to go to the university or anything.

Here, Hasel refers to the hierarchy between university and college degrees on the one hand and degrees in vocational education on the other. The hierarchy exists in Germany, but it is not nearly as pronounced as in the U.S. Many careers are made from inside companies, and often people who have learned from the ground up are preferred for upper management positions.

The possibility of a professional career in sales, vocational training that offers applicable knowledge, and the prospect of personal and career growth on the job, all make sales positions potentially long-term jobs in Germany. All of the German interviewees just profiled are examples of "settlers" who remain in their jobs because they are satisfied with them. In contrast to Ben Johnson and Victor Mejia, Kerstin Jansen, Kerstin Keller, Tobias Emons, and Nils Hasel do not plan to quit their jobs for other jobs or for further education. As Emons states: "In all these years I have been at probably three or four different branches, and yes, I could imagine staying here a very, very long time or not leaving at all. It's currently the case that I really like my colleagues and how well we get along with each other." Apart from Kerstin Jansen, all of the other German salespeople are also very content with their jobs. For Jansen, it was a struggle to work things out at her job. This related to her situation as a single mother of a sick child without any support from her firm. In Chapter 7 I will return to her and her process of coming to terms with her job after a period of disillusionment. But Emons ends his interview with the statement, "Basically, I feel balanced."

To sum up, the degree of recognition accorded an occupation relates to employees' rejecting or affirming attitudes toward the job. If the job is seen as an entry-level job that leads nowhere, employees in that position will most likely want to move on as soon as possible. Staying will be interpreted as failure unless remaining on the job is framed as a way of funding objectives or ambitions beyond the workplace. Only people with little in the way of resources and possibilities are likely to find a "fit" with a low-end job. It may be that some people are happy to have any employment at all and see that as a form of "fitting." In contrast, in cases where the occupation does hold a certain level of recognition and offers room for growth, this enables people to relate to and identify with their job, thus settling into it in an affirmative way.

## NOTES

1.  This interview was conducted in Spanish. All quotes from interviews in Spanish are translated by myself.
2.  I am using male pronouns here as the two cases I present feature men. Without being able to generalize in terms of numbers due to my small sample, it could be argued that the unsettled clerk is more likely to be a man than a woman as it might be more difficult for men to accept the job's low social status in a patriarchal society than for women.

# 6. Modes of use value constituting work appropriation

This chapter concentrates on interviewees' responses to questions about their perceptions of the tasks and content comprising their work. As the literature review revealed, use value forms an important part of workers' and employees' thinking about their jobs since it is a major aspect of work motivation and has to do with vocational and professional identity. Thus, Nies (2015) has identified working conditions that impede the realization of work tasks and content that benefit others as a major reason for workplace conflicts. In this chapter, I will use the interviewees' responses to illustrate how use value forms work appropriation, identifying three different modes. The first mode consists of explicit references to use value in interviewees' remarks. In all cases, professional knowledge is crucial for carrying out tasks adequately and meeting customers' needs. The second mode ties in with the fact that labor power itself becomes a use value for the companies' owners. The cases I will use are characterized by interviewees' strong identification with the economic system they affirm – albeit with different motives. Here, a crucial role is played by institutional conditions, such as the existence or lack of career paths. The third mode is one I call work ethos, which was widely detectable among my interviewees. A strong work ethos results in good performance, which increases the use value of the labor power. On a subject level, a strong work ethos serves to increase self-esteem, which is especially required in low-wage work. Here, my work might tie in with Voswinkel's (2005) list of framings employees used in order to upgrade the social recognition of their work as outlined in Chapter 2. I will show how supermarket clerks use their strong work ethos to appreciate and acknowledge themselves and their work in the absence of appreciation from supervisors and customers. In doing so, they often even take on new tasks that are not their responsibility – a typical feature of neoliberalism in which workers contribute to their self-exploitation.

## EXPLICIT USE VALUE ORIENTATION

The first mode is characterized by the employees' deep and profound knowledge of the products they sell. This knowledge is generally acquired either in the kind of vocational education required in Germany or through specific

certification processes, as in the case of a clerk in one of the high-end supermarkets in the U.S.

I will start with Kerstin Keller, whom I have already introduced in the previous chapter, in the section on social status and career aspirations of becoming
a clerk. Her aspiration to become a supermarket clerk reflected the societal
classification of the occupation as a professional one. This classification pre-
supposes an evaluation of the content of that work as requiring a vocational
education, whereas in the U.S. the content of that work is mostly categorized
as tasks that can be carried out after completing on-the-job training. The difference in classification leads to a difference in the clerks' social status, as I have
laid out above. Here, concerning the content of the work, it is noteworthy that
Keller argues that an apprenticeship is necessary to meet the legitimate expectations of customers:

> No. So, if a person comes into my shop, he has a legitimate claim [to being able to
> speak with knowledgeable salespeople], and the expectation is there as well. And
> of course, I had already read a lot about organics and also knew about them because
> I would buy them myself, but that is nothing like a sufficient background. So it was
> important for me to get a really sound education on this stuff.

The vocational education as a natural foods specialist Keller received was one
that focused mainly on the products themselves and less on retail. She explains:

> So this was basically about expertise in organic products. It was less the business
> end of things, although of course that also plays a role. Things have to be sold some-
> where, of course. But it was basically about how the items were being produced,
> what the underlying conditions of their production were, and how they differed
> from conventional products. This was very essential. And the entirety of nutritional
> science was also essential background for this job. To be clear, people who go to
> natural and organic food stores have very specific backgrounds and have various
> reasons for being there. Those reasons can be ethical or of course health-related.
> And one simply needs to have this background knowledge. So, it was really impor-
> tant mainly to know everything about organics and a lot about healthy eating and
> organic farming.

This kind of vocational education fits well with the organizational model of
the cooperative where she works because her training is not profit-oriented.
Thus, the store's nonprofit orientation contributes to a large extent to her use
value orientation and harmonizes with her views: "And yes, the co-op in itself
is something that makes me say, okay, I am getting both – a job and something
that eases my bad conscience as a human being at the same time because I'm
helping to save the planet. This is a very practical concern." Overall, Keller's
use value orientation is embedded in social contexts that do not invalidate her
motivations. In fact, quite the contrary: she is able to develop an unbroken

identification with her work and affirmation through her job because the products she sells are healthy and the profit goes to the cooperative's community of customers, and not into the wallets of corporate leaders and shareholders.

In contrast to Kerstin Keller, Axel Conradi does not work in a corporation that supports his use value orientation where the content of his work is concerned. Quite the contrary: He has found himself at odds with his company's policies and struggling to maintain his use value orientation. At the time of the interview, his company, Real (a large warehouse with food, electronics, and other departments), was in danger of being sold, and working conditions were deteriorating. His employer left the network of companies under a collective agreement, and the company was now under an agreement that allowed money to be clawed back from employee holiday paychecks in support of the company's efforts to recover. Under the agreement, newly hired staff would work more hours but earn about 20–30% less than existing staff. Conradi is a member of the workers' union council, serving his second four-year term, and he participates in the bargaining committee. His story is dominated by descriptions of bad and deteriorating working conditions. In addition, he describes his boss as abusive and bullying to coworkers. Against this background, Conradi's attitude toward the content of his work, which he describes as explicitly customer oriented, could be described as almost heroic, but it is clear that his use value orientation contributes to a mode of work appropriation that is consistent with his self-image as a professional. In contrast to Keller, he frames his work with customers as a needed break from the social context and conditions at his company and something that allows him to uphold his self-respect. Furthermore, as a member of the union workers' council, he obtains a critical attitude toward his corporation's politics and is aware of workers' and employees' rights, leading to conflicts with his supervisor. Conradi is 56 years old and grew up in a rural area in the south of the former GDR. His father was a teacher and his mother a childcare worker. His parents separated, and he grew up with his father. He has two older sisters who have both also worked in retail. As a child, he fixed a broken TV and was then allowed to keep it in his room, which was rather unusual for that time. After finishing compulsory school, he started an apprenticeship in communications engineering ("Nachrichtentechnik") in Karl-Marx-Stadt (now Chemnitz). Due to a staff shortage, he was sent to X to work for half a year and stayed there after falling in love. He later married and had a son. After reunification, he was laid off, but he obtained employment first in one and later in a second company. When his work there ended, he looked for another occupation and started working in retail in 1997. His company was later bought by another one, which mostly sold food but maintained an electronics department. Conradi has a three-year-old granddaughter whom he sees regularly, picking her up from his divorced daughter-in-law.

In general, Conradi maintains a strong work ethos, but his case is especially instructive for highlighting use value as an aspect of work appropriation. His company has adopted a policy of employing more workers with less training for lower salaries so that it can save money. The two-year vocational education for their workplace does not include specialized knowledge about electronics, so customers and even employees from other departments and branches of his company come to Conradi for information and advice. As he notes:

> Customers see us as a specialty store. That's how it is now, and several customers have told me that. They make a special point of coming to us because our competitors don't have a specialized sales staff. They just have salespeople with no knowledge of what they are selling. Above our store is X, which is a specialty store for electronics. Their customers (laughs) come down to us and say to me: 'Hi, I can get better advice from you. Tell me the difference between these two devices' (laughs). Yes, this is of course nice for me, of course I am happy. It is good for my ego. But I am not always able to get my work done.

Apart from falling behind in performing other tasks with less use value while serving customers and advising them on products, Conradi also provides a service to customers by steering them away from products they do not need. He is quite conscious that his company is not pleased about this, but he suffers no repercussions and is able to maintain his use value orientation. As he explains:

> When a customer buys a product, X sells an insurance so that instead of a two-year warranty the customer buys a five-year warranty. Uh, washing machines generally work for five years. They mostly break after five years. But if I'm buying a TV, it makes more sense, say, if I have kids at home, who, I am going to be mean now and say, if I have kids at home who are being brought up badly and throw things around, hitting the windows, and something could hit the TV and break the screen, then it would be useful, because then the TV would be insured. The warranty doesn't cover breakage, but the insurance does. But otherwise, it's just not so that every customer needs the insurance – that's nonsense. So I tell the customer, 'You really don't need it.' So, just the way I told you now, I say to the customer: 'You only need it if you have rambunctious kids at home.' These TVs hold up, and if one buys a better brand, X or Y, they hold up for longer than five years. There's no need for an insurance that costs an additional 100 Euros. That's complete nonsense. Of course, management doesn't look kindly on this. But the customers like me because I give them objective advice. Luckily, we are not paid by commission, so I don't have my salary tied to sales. And especially for that reason, customers are happy to see me and come to our department, because that's how we work.

Like Kerstin Keller, Axel Conradi gets satisfaction from realizing his work content expectations related to use value. But in contrast to Keller, he struggles to realize these expectations, which put him at odds with the company's interest in generating profits instead of use value.

While Conradi's use value orientation works against his company's interest in selling useless things such as warranties, Steven Hill's use value orientation fits well with the company's interest in raising profits. Hill is a white, 30-year-old wine section manager at TJ's. He has worked part time at the company for four years, 30 hours per week, and at the time of the interview was earning an income of $16.30 per hour. In addition, he had complete health care, vision, and dental coverage and a gym membership at a particular recreation center. He has a BSc. from a public college and considers his main occupation to be his work as a voice actor, even though he only works at it for about eight to ten hours per week. After graduation, he faced difficulties in finding a job during the financial crisis of 2007-2008 and paying back his college loans. He moved to California and then back to Massachusetts, where a college friend suggested he apply at this supermarket chain. After one year working, Hill was promoted to section manager. He received training in the layout of the store and in working at the register together with other people from winecentric cities and towns. Having developed an interest in wine, he studied wine and went to wine tastings with people he worked with. Their store has a separate room for wine tastings. Hill has become knowledgeable about wines and knows most of the wines stocked by his store. Wine is the only product he sells, and he would not recommend a wine he has not tasted himself. Wine customers expect wine purveyors to know their wines and be able to tell which wine would complement a certain meal, and Steven is able to do that. As section manager, he orders the wine, creates the wine display, and decides which wine to offer the customers for tastings. He also trains people. According to Hill, the wine section brings in about 30% of his company's profit, so it is quite important. This contributes to his job satisfaction. When asked how other people see his work, he answers that he hasn't received any open disrespect, but he thinks that many people see it as a temporary job. So he feels he needs to add that he is working in wines as this "adds a little bit more of the gravitas to the job itself." In sum, Hill's value orientation is closely connected to his knowledge of one product that contributes substantially to the company's profits. There is no conflict between his use value orientation and his company's interest in enlarging profits. His aspirations as a voice actor do not diminish his use value orientation in the supermarket either.

Hill is an exception among the U.S. supermarket clerks I spoke with in terms of his satisfactory working conditions and wages, as well as his opportunities to take on responsibilities in decision-making and to use and expand his knowledge about a specific product. Most supermarket clerks in the U.S. articulated a less specific use value orientation by saying that they wanted to help customers. Robert Clark, a 24-year-old white Scan-IT clerk working 22 hours weekly at Stop & Shop and studying chemical engineering, refers to "helping the customers with all their different needs." Customers' needs could refer to a variety of things, such as finding products, using self-checkout registers, or loading purchases into cars, especially in the case of older customers. Even clerks who otherwise received no training for their supermarket jobs, including students and part-time staff working only a few hours per week, generally received an orientation on helping customers. This indicates that vocational education and professional knowledge are not the only means of finding value in one's work. However, obtaining knowledge often increases the ability to fulfill customers' needs.

## EXPLICIT EXCHANGE VALUE ORIENTATION

As I have outlined above, one aspect of use value is that in capitalist societies, the use value of the labor force creates surplus value. Thus, in capitalist systems exchange value is inevitably a part of use value, and for that reason we see workers and employees referring to exchange value explicitly in their work-related demands. One motivation for workers' references to exchange value is the desire to enhance their own social status (Kupfer et al. 2019). By pointing to supermarkets' large profits, clerks address the fundamental and widely recognized value of profits and competition in the capitalist systems to which they contribute with their work. The content of tasks might not require much training, and wages may be low, resulting in a devaluation of employees' status, but affirming that one is boosting efficiency and productivity without sharing in profits is a way to argue for a higher social position and more respect in the social hierarchy.

Here I will point to two additional ways of orienting one's work toward exchange value and appropriation. Starting with the German example, I focus on Andreas Meiners, a 26-year-old manager of an Aldi store who has vocational training. His aim is to become a shop owner as some chains offer franchises to be run independently. The objective of becoming a self-employed supermarket owner is the classic professional goal for supermarket clerks in Germany. Vocational training in supermarket retail therefore includes not only a customer service orientation, but also a business orientation. Meiners grew up in a small town in northeastern Germany with his mother, who worked as a cashier in a discount store, and his sister. Meiners repeated ninth grade in school and completed regular high school (the non-college-bound track). He had to complete an internship and opted for one in a supermarket close to his home for convenience. His boss appreciated his work and offered him a three-year apprenticeship right away. This is an honor, since many vocational apprenticeships start with a two-year contract that can be extended if the apprentice performs well. Vocational education was easy for him, and in his third year he was already promoted to deputy shop manager. After his apprenticeship, he worked for two years in that supermarket and then, with the help of a personal contact, switched to another company as his own company would have sent him to a branch that was not reachable without a car. Later he moved to another city, where he was offered the position of shop manager. "I am a salesman through and through!" states Meiners. Asked about his motivation to become a trained retail salesclerk, he answers: "to sell at high volumes." He enjoys selling as a way of increasing profits, not as a means of satisfying customers. Selling means influencing customers through aspects such as placement and layout of the items in the store, and mastering this art can lead to a feeling of efficacy. He is not at all critical of the capitalist system, but rather aims at becoming an entrepreneur himself. His case is embedded in the German system of career paths from employed clerks to shop owners.

A special case is Andrew Harris, a 49-year-old white former manager and now supermarket clerk at TJ's who has worked in a highly ranked supermarket for five years. He grew up in the state of X, studied business management with a focus on human resources, and earned a four-year degree from a college in the state. He has been a retail manager for over 20 years, with experiences in various areas such as rental cars, book and video stores, high-end gift stores, and restaurants. Harris was arrested and spent time in prison on drug charges and since then has not been able to work in managerial positions. He explains: "I'm handicapped and can't work [in] my real profession which is management." Although Harris works as a supermarket clerk, his perspective is one of a manager. He has been educated and socialized from an exchange value perspective. Similar to Andreas Meiners, Harris is less interested in customer satisfaction than in the functioning of the whole store.

> I have a different perspective, so when the store does well I get excited. We break records or we have a record-setting weekend or the store looks good after we get hammered. I said to the manager the other day, 'We've got a great crew right now.' We just had one of our busiest weekends of all time, and the store Monday morning looked perfect, and so stuff like that I like.

His managerial perspective trumps impulse toward adopting a customer-serving attitude. It may come as no surprise that I met men who referred to exchange value, but not women. One reason could be that women more than men tend to be trained and socialized to serve others, to detect and respond to other people's needs. Because of socialization, women's labor capacity might lean more toward use value orientation. A second reason for this imbalance might be that women feel less devalued doing work considered feminine or focused on others than men might feel, and some men might react to those feelings by trying to boost their egos or self-confidence by touting the exchange value of their work. Finally, since the exchange value perspective is sometimes linked with upper career positions, which are more likely to be held by men, this might be a reason for fewer women expressing such an attitude.

## WORK ETHOS

In the final section on modes by which use value impacts work appropriation, I look at work ethos. As I have explained above, the connection of work ethos to use value lies in the fact that a strong work ethos leads to good performance, from which customers (and corporations) benefit. In this section, I want to focus on another aspect of a strong work ethos that is crucial for work appropriation: its contribution to self-esteem, joy, well-being, and a sense of accomplishment. Thus, workers and employees benefit from use value orientations.

The first case relates to self-esteem. Baptiste Laguerre is a 32-year-old black produce clerk from Haiti working at Star Market. He immigrated to the U.S. to live with his wife, a U.S. citizen with Haitian roots whom he met in Haiti. His wife is working in a nursing home. They have one child. Back in Haiti, Laguerre was a French and social science teacher at a high school. At the time of the interview, he has lived for ten months in the U.S. In the interview, Laguerre notes that at the supermarket where he is employed, "the schedule is full time but on the paper I'm part time." He earns $9 per hour. Laguerre has received three days of training from a coworker who instructed him in Creole, since he couldn't speak English yet. His job is to carry produce inside the store and lay it out, sorting it according to expiration dates and removing whatever is going bad. "You need to care about what you're doing," he says. Laguerre is not looking for another job right away "because I respect that I have an experience with a job, I still want to work in this job." Here Laguerre brings up the double significance of work experience: carrying out good work, on one hand, and feeling good about honoring the experience, on the other. His work ethos supports his self-esteem. In putting care into what he is doing, he takes care of himself. However, his self-care is problematic as it contributes to the perpetuation of a situation in which he is robbed of self-esteem by being exploited as cheap labor.

The next portrait is of a clerk who derives joy from his strong work ethos. Brian Mwangi is a black, 44-year-old, experienced full-time cashier at Whole Foods earning $15 per hour. He was born in Nairobi, Kenya, where he finished high school before immigrating to the U.S. at the age of 22. One of his siblings already lived there, but in another state. In America, Brian Mwangi attended a professional school and worked several sales jobs outside and inside supermarkets but wanted to sell used cars instead. Another aim was to find a partner and to marry. Mwangi has a radiant, playful, and easy manner and a positive work ethos. His description resonates with Studs Terkel's (2004 [1972]) study on work containing workers' descriptions of flow, mentioned in the literature review. When talking about performing his tasks, he speaks of enjoyment: "I enjoyed it. And with cashiering, it's one of those things you get into a rhythm. As a matter of fact, I enjoyed more when it was busy. The busier it was the quicker the time went by and the more fun the job was. When it's slow, it's lagging." For Mwangi, work can be fun and at the same time very efficient: "Like when you have a long line and you don't want the customers to walk away. So the more you take care of the time, the more patient they'll wait." A bit later, he returns to the pleasantness of feeling at one with the tasks he performs:

> Yes, like when it's very busy and your register comes up perfect. You feel proud of yourself especially there are days where you could ... Your mind could be pre-occupied and you still are able to get the rhythm. You see every cashier arranges the register his own way. And you go systematically. It's part of you. That way even when you're spaced out and you're not even paying attention, because of your organization it just flows. And that's how you prevent errors because you're organized and you're working on a certain rhythm.

Ava Smith is a 50-year-old woman of color who grew up in Somerville, Massachusetts. She has five siblings and was raised by her single mother. Smith has five children and dropped out of high school when she started a family. She earned her GED, a high school diploma equivalent, when she was about 30 years old. Two of her children (aged 12 and 14) are still at home at the time of the interview. Smith lived for about five years in Florida, where she and her husband took care of properties and small landscapes (cutting grass, etc.). After they separated, Smith started working as a cashier and later moved back to Massachusetts. There her tasks consisted additionally of ringing up for customers, restocking, bagging, and collecting shopping carts at the ends of shifts. In addition to her two at-home children, Smith also takes care of her four-year-old grandson. Nursery school is too expensive and far away, so her own children, her sister, and her mother take care of her grandson. She says about her work ethos:

> I think in anything that I do, I give it my all. So if I can't be the best that I can, honestly, I won't do it. If I can't give it my all, I don't like to go in halfway. So, if I'm doing something, a job or whatever, I want to be 100% at it. I'm not saying that I'm perfect by no means but I try to do the best that I can ... I just feel that if it's not something that I want to give my all to, why do it?

Her work ethos is connected to the meaning of work and leads her to perform well, and that in turn gives her joy: "Just leaving when I go at the end of the day and my drawer was correct. Things like that made me feel happy. No mistakes." Smith urgently needed an income and could not choose her shifts, which were scheduled weekly and changed when someone called in sick.

"Whatever shift they chose me for, that's what I worked." Here, her strong work ethic is linked to her urgent necessity of obtaining a job for an income.

Another example of a generally strong work ethic can be found in the interview responses of Charles West. He is a black 51-year-old clerk who grew up in X. He finds food important because "I didn't have everything growing up. I mean my mother took care of us. My father worked. Stuff like that, but it's like, you know I mean ... ." West went to public school. He became a father at age 16 and has five children and five grandchildren. He has worked as a meat packer and has held several other jobs, including working in a restaurant and in a large hospital. At the supermarket, his job is to wrap meat in cellophane, weigh and price items, clean, answer customers' questions, and put items in the bakery department freezer. He says: "You know, I like having things organized. You know in the right way it's supposed to be." West likes dealing with customers and puts effort into serving them well: "[I] try to explain to the best of my ability what they want [to know]."

> I can just look at something and know what it is in there. The bread, I know all that stuff. What kind we got, everything. So after a while I would know from listening to other people explaining stuff ... Like coworkers. And then I would know, you know just what, you know ingredients that are in it. Some people want to know, you know how much sugar and sodium, you know stuff like that. So I would try to get education on what's going on with the products.

He also likes creating a pleasant experience for customers:

> Well I feel proud when a person can come [into the store] and they leave happy and I can help them with what they want and explain to them what they're shopping for or something. I like that to help, you know ... I mean some people ... Like I get comments now where a lady was so happy that when she came in she was feeling so sad and stuff, wasn't feeling that good. And when she left, she left with a smile, and you know she was happy. You know after you know coming into the [store].

Here, West indicates that through his work, he can make a difference in people's life.

Another example of a strong work ethos that leads both to quality work and to the employee's sense of well-being can be found in the interview responses by Alexander Jones, a 46-year-old former produce clerk employed part time for 36 hours per week at Star Market. Since this interview was conducted via phone and I didn't ask, I do not the know his skin color. Jones grew up in X, and went to community college, attending a nursing program. Jones has worked in nursing, but also in student loan collection over the phone. After a car accident, he was unemployed for a time but then started working at a supermarket. He took a medical leave and was promised that he could return, but by the time he had recovered, other people had been hired and he was offered nothing more than a good reference. This was a very painful experience for him:

> I went on medical leave, they told me everything was okay and then when I came back to work at my job, they said 'oh we don't have ... We can't find the paperwork (background noise). And we hired other people and we can't use you right now. But we'll give you a good reference.' And I wasn't happy about that. I thought this was the (background noise). And then that all came from the store director. Because my manager wanted me back. But other than that I was very happy there.

He had had expectations of moving up and making a career in the supermarket: "It's a big company and there's a lot of room for growth potential. And so I might have to work for a low wage now but it's going to go up, you know." Now, Jones would like to start a meat cutter apprenticeship, because "I like meat and the pay is better." At the supermarket, he had to cut fruit and vegetables, put these into containers for sale, and label them. Sometimes he had to prepare special platters for parties and help out in the floral department next to produce. He earned $9.25 per hour. Like Ava Smith and Baptiste Laguerre, Alexander Jones expresses a strong work ethos that is closely connected with his well-being: "I mean I like to do a good job with work. I like that. I take pride in my work no matter what I'm doing." His work ethos includes special efforts to deliver high-quality work and reap the emotional rewards:

> One time I was in (background noise) fruit platter for a Harvard University party and I had no idea how to do it. And they just gave me a picture out of a magazine and said just do the best you can. So it was kind of like a scene with a tree, you know all kinds of like (background noise), like a kind of like an outdoor scene (background noise). So I was proud that I was able to replicate what they wanted.

His strong work ethos clearly serves his employer, who pays very little for his committed efforts, but it also serves him. He states explicitly what needs work fulfills for him: it provides a paycheck, a purpose, and feelings of self-worth.

> I can't survive without having money ... I don't want to say as a man, but as a person I feel I should be working. And it gives me a sense of who I am ... Just because, I don't know. When people ask 'oh, what do you do for work?' And I don't want to say nothing. Or I'm unemployed. You know. I'd rather say I work in a supermarket and you know I'm working my way up to be ... (background noise) wanted me to be an assistant manager of produce or go into the meat apprentice program. So I felt good about [it]. And I was working my way up until I got sick.

Alexander Jones's case illustrates the close connection between work ethos and subjectivity. Here, my study adds to the literature on workers' and employees' subjectivity in demonstrating how crucial a work ethos is for the formation of confidence and a sense of personhood.

An outcome of Mwangi's and others' work ethos is a sense of accomplishment, such as the feeling a salesclerk can have upon quickly ringing up a long queue of customers, contributing to a store's smooth operation. This is the facet of a strong work ethic I turn to now because it came up in several narratives about tasks and work content. Hard work and well-performed tasks generally lead to results. Work aspirations can be directed toward creating output and achieving goals (see Becker-Schmidt [1983] on activity as one of the subject's fundamental interests). As described above, Bahl (2018) links accomplishment to pride and differentiates between the production and service sectors. For low-waged labor apart from the care sector, according to her, a majority of employees perceive pride in their work ("Arbeitsstolz") as something to be performed consciously and physically. Some of my interviewees (e.g., Jones) linked a sense of accomplishment and pride to completing special or extraordinary tasks (in most cases cognitive ones). But for the most part, accomplishments are directed at maintaining a well-run supermarket through the successful fulfillment of daily tasks. While some clerks enjoy these accomplishments, others find them routine. In terms of use value, clerks' accomplishments fulfill the customers' needs: items are stocked and available, cash registers are open, and purchases can be made efficiently. In these cases, accomplishment is closely connected to use value as it relates to satisfying customers' needs. In times of neoliberalism, when staff is cut, achieving a sense of accomplishment and meeting customers' needs becomes a challenge that requires effort for workers and employees.

Gabriele Sibelius is a 48-year-old trained saleswoman working part time as a deputy shop manager at Lidl (contracted for 30 hours per week but actually working 35 hours, for which she is paid). She grew up in a provincial capital of one of the so-called new federal states of the former GDR. She has a brother who is ten years younger. Her parents worked in an agricultural cooperative headed by her grandfather. Her mother was a professional meat and sausage saleswoman and her father was a professional bricklayer. He built their house, which was quite difficult given the lack of construction materials. Sibelius completed a polytechnic comprehensive school education up to tenth grade. Her grandfather, who was the head of the family, wanted her to become a florist, but her grades were insufficient, so she started an apprenticeship at a tree nursery. Her apprenticeship ended half a year before reunification, when, together with a friend, she moved to West Germany and lived at first in federal housing. Later, when she met her first husband, she moved in with him. At age 21, she had her first daughter. When her daughter started kindergarten, Sibelius worked a 400-Euros (maximum per month) job in a small supermarket. She separated and started a new relationship, moved in with her new partner, and had a second daughter. After a while, she returned to work and after almost two years was offered a position working evenings doing the invoices and orders. After living there in the same city for 17 years, she moved to another city, where she worked in a supermarket chain. At the time of the interview, she still works there, earning 19 Euros per hour.

> The most fun is on Saturdays, when a number of my coworkers are there in the shop. Then there are four or five of us together, and it's really fun or really nice getting things done together. When the goods arrive, the storage is extremely packed once the driver has offloaded. And then we go to town, stocking those shelves, and after the shift we say, 'Yes, that storage is empty now, and all the shelves are stocked the way they're supposed to be.' Yes, and this is always a really good feeling. So then we drink a small glass of Prosecco together after the shift because we are just happy that everything worked out so well. And then everyone just says, 'Hey, it's really fun to work with you.' And yes, it's a good feeling, and it makes the others keep up, when everything just runs smoothly.

Saturdays are the busiest days, and Sibelius likes to work hard. An important part of her joy is working in a good team. Their work is directed at running a small and busy shop, an accomplishment that is an enjoyable challenge for a successful team. As in the study by Nies (2015) on engineers and bank clerks, work content orientation is not directed toward personal development, but rather toward running the operation and serving customers. Work carried out in a team can lead to mutual recognition and increased work satisfaction. Even strenuous work of this nature, if the strenuousness has to do with the content of the work and not poor conditions or corporate cost-saving measures, can run smoothly in a team, without giving rise to feelings of resistance from workers.

Jochen Hilmer has had a very different experience at his workplace and is much more critical toward the working conditions there. He is a 27-year-old graduate with a master's degree and an engineering background who works in an organic supermarket because he has not found a job in his profession yet. After one and a half years of working there, he was offered a deputy store manager position in another branch without an increase in salary. At the time of the interview, he was negotiating for a possible change. For the long term, he does not want to stay in the supermarket business. He feels flattered and frustrated at the same time. Hilmer describes his job tasks as primarily accomplishment oriented: ordering and managing sales items, managing time, imposing cleanliness, and working under pressure. He mentions several times that staff has been cut and that working conditions are stressful as tasks are concentrated among fewer workers. Nevertheless, thanks to the workers' commitment, the shop runs smoothly: "And so the commitment to the job among employees that may not feel totally behind their employer is extreme. So I don't know, that employer is really lucky that we are all busy and somehow try to pull together to keep the shop running. So yes, in this respect the commitment of the employees is really strong." His feelings about accomplishing the tasks that are set for him are ambivalent. On the one hand, he is proud of having been offered the position of deputy manager, but on the other hand, he is frustrated:

A feeling of pride? Yes, actually, often on those days when I have the late shift and the boss has left me a to-do list and I think, I'll never be able to do all of this, and then I really knuckle down and get it done, everything that needed to be done that day, then I leave the market with a feeling of pride and say, 'Okay, today I really accomplished everything.' And then maybe the next day I show up at the shop, feeling proud, and not a word of gratitude. We talked about this earlier. So then I just have to be proud for myself (laughs), I don't know – there's no one to share the feeling with. I guess this is generally the case in retail, you don't ever really finish everything, it's a continuing process of repetitive tasks ... You always start again at the beginning, and it's always the same scenarios.

Hilmer describes the tasks as repetitive and never-ending. On days when his to-do list is so long that he feels unable to complete everything but still does finally accomplish it all, he feels proud. However, this experience does not change the feeling that the tasks are endless and much the same, a sense that mitigates his pride in his accomplishments. In addition to his accomplishment orientation, he is inclined toward a use value orientation when talking about his work in that he mentions more than once the importance of offering consultation to customers. Asked about the ideal working conditions, he mentions having enough time to advise customers. In addition, he talks about the essential work they do in feeding the population: "In any case, we do a job that is essential because without food retail, people will be unable to buy food. But it is not seen that way. Instead, food retail is taken for granted." Hilmer's work appropriation is characterized by ambivalences. His master's degree makes him overqualified for a position in retail, but at the same time he lacks knowledge of the field. He would rather work elsewhere, but his current path has offered him a chance to climb the career ladder. He acknowledges the importance of his work in terms of providing food for the population, but he is also aware of how little value society places on what he does.

Asiye Kaya's responses about her work also resonate with Bahl (2018) in that she implies a link between pride and accomplishment. Referring to the end of a working day, she notes that she feels proud

when work is done: items are shelved, perfectly, in a line at the front, everything in the basement, put signs to it, shop is swept, garbage emptied, doors, windows closed: accomplished! When cup is lined next to cup and not to saltcellar [she pushes a cup and a saltcellar on the table where we are sitting during the interview], as an example. I step back: I have put away beautifully. Very beautiful! One watches it: looks beautiful! Then more motivation to continue.

Kaya is a 28-year-old deputy store manager of Pfennigland, working full time with a net wage of 1,200 Euros a month. Her parents immigrated from Turkey, and she grew up in X. She started working six years ago and was promoted four years ago. She does not want to become a store manager: "No! not a manager! Then too much responsibility: coworkers, if items arrive, decide, if boss arrives and talks: always say, everything is okay." She recently married a man who arrived from Turkey. She attended school for ten years and completed an apprenticeship in social work with public funding through a private vocational school with fees, but she received public funding. During her vocational education, she had three internships: one in a kindergarten, a second in a care facility, and the third in housekeeping. After her internships, she wanted to work in a kindergarten, but for that she needed a four-year vocational education, and she found that too long. She did not want to work in care, so after six months of unemployment upon graduating and applying for several jobs, she found employment at a discount store. Her mother was very relieved as she always told her to work ("my mom: 'work, work, demonstrate that you work!'"), to earn money. Kaya has a twin sister who works part time as a pediatrician's receptionist and earns more than Kaya and her younger brother, who receives 600 Euros per month for his vocational education. She had received less during her vocational education. Money is central to Kaya's narration because it serves as an important motivator. She suffers from earning a low wage and states, "it would be good to receive Christmas money separately, so it is not deducted, but received in my hand." In general, an increase in salary would be important as "one works a lot." Despite her low wage, Kaya is very patient with customers. If they look for something they are unable to name in German or Turkish, she asks for a photo or offers a pad and pen to draw the desired item. Kaya feels a constant need to accomplish that is linked to her work ethos: she feels compelled to leave her register if items need to be inspected, checked, or shelved, or if tables need to be cleaned and floors swept. "I am unable to stay; I lift it up if an item is placed wrongly. I feel guilty if I do not do nothing, five minutes, I think, if work remains, I get up." Her "parents are happy that I am employed: main thing earn money. Mom: 'thanks god!' She is happy that we work, it is important to work, to earn money." Kaya's work ethos is oriented toward accomplishment while avoiding conflicts, stress, and exhaustion. When an item is priced at 1.49 Euros and the cashier says it should be marked as 1.79 Euros and customers complain, she simply rings the item up at the lower price: "the customer is happy, and I am not stressed." Serenity is what she radiates. She is secure in her place, in terms of both work content accomplishment and her job position.

Stefanie Moser is a 50-year-old clerk who mainly works as a cashier at Rewe. She is also a first deputy workers' council member, stepping in to attend workers' council meetings and activities to fill in for any of the five elected regular members. She previously held the position of workers' council member. Moser grew up in X. She is the only child of adopted parents (and is not in contact with her biological family). Her adoptive mother also worked in retail, selling furs, and her adoptive father was a professor of physics at a college for applied sciences in engineering. Moser attended compulsory polytechnical school for ten years, as was common in the GDR. During her childhood she had back problems and could not choose her later profession. In the GDR, the job center played a crucial role in deciding who is assigned to which vocational education. In the mid-1980s she completed vocational education for working in a post office. She had an inclination to this work because her father had taken her often to the post office when she was small, and she had been allowed to sit behind the desk. Until the fall of the Berlin Wall, she worked in her profession. The reunification entailed a reorganization of the post office, and she would have to become a civil servant in order to continue her job. She decided not to do so as she saw herself as more of a worker than a bureaucrat. She therefore left the post office to sell newspapers for three years. She started a relationship with a man who had three children, and as a consequence she wanted a more family-friendly work schedule. Also, she aimed for a higher income and more responsibility in her job. Since the mid-1990s, she has worked at a mid-range supermarket – not a discounter, but also not a high-end store. At the time of the interview, she is still employed by the same company. Similar to Asiye Kaya, she is not a professionally educated supermarket clerk. However, her professional training and work experience were crucial for being hired at the supermarket, mainly as a cashier, for whom contact and communication with customers and handling money are crucial. Her narrative is shaped by a hurtful experience at work, which she chose not to discuss in detail, but which caused her to be transferred to another branch and fight to return. She is now employed part time and has lost her position as head cashier, which entailed the responsibility for ensuring a correct balance for all of the cashiers and counting all of the proceeds at the end of the shift.

Moser emphasizes that she doesn't mind working part time and having peace of mind without the extra responsibilities (for which clerks are not paid). The tone running through her narration conveys what might be called "frustrated detachment," which entails placing boundaries on one's emotional involvement and achieving a state of relative equanimity. Her work ethos is reflected in her commitment, but she also follows her own interests in warding off her employers' demands and not going beyond the duties specified in her contract. Her negative work experience contributed to a special feature of her case, her determination to meet the requirements of work and accomplish her assigned tasks without aiming for top-level performance:

> And on Christmas Eve people are queuing through the whole shop. Yes. You can't get around that. But it doesn't bother me: I just get slower and work more precisely. I'm not going to get rid of these people one way or another, so there's no need to knock myself out. The way I see it, I work my hours and earn an hourly wage. I don't have a performance-based salary. Full stop. Other colleagues hold other views. But everybody has to manage for him- or herself.

In contrast to several other interviewee narratives in which accomplishment is described as only reachable through extraordinary effort and faster performance, Moser points to another kind of accomplishment: executing her duties deliberately and with precision. She justifies her attitude by pointing to her remuneration in the form of an hourly wage that is not tied to performance, but her approach is also functional, directed toward purpose and usefulness. Apart from extraordinarily busy days, such as during the Christmas season, Moser describes her work content and tasks as being directed toward accomplishment:

> I am kind of a gofer, I would say. So, I am not just standing behind the register … Someone might say, 'Please unpack the milk,' 'Put the sandwich rolls away,' or 'Clear the empty bottles from the belt and put them with the recycling.' So I'm in multifunction mode. It's not that I am just sitting there for eight hours. You're getting up and doing this and that. Or: 'Could you step in as deputy?' 'Could you unpack milk?' Well, then I just might spend a whole shift unpacking and shelving milk. I don't have a problem with that. All of this is part of my job description: I'm a store clerk with cashier duties. It is not a problem, no, and simply all the tasks that arise … And everybody has his hobbyhorse. As I said, I do dairy, cleaning up, rummaging, cleaning up eggs, and so on. The next person takes care of newspapers; everyone has his special thing.

The distribution of tasks is flexible at her workplace, an arrangement that goes against Frey's (2009) assertion that employees lose autonomy when the use value of their labor power increases. It seems that in her case, the organization has successfully combined autonomy with making profits. Moser achieves a measure of autonomy in being able to make her own decisions about which tasks to perform or prioritize. "If the flow of customers allows, I can get up and leave. But the customer comes first, and when it's crowded, I can't just say, 'I'm going to close the register and go put something away.'" She also defines accomplishment in terms of her motivation to satisfy customers' needs:

> Uh, I am a person you seldom see sitting around with a nasty look on my face. If I'm running around the shop, I'm still always approachable, even if I'm on break. I try to apply the Rewe philosophy. Go with the customer to the shelf and show them where the item is, don't just say 'row 7, spot 35.' Yes, I really try to go along

with the customer, or if there are problems, to solve it together, in the interest of the customer, even if others say, 'Hey, what are you doing?' I mean, this is the way it is, there's a problem that needs solving. So, I try to do that, and the customers in this store and previous ones I've worked in have really appreciated that, the fact that they can always ask me and know they'll get a pleasant, polite answer. That I'll help them and not drag my feet.

The last quote goes beyond an accomplishment orientation and expresses Moser's work ethos. For her, the use value of her work consists in direct and immediate fulfillment of customers' articulated needs. In people-oriented rather than task-oriented attitudes as well as in achieving accomplishment without exhaustion, the narrations of Asiye Kaya and Stefanie Moser are similar. Moser's statements resonate partly with Bahl's (2018) account of taking pride in accomplishment:

> Yeah, there are always days when my register is kind of getting the job done. It's not much different from when you are so busy you have no time to look up. Like on a really stressful day, like during the Christmas season. Where people – the customers – are not in a good mood, because they're stressed out themselves. Yes, on days like that I am really like, 'Man, today the day went really well.' Now you are looking forward to going home to your couch [incomprehensible] or spending the evening at the theater or doing whatever you have planned.

But Moser also goes beyond Bahl's observations in connecting her feelings of pride at a job well done with extraordinary performance, not just accomplishing the required tasks.

I want to finish the section on work ethos with the account given by Wolfgang Gerke. His narrative serves as an important contribution to understanding use value formation as a dimension of work appropriation. His story demonstrates more clearly than others the dilemma of the use value of the labor force itself. His childhood was much harder than that of many others I interviewed because of his mental illness: his social anxiety and depression are a very heavy burden on his life and make it difficult for him to function in the workplace. But I refrain from categorizing his case as "special" as there were other interviewees who have experienced difficult childhoods and who also struggled with mental illness. In general, child abuse and depression are widespread social problems. What makes his case intriguing is the extent to which he contributes to his own exploitation by framing his commitment to work as medicine. Even exploitative work helps him to cope with his personal difficulties. There are three aspects of Gerke's labor power that result in use value for his employer: his motivation, his availability, and his overqualification. All three are consequences of his illness and rooted in vulnerability. His case offers insights into how employees' feelings of inferiority can be exploited by employers. I will start with a short overview of his biography and continue with an account of three ways in which work and work ethos can become forms of use value.

Gerke is 33 years old and by contract works 60 hours per month at Edeka. He receives a reduced earning capacity pension. He grew up in a small town in Bavaria, in a working-class family. His older half-sister is also being treated for mental health issues. He also has a younger sister. His mother is genetically predisposed to depression. Gerke has had various difficulties with his father, on which he does not elaborate further, and he felt let down by his mother when she returned to his father and the family broke apart. Gerke went to live with a foster family at the age of 16 and stayed until he was 21. His foster parents had biological and more foster children, and it was an "ongoing coming and going." Gerke attended a special-needs school, elementary school, and high school (college preparatory). He repeated the tenth grade because of depression but still did not pass. So, he left and attended a vocational-track school with a focus on social work. After graduation, he moved with a friend from school to X. He worked in several "one-Euro-jobs" (additional cost compensation jobs) and later attended a one-year vocational course in a technical area and then started vocational education (3.5 years) as a device and system electronic technician. After graduating, he worked for two-and-a-half weeks at a full-time post and had a breakdown. The job had entailed working at a piece rate, checking devices in seconds. In addition, he had a commute of two hours each way. Another job was in sight, but when a colleague got preference, Gerke became frustrated. He returned to his foster parents to care for them for two years, and after both died he spent the next four years distributing advertisements and newspapers. At the time of the interview, he has been working mainly as a cashier for six months.

From a distance I could spot Gerke, as we agreed to meet on a Sunday afternoon for the interview outside a café: he wore a sweater with large letters from his corporation. He explained immediately:

> like today, it is "open-for-business Sunday," and although I am not on the schedule, I still did the whole thing of getting up, showering, and so on. So, just being at the ready. I've been doing this, actually since October, since my trial period, where it started with overtime or filling in for others. Because they know they can rely on me all the time and I live the closest to work.

The shop where he works is part of a chain, but privately owned. It is one of the "better" supermarkets. Gerke is extraordinarily committed to his work: "After my shift, I walk through the aisles without somebody telling me and make sure everything is tidy. I collect the shopping baskets and of course the goods that customers didn't want to buy, and I put them back on the shelves." He also arrives early to collect shopping carts from the parking lot. Gerke makes explicit reference to his extraordinary motivation as he talks about his work: "Well, I am the kind of guy where people think they have never seen someone so friendly, so accommodating, and so highly motivated. They're not used to seeing this in a salesclerk. They think I must have been put in the wrong job." But: "it motivates me to work ... Work is actually like medicine for me." Because of his illness he has an exemption from work, but he nevertheless works to feel better. His 3.5-year vocational education qualifies him for a job far beyond his responsibilities as a cashier with the lowest level of authorization. The work he performs required only a brief introduction to the cash register and payment by credit card or with food stamps, along with other issues such as canceling a sale or selling fireworks or alcohol. "I already learned that on my own or knew it already, even from my teenage years. I apply what I know and, let's say, even though no one showed me how, I do it. But if I observe things in other cashiers, a system for the register or whatever they do, I just copy what they do." Gerke burns for his work and is adjusting to having a job again and being around other people, working up to his goal of becoming a professional clerk but moving at his own pace: "the largest benefit I have is the personal training in dealing with people and of course with work in general." But for the moment, "I am scheduled for a rhythm of 60 hours [per month]. I wouldn't want to do more. The amount of pressure from work is exactly right." Gerke receives a low wage: "Payment is actually better than good, I feel. I'm grossing 10.20 Euros now instead of 8.82 Euros," he says.

His case illustrates a dilemma: his work appropriation is both healing and (self-) exploitation. He compensates for the burden of his personal struggles through extreme commitment and the efforts he puts in at work. But although the work brings health benefits to him, he is paid very little, and nearly all of the financial benefits of the arrangement accrue to the shop owner.

# 7. Activity, coming to terms with the job

In this chapter, I offer results on my analysis of work activity as part of the interviewees' process of coming to terms with their jobs. I have found two broad patterns of work activity: one relates to change and the other to continuity. These two patterns largely correspond to the two countries under investigation. The activity pattern involving change relates more to German contexts, and the pattern of continuity relates more to U.S. contexts.

As I explained in the theory chapter, activity leads to subject formation. Therefore, it is a dimension of work appropriation that unfolds over a longer work experience in social contexts. This section focuses on the parts of the interviewees' responses in which they reflect upon their many years in retail, creating portraits of change and continuity. I will demonstrate how these experiences contributed to a personal reconstruction or reconfiguration, which Leontjew (2012 [1975]) referred to as "Umbau." How these personal experiences are received and processed in relation to supermarket clerks' living conditions, and how they result in Umbau, will be the focus of my analysis. The necessity of personal reconstruction stems from the need to appropriate the world actively, as Leontjew (2012 [1975]) has stated. This reconstruction requires gradual interiorization that unfolds interdependently with living conditions. Activity in the context of work appropriation is both individual and social. It is individual since the activity is bound to an individual human being, and it is social since the meaning of tasks and the ways they are organized necessarily involve more than one person. This leads to an endless variety of activities unfolding in multiple possible patterns. My study singles out patterns of change and continuity. The pattern of change prevails in Germany as there the forms of processing are more manifold than in the U.S. because in Germany employees have more knowledge, more rights, a greater variety of tasks, and more flexibility. Nevertheless, two of the U.S. clerks I interviewed also underwent change, even though it was substantially different from what the German clerks experienced. I will discuss these country-specific differences later, but first I will introduce processes of change that emerged from the interviews.

## PROCESSES OF CHANGE

The five portraits of change in this section differ in terms of the reasons and circumstances behind the nature and direction of those changes. What unites these examples are fundamental processes of reconstructing individual subjectivities. As a result, the attitudes toward and significance of the occupation for the supermarket clerks changed over the years.

## Simone Koch

An important factor that can lead to processes of change is the deterioration of working conditions. The example of Simone Koch could be represented using a satisfaction curve that rises at the beginning of her vocational education and remains high as she begins to work but after a couple of years, as she becomes disenchanted, traces a path downward. During her apprenticeship, she developed a positive professional identity leading to a satisfactory work life, but when working conditions worsened, her satisfaction declined, and she ended up leaving the job.

Simone Koch was born in 1977 in a small town in Thuringia. She grew up with her parents and grandparents in the same house. At the age of 12, the GDR collapsed, and teachers no longer knew what to teach in the schools. A year later, when the GDR reunited with the Federal Republic of Germany, Koch was in the ninth grade and realized that she disliked school. She decided against going to a college-preparatory high school, which was something previously unknown in the former GDR, and ended her studies with a secondary school certificate. It was a time of great turmoil and insecurity, and Koch had no concrete plans for her own future. She applied for various apprenticeships in an arbitrary way, from plumbing to auto repair, and also retail. Having grown up in East Germany, she had been socialized in a society in which women were oriented toward employment and earning their own incomes and being independent. She received an invitation for an interview with a supermarket chain. "And I went there with red torn jeans and in a checkered shirt. So, no idea. There I was having a chat with the boss, and then I asked: 'Well, what's next?' 'Well, we'll send you a contract of apprenticeship.'" From 1993–1996, Koch worked as a retail salesclerk apprentice. The supermarket was very close to her home. In the mornings, she worked there for four hours stocking shelves. In the evenings she put away fruits and vegetables. During the break, she would return home. In vocational school, two days a week, 20 kilometers from her home, changes due to reunification were perceptible. In the economics and law classes, teachers "had just learned what to teach us. This was still very theoretical."

Koch presents herself as having been an aimless, rather lazy teenager in a time of great societal transformation. During the apprenticeship, she changed and became a responsible professional. Thus, her vocational education was a period of important socialization, in terms of both personality and professionalism. An important precondition for enjoying her apprenticeship was the experience of being respected.

> I was also always recognized as equal compared to others. Well, I know of many other apprentices among my friends who have learned to become electricians, for example, and if you visited them on the weekends, they were shoveling snow for the master they were apprenticing with. This made me think: 'Yes, they may be apprentices, but actually, no, this is not the meaning and purpose of an apprentice-ship.' I was taught that I was supposed to have fun and they would too. Yes, we were not on a first-name basis in the beginning, but later we would be together at a wedding-eve party and everybody offered to start going by first names. Exactly. And after that, we belonged together, one was part of a team. Like: 'Here come the Tengelmann [grocery chain] workers.' Something like that, and you knew you were part of it.

She talks about experiencing a mixture of being taken seriously as an apprentice who is learning and being treated as a colleague who is working. In her account, the integrative power of apprenticeships becomes obvious. At the supermarket, she is systematically instructed in every section, and at the same time her needs and wishes for schedules are taken into account as well.

> In the early morning, one waited in front of the supermarket until everybody arrived. Then the supermarket opened. Then everyone started quite normally, some setting up their cash registers. And if I, for example, was working in produce, the first day, you actually had to just work according to instructions. Sort of like you didn't even know what a lime was, you know? And early on you started working alongside somebody and they'd tell you, 'No, you need to turn it this way, because … .' Actually everything was explained to everybody. And after three months you got transferred to, say, dairy products. There you related a few things in the early morning and then later you're told, 'If you stock this, you need to take care of this or have that in mind.' And you started by checking expiration dates to see if anything on the shelves had expired. You checked every yogurt daily. Then you'd develop a routine, and eventually the person who's been teaching you all of this stuff says, 'You are ready, you can move on to the next thing. You know it now.' And so it went from shelf to shelf, department to department.

Every three months she switched to a new department where she would receive first explanations and instructions and later the chance to work autonomously.

> Yes, later I was in the meat section and I said, 'Three months in the meat department is too short.' They have cheese. They prepared salads themselves. They have a fish section. And I would like to spend more time on meat and sausages. And therefore I really only filled up a deep freezer for an hour and then headed through the crowd, behind the sales counter and was preparing salads myself. I worked at the cheese counter. There were customers. Well, because I said I would like to spend longer on meats, we went more into detail. I am not a trained sales clerk for meat and sausages, but I think in the meantime I'm becoming as good in this area as in the others.

To learn more about the degree of autonomy she experienced during her apprenticeship, I asked her whether she really had influence to focus on her interests and pose questions, and Koch answered: "Yes. Hm. And I have had always colleagues around who said 'yes' and didn't obstruct or say 'No time!' No, they their took time, which they actually had." Koch talks about how she learned what clockwise yogurt was and also learned that a strawberry yogurt contains 0.5 grams of strawberry. Koch acquires knowledge of the products and the organization of a supermarket. There are internal exams. She values her apprenticeship "This was really very well structured, hm, especially the cash register and office work training. There's a bit more there and you don't really get a routine going: orders before Christmas are different from after-Christmas orders. And so, well, the plan made sense, I would say." At vocational school, she learns background knowledge: "You understand why this product is so expensive or how it could be made cheaper or so. Because you understand the whole background connected to it, it's not just that the shop is there. There's a lot more to it, and you understand that." Recalling the final exam, which takes place with examiners of the Chamber of Industry and Commerce (IHK), she is indignant about the questions she had to choose from as she identifies with her field of expertise, which was not touched upon:

> No, the exam took place at IHK and it's almost like a game of chance. You never know how the examiners will be. For example, I got the topic ... [one has to draw from three topics] 'You're selling a cashmere sweater! And I have washed it at home without following instructions, and now I want to return it!' And I read the piece of paper and said to myself, 'Cashmere. Hmm.' And then I went in and said: 'Yes, good morning, I am sorry, but I'm afraid I can't exchange your cashmere sweater because I work at Tengelmann, and we don't sell sweaters! I'm not sure where you bought it.' They looked at me and smiled, and then one of the examiners said, 'Well, while I'm here, maybe you can tell me: when I make fruit salad, it always turns brown! Can you give me a tip on what to do about that?' And I said 'Why, lemon juice, my dear!' I got a B! But that could have gone badly, that's for sure.

At the end of her apprenticeship, Koch was a professional supermarket clerk. This sequence demonstrates her identification with the content of her job. What was arbitrary three years ago is now an important part of her subjectivity.

After her apprenticeship, Koch was hired by the supermarket, and when her store closed, she switched to another from the same chain 30 kilometers away together with her colleagues, who commute with her. Soon she developed the desire to leave the area and move away. She asked her boss for a job elsewhere and received an offer in Hamburg.

> Yes, and then we moved to Hamburg, Friday evening. And there I had a young female boss. I went in and thought, 'Jesus! A young – let me say it straight – Hamburg bitch!' And she saw me and said, 'Oh, here comes my Ossi [East

German]!' The first week this was a real pain, because of our prejudices. She was also a vegetarian, and there I was around noon thinking about what kind of meat I would have for dinner, so it didn't look as if there was any common denominator there. And I thought, 'Is this how it's going to be?' And then she came to me and said, 'Well, I need to tell you something.' Because I had done nothing but work the register in the first week. 'No one working the register here has ever gone and done other work to the side.' And I said 'Otherwise it's boring just sitting there!' In between customers I had been restocking the fruits and vegetables or taking a look to see what needed doing. Nobody had done that before. And then we started to chat. And in the evening, the door wouldn't lock and we were waiting for security, and we stood there, the two of us. And really, this was still a tense relationship, and I said: 'You know, this is really stupid!' – 'How do you mean?' I said, 'Well, you come here as an "Ossi," and then nobody wants to talk to you!' I was goading her a bit. And she said, 'Hm, hm. But I think we'll work it out. I actually like you!' she said later. And I said, 'Yeah, me too, somehow!' and since then, that evening, we've been inseparable.

After this difficult start, Koch felt better at work. Another incident further demonstrated her knowledge and professionalism. Her cash register has a special form that needs to be filled out, and she couldn't find one in the file. She mentioned to her colleagues that more needed to be printed up, and they didn't know anything about it because whenever they encountered the same problem, they would just call the boss.

Another aspect of her work that she appreciated was being part of a committed team. She and her colleagues drew close through their shared experiences:

> … there were five or six of us there regularly, sometimes fewer, depending on the day. When goods arrived, there were more of us. When there was nothing to clear away, why should five of us work? And later we also met privately, or when there was the Alster Festival: 'Today we close an hour earlier!' But nobody was supposed to know that, for heaven's sake!

Quiet subversion of the normal rules – sometimes favoring the staff, like closing early, or the customers, like just leaving a pallet with goods on the floor to offer more of them at once in the scarce space of an inner-city supermarket – brought the team closer together. Simone Koch describes herself as working at times like this with joy. She even enjoys being called upon by her colleagues for her ability to work with especially difficult customers. "They'd send me to deal with them and say, 'Have at it, Simone!' I know how to keep my cool. ('Be calm!' as the customers say. I love that.) Because I had learned how to do that. We practiced all kinds of situations."

When her first son was about two or three, she decided she wanted him to grow up the way she had, in the countryside and close to grandparents. So her family moved back to Thuringia. She was offered a job as manager of the butcher's shop, but she turned it down because she hadn't worked in such a department for five years. Instead, she started in a lower-level, part-time position in the same department. From about 2005 onward, retail changed. Cost efficiency measures became more prominent, and this meant a reduction in staff. As a result, there was less time for customer service and consultation. This went along with a reduction in clerks' participation in making decisions. She began to have less autonomy, and orders came increasingly from above.

It started, I would say: what year is it now? It was about ten years ago. And suddenly, going through instructions, it was like: 'What is this now?' There is someone above us who has no idea about meat. Somehow. And we had been having super good inventories and super good sales figures. But these really went down later. And suddenly you no longer had time for the customers. At some point they say, 'Well, I am just getting into line so that you are being served faster at some point.' And issues like when you're offering beef roulade, there's a lot left over that you can use to make ground beef. No, ground pork was on sale – who was going to buy ground beef? Even though you told them, in the end, you'd still have to throw the leftover beef away. You weren't allowed to make decisions, like putting ground beef on special along with ground pork. For God's sake! This was something where I thought, 'Wow, you really have to start fighting with yourself because it just makes no sense!' They just went against everything we learned in vocational school.

This sequence illustrates how changes in the work structure injured Koch's sense of her professional identity. New organizational regulations impeded her ability to act as a professional clerk, leading her to develop negative feelings and a resistant attitude toward work. Sarah Nies (2015) describes a similar impact in relation to impediments to realizing use value. Koch's expectations for work, based on the professional socialization that she had internalized in practice, were not met. Her former ability to make decisions at work was taken away. The company's interests were defined rigidly, and individual initiative was now discouraged. She was forced to carry out orders without contributing more:

Before you knew, from Monday onward this and that is on sale, so you do this and that on Saturday. As preparation. Now you receive a note on Friday: 'This must be prepared tomorrow for Monday! In exactly this way!' So, you do not need brains anymore, if you follow the note to a tee. Because if you would switch on your brain you would say, 'Doing this at the time designated in this note is impossible, you can't do it!' Because there just might be a customer or two who wants to buy something.

Simone Koch describes feeling demoralized at being asked to carry out orders that make no sense. Having decisions taken away from her and her coworkers results in feelings of being undervalued. At the same time, the workload and hours increase without a corresponding increase in pay. "It says on the schedule 6:30 a.m., but you got a dirty look if you arrived at 6:30 a.m. [They expected you at] 5:30 a.m. You'd also go later than the official 4 p.m. quitting time. At home you would say, 'well, I should be home about 5:30 or 6 p.m., with any luck.'" The increased workload affected her health: "During this time, I lost 10 kilos. I was working all day because I had almost no staff and then I realized, I should go to the gynecologist, something is wrong. And I was six months pregnant." Long working hours and having two children was leading to further exhaustion. However, when the second child was two years old, Koch accepted an offer from the company to return and work as floor manager. "'So, my dear Ms. Koch, your child has grown up. Now we need a floor manager again!' And I said, 'This is the last time you transfer me, because within the company, there are fires to put out everywhere and your dear Ms. Koch will take care of it!'" She started working, but not to the same extent as before. Her private life changed now too, with two children in the picture.

> I started early in the morning, at 6 a.m., and worked until 4 p.m. And I would write down the hours I was working, with half an hour break. Suddenly, they came to me and said, 'Well, Ms. Koch, half an hour break – you are entitled to two hours break time!" I say: 'Well, then see where you can spare me for two hours!' – 'Well, it is not so busy, you can always just keep watch now and then!' I said: 'Well, then I will go to the hairdresser for two hours and someone else can keep watch now and then!' And then inside I was thinking, 'Screw you! Now I'm on a crusade, for law and order,' as they say. I said, 'No way!'

Koch is not willing to *lie* about the work schedule, but she was willing to work an hour and a half extra every day without being paid. Her attitude makes it clear that she is still very committed to her work and wants the shop to function. The conflict culminates because, as line manager, she is not willing to sign work schedules for her colleagues lying about the actual break time. She argues that her colleagues could turn her in for that. For a year and half, Koch would begin her early morning shifts and expect a call in the evening, which came. "And at some stage the air went out of the balloon." She was exhausted from the internal strain of hurt feelings and disillusionment and from the stress of her ambivalent leadership position, in which she acquired responsibility but not power. She also had a family to attend to. Her insistence on correct behavior at work fed into the perception that she was resisting management. Eventually, she received a warning. Her lawyer was optimistic, but the company is powerful, and after a couple of months, she received a severance payment.

Her reaction was one of exhausted frustration: "One cannot laugh about it, where I say: 'Gosh!' and quietness, simply quietness." Koch's life trajectory shows very sharp shifts, from joy at acquiring knowledge and skills, through satisfaction over working successfully and professionally in a team, to finally becoming completely frustrated and demoralized by her working conditions.

This process of change in her subjective experience of her activity is mainly influenced by the deterioration in working conditions that occurred over the years in her places of work.

Koch's case could be described using Giegel's (1989, see above) perspective as one in which the person adheres to her unconsciously acquired values during vocational education and socialization to maintain her identity, even if it is detrimental to her. She remains faithful to herself at the cost of losing her job – but not her soul.

A similar example of starting with very positive experiences and joy at work to struggling hard and finally leaving is illustrated in the following life history. However, in this case the content of interiorization, the focus of the work activity, is very different.

## Peter Swing

Peter Swing is a white 28-year-old man at the time of the interview. His narrative contains two very different parts: the first consists of warm reflections on his time at the supermarket where he worked contentedly for ten years. The second part covers the last year and a half at the store, when working conditions made his life miserable. His experience can be rendered as a curve similar to the one identified with Simone Koch's story, but in his case the reasons for his initial satisfaction with his job are quite different from those of Koch.

Swing grew up with his mother and a brother who was ten years older; he had a close relationship with both. His father died when he was still young, and his mother died when he was 19. The supermarket where he has worked since the age of 14 is right across the street from his house. He was still in school when he began working there, but he later dropped out. He recalls: "So it was a fascinating place to work. So when I first started working there I was this stupid immature high school kid, and my first year there was really tough, and it was the first job I ever had. And I goofed around a lot." Swing describes himself as a young person who is not used to work and has trouble taking orders and maintaining discipline. This was the case in school, but at work this changed because he felt he was being treated fairly.

> Well I'd had a really tough time in high school and my public school education. I did not have respect for authority. Anyone outside of my mother. I loved my mother and her voice was the one I listened to, and that [had an] (…) effect at Shaw's too. I think I said I didn't get along with my bosses at first, but the difference between school and Shaw's was I felt like they treated me for the most part fairly. Whereas at school I didn't.

For him, this made all the difference in the way he related to his work. He developed an attitude of openness toward learning, cooperating, and performing well. The following section demonstrates this development:

> And then we got an assistant grocery manager whose name was Bill ... And at first I was the goofy immature kid, so Bill didn't like me at first at all and he actually cut me down to three hours a week for an entire summer, but he wanted me to quit and he told me, 'I want you to quit, I don't need an immature kid around here,' and he was really tough on me too, which was good. I remember one of the first times that I met him we were in the back and we were unloading a truck. We were opening up a truck and I was opening it up and I looked up and I [said], 'Hey Bill, how's it going?' and he was focusing on everything outside and he [went], 'Get used to being down there because you're going to be working on your knees for the rest of your life,' and I was [like], 'It's good to meet you, too!' But getting my hours cut to three hours a week made me work harder because I wanted to get more hours and I wanted to show them that I could do it. I was actually going to ask for a transfer to another store, but the weekend when I went in to ask for it, I got more hours. It was just a really weird coincidence, and Bill started giving me more hours because I was working harder, and he's treating me a lot nicer, and me and him became really good friends. I still talk to him to this day. He's moved out of town and he doesn't work for the company anymore, but he had been working there for a long time, and the guy is like a brother to me at this point. That's how close our department was.

Swing experienced that an improvement in his performance resulted in an improvement in his working hours and recognition. For him, working well is inseparably connected to the emotional dimension of being respected. He experienced work as a form of probation that he could weather successfully, gaining recognition.

> They always made sure that I had good hours, and during the summer I was working 40 hours a week. There was one time I worked for 50 hours during the week, so during the summer I would actually work more than them. So we took care of each other when they knew and when they needed somebody to come in, I would come in because really, I looked up to these guys, especially Bill, and they knew I was reliable.

The growing emotional bond goes very deep: "There was so much we had to do. It was hard work, but we would come in and then we would all get lunch at the same time. We would order food from Chinese food or a pizza place or whatever. It was really like we were a family and we took care of each other too." The fatherless and later also motherless, resistant teenager became a hard-working colleague and acquired a family with caring brothers who were role models for him. During this time, Swing went back to school, but not to an ordinary high school. It was a community learning center without grades and with supportive staff. He completed his high school equivalent and began attending college part time to study communication for a two-year associates degree. Here one of the three biographical patterns Brose (1983) identifies in his research on work experiences, the pattern of further qualification, is observable. Swing then moved on to another college for general studies. Like Simone Koch, Swing experiences work as becoming a member of a community. But unlike her, his focus is on the social relations he builds through work rather than on taking pride in applying his vocational knowledge and acting professionally. His motivation is aimed at his coworkers' well-being:

> I grew up in that store and because those guys treated me well when I worked hard because I wanted to work hard for them because I loved them and I didn't want to not do well in my job and then have them come in the next day because I had been there. Like I said, on Sundays I was there on my own, so I saw what happened when we fell behind in work, and [I didn't want] for that to happen to them.

Part of this mutuality was a slight increase in his wage, which helped him to get through college.

These positive experiences ended when working conditions declined. Swing narrates in detail a whole list of incidents that lead to him losing his motivation and satisfaction at work and starting to "slack off." It started during a recession, when full-timers were told, "'You can either take a buyout and get laid off or you can go part-time,' and the ones that were dumb enough to go part-time got their hours cut after that, and a lot of people got laid off, so morale went down really low." Not only were staff cut, but long-term managers left and the new policy of changing managers started. "They usually transfer them out because the company doesn't want people to feel too comfortable in one store, so they will transfer full-timers, management." The store manager, who "didn't want to micro-manage you," was replaced by a woman who "had to be involved in everything … she bothered the department heads and they got really stressed out." Swing describes micro-management as an increase in control over employees: "managers were breathing down their back all of the time. They were watching them. Telling them what to do." He remembers a so-called efficiency policy that aimed at organizing the work space better through labeling.

> So some of it made sense. There was a certain section in the back room where you store water and they put a sign that said, "Water," so everyone knew where to put the water, but they went nuts with it. I remember opening up the freezer one time and a pallet of ice had a sticker on it that said "Ice" and I remember hearing from one of the boys who was at my store that had put a sign that said "Clock" at the clock.

While these changes might be seen as harmless or just funny, they undermined respect for employees. Other measures such as blocking, which is stocking shelves so that they look full without actually being full, were consequences of the lack of staff, for example the night crew. The remaining clerks tried to offer enough items to customers by leaving pallets on floors, as they had done in Simone Koch's store. The new management policies included new rules for clothing. Up until then it had been acceptable to show up in jeans, shoes, and a polo shirt, but now clerks had to tuck their shirts into black pants and wear full-length aprons and black shoes. Staff had to buy the clothes themselves. The dress code created uniformed staff, which Swing considered humiliating, echoing Ehrenreich's (2011 [2001]) findings on ways in which low-wage jobs impose measures that erode workers' dignity. As Swing relates:

> They wouldn't buy them for you, and black shoes. So these shoes weren't black enough. They had to be completely black and no logos. So I fought this for a while because I'm getting paid 10.66 an hour and I don't want to have to go out and buy shoes just for work. So most of my department (inaudible) he just wanted to get the job done. The store manager didn't even really care that much, but her assistant did because he was working his way up the ladder and he wanted to (inaudible), so nobody said anything until he walked up to me and he was, 'Your shoes aren't black enough!' and I was, 'Okay, what do you want me to do?' and he was like, 'You need to get a pair of shoes' and I said, 'I'm not getting black shoes because I can't afford them and I'm not going to do it,' and he said, 'Well you can't work here,' and I said, 'Well I guess I'm not working here anymore.' So then Susan the store manager walked out to me and she was like I said, she wasn't a bad person but she's very manipulative and she goes, 'You have to wear black shoes or we can't schedule you,' and I said, 'What do you want me to do?' and she was alright and I'll never forget this, she goes, 'Come with me upstairs' and I go upstairs and she goes, 'Take your shoes off,' and I took my shoes off and put them on the table and they spray painted them black. They spray painted – I still have them. In fact, once the spray paint started wearing off, they started saying, 'The shoes aren't black enough anymore.' Spray painted them black to go by this code. So I started to get that I could go in and work my butt off but it didn't matter how hard I worked. What they were really focused on was I'm wearing my apron or my shoes are black, or was my shirt tucked in and that sort of thing. And on top of that they called it the 'Grand reopening' of the stores.

The humiliation extended to the customers, too. Swing, who knew the store like the back of his hand and sent customers to exactly the right place when they asked where items were ("'where's sugar?' 'The front half of isle 7 on the left-hand side bottom shelf'") now had to walk customers to the item. The understaffed store employed a "customer service sales manager" who had to stand in the middle of the store greeting customers and asking them all the time if they needed any help.

All of this together led Swing to conclude, "They didn't appreciate their employees very much [and] I started really slacking off." It is the lack of respect that initiated a sharp change in his attitude toward work. He started taking long breaks, reading the newspaper at work. Swing no longer enjoys his work as an activity and seems rather defensive about his attitude: "But

I couldn't deal with it anymore. It got to a point where I wasn't doing anything and I would just come in and literally sit around for hours at a time." Working well is tightly connected to being treated well. Swing's expectations are mainly directed toward relationships rather than work content. "My philosophy is if they want me to work hard for them, they've got to treat me with respect and they're going to treat me well and value [me] to at least some extent. I'm not looking for pats on the back or anything, but to some extent value the work that I'm putting in for them, and let me do my job if I'm doing it well. New Management wasn't good at that." Swing's narration affirms the research findings by Nies (2015) on conflicts originating in impediments to work following a use value orientation. Swing does not share any of the corporation's aims, nor does he hold a critical attitude toward management itself. His conflict with management takes place on a relational and emotional level, when he feels disrespected and undervalued because of being forced to focus on nonsense. By the time he experienced and reacted to the feeling of being treated badly, he had already grown up and graduated. He was no longer dependent on adults. Still, his rebellious streak remained: "I have a healthy disrespect for authority. I'm the type of person that if people treat me fairly, I'm good, and if they don't, I'm going to give them a hard time and I'm going to act out certain ways." Swing's history describes an arc of change: from building up respectful and appreciative relationships to being exposed to disrespect and finally quitting the supermarket. Compared to Simone Koch, he held out for a shorter time through conditions that had changed for the worse. While her dependency on the job grew with having two children, his dependency decreased because he acquired a college degree. In extending Brose's (1983) assumption that for a reconstruction of biographical developments one needs to take the company, the sector, and the occupation into account, it becomes clear that life contexts also need to be included in the analysis. Both interviewees finally left their supermarket work. The following three portraits are of supermarket clerks who undergo change in their activities despite still working at the supermarket at the time of the interview.

**Vasiliki Papadopoulos**

Vasiliki Papadopoulos is a 47-year-old white woman at the time of the interview. She has worked for six years in a supermarket. She is a part-timer working 21 to 22 hours a week, mainly in the evenings. Her first job was in medical billing. Papadopoulos's process of change could be summed up as frustration and disillusion. Her frustration has a range of causes from an increased workload after cuts in staff and loss of solidarity among coworkers to lower levels of appreciation from managers, culminating in a disturbing feeling of working regressively in terms of a long-term, generation-spanning perspective meant to lead to upward social mobility.

Papadopoulos is the daughter of Greek immigrants but was herself born in the U.S. She is married to a Greek who came to the U.S. at age ten. They have three children. At home, they speak Greek. Her father dropped out of school after the fifth grade and since then "worked two jobs coming to this country and just never taking a sick day or anything and just work, work, work." Her mother has also worked hard. Papadopoulos grew up in a household in which her parents had little formal education but devoted themselves to supporting the family. She did not attend college. Work is of "very high significance" in her life, and her children are her motivators: "I want better for them. And I try to work really hard to make it easier for them. Having a certain standard of life I want to live." Her husband didn't attend college either and is an electrician.

As was true of Simone Koch and Peter Swing, there was a time when Papadopoulos enjoyed working in a Target supermarket. She, too, went through a process of change.

> I mean, when I first started working there: wonderful boss, absolutely wonderful, and he had all kinds of incentives to … Again, when I (inaudible) area he felt was the best he would give a prize out, it was like $25 gift cards, so it was kind of like 'Oh, let me get my area …' and they would have different themes: hot chocolate day and they would have everything you needed to make hot chocolate, or popcorn, or peanut butter; just little different things that made you feel appreciated and stuff, which was very nice. They've done away with all that now.

She remembers that someone from human resources would come and sit down and talk with them about what could be done better for the clerks. There was a lot of communication, while now there are online surveys for feedback without any consequences. When Papadopoulos started working in the supermarket, she was surprised by the efforts at motivating workers by management, thinking this was unnecessary. What counted was getting the work done. That's the area in which she took pride. So much of her frustration now is over not being able to finish all her tasks, which have mounted in number in recent years while staffing has been reduced. "It's the time expected of you kind of generally – what they want, there is no way you would ever get your work done." Even renouncing breaks would not enable her to finish her work. "I mean, especially with the bosses; you're giving 100% and you couldn't be doing any more, and then to feel that they still want more from you; and it's just frustrating because you know you're putting in all that you can possibly do, and they don't see that." Staffing has been reduced from usually two people for each area to one. A coworker's job collecting items that have been left out of place by customers has been rationalized. Therefore, she needs to reshelve wrongly shelved items herself. "Before you'd have the cashiers who did cashier and we had the backroom and now it's like we have to do all of that now." In the beginning, Papadopoulos liked to help customers. She is working in the pharmacy section, and many customers approach her to ask for advice. She started having conversations in which she would advise them to see their doctors. From being open and attentive, she has "come to see people in a different light … you become immune to it, it's just like, 'okay.'" This demonstrates that Papadopoulos herself changed in the way she used to work. She became emotionally disengaged and less customer oriented. There is another section of her response in which she describes changing the way she works – not as Peter Swing did when he turned rebellious, but rather by holding back and legitimizing her lack of engagement by accusing her cow-orkers of working badly. "Like before it was … which was very (inaudible) everybody had their own section so when you finished your section if there is somebody else who hasn't done their section everybody goes over to help and it's just like, 'Well, why should I go over and help somebody who has spent all of their time walking around talking to the other employees and not putting (inaudible)?'" Part of this change has to do with diminishing solidarity among the staff. Being exposed to working conditions in which she is unable to finish her work, and in which her extra efforts to work through break times and give her all are not recognized by managers, leads in the case of Papadopoulos to a distant attitude toward her colleagues. This distance is also fueled by a high turnover rate. "I mean it's just also too it's terrible because the turnover rate is so much, you see a face then they're gone and it's like you never really know who is working or what happened to the person you were working with, so it's kind of hard to form any kind of friendships with your coworkers; it's like we're all strangers, kind of." Despite suffering in her job, she is more worried about unemployment than the consequences of staying. "As bad as it is, you know you're getting that paycheck. We currently have someone who is trying to get fired because if he quits, he doesn't get benefits, so he's trying to get fired himself." Papadopoulos pays a high price for supporting her children and trying to secure a certain living standard. The social ascent of her family has taken two generations, and its continuation is not certain. She raises doubts: "I mean the terrible thing is I grew up … with my parents being from Greece you just … you work backwards [are socially descending], it just (inaudible) I want to do a good job no matter what; it's a reflection on me." Her confidence about leveraging her strong work ethic to support her children has suffered some blows. Processing the work experience through an intergenerational perspective, which includes her children's and parents' viewpoints, she finds the promise of the American Dream, prosperity through hard work, somewhat elusive. At the same time, she is stuck with no alternative in sight. Without a college degree, it is unlikely that she will find a job with better working conditions, and becoming unemployed and forgoing a paycheck would be worse. Faced with this dead end, she undergoes a change in the personality she projects at work, from being a caring coworker to an "immune" sales clerk.

**Kerstin Jansen**

Kerstin Jansen (introduced in Chapter 5) is a supermarket clerk whose activity and work appropriation led to different stages of subject formation. She is a trained retail saleswoman who was wholly committed to her work but then became disillusioned. Since then, she has actively seen to it that she has satisfying work. In contrast to Simone Koch and Peter Swing, she has not quit, and in contrast to Papadopoulos, she is focused on the content of her work, having processed her disillusionment. She serves as another example of how the interviewees describe their process of coming to terms with their job despite setbacks and frustrations.

Jansen emphasizes the significance of vocational education for identification, which is crucial for commitment to one's work. "I learn the job, I learn something because I want to learn it. And consequently, I convey it differently, I identify with it." This is a description of the process of internalization, which is crucial for any meaningful activity. Comparing vocationally educated and non-vocationally educated staff, she notes:

> Funnily enough, one still needs vocationally educated staff, yes? And also at the cash register – the cashier should be a vocationally educated clerk who identifies with the firm, with the company in which she is employed and backs up the company, and I can't expect this from temporary staff earning a little bit after school.

After reunification, her shop closed and she was unemployed for three weeks – a very short period, as she notes with pride. She started working in one of the more prestigious supermarket chains of West Germany, "so to speak, the Mercedes Benz among the supermarkets." It has a meat department, and after a further education course, she will be qualified to become a floor manager there.

The main narration in her interview is about the repeated process of going from being very committed to facing disillusionment but learning to deal with it, after which she is able to work happily again. Jansen is committed not only to her company, but also to her colleagues. She tells the story of how she advocated for a coworker as a young clerk:

> And I had a colleague who told me she urgently needed to have Saturday off because her father-in-law was having his seventieth birthday. And I went to the boss and said, 'You need to change the schedule, and she needs to be off. Her father-in-law becomes 70 and you didn't make a note of that.' And so forth. And then I return from break and my boss says, 'I don't know what that was about. She said she'd

make an exception this time and work.' So. And there I thought, 'well, super, great.' And these are things you just have to learn in life.

Her intervention is unsuccessful because the colleague she tries to stand up for retreats. Jansen repeatedly goes through experiences of this kind.

As a single mother, Jansen struggles to manage her paid and unpaid work. Having grown up in the GDR, with its comprehensive public childcare system, she once called the central office of the company employing her to ask whether the company hosts a vacation camp for its employees' children. The only answer she received was a laugh. Her biggest work-related disappointment was the lack of support from her workplace when she needed time off to care for her sick son. When no support was forthcoming, she felt less committed to her job:

> If somebody called and I had no plans, I would go to work, if someone was needed. The difference between this and former times is that formerly, if I had another appointment, I would have rescheduled it to go to work. Today not. And this is because I don't get any gratitude either way. I needed to have this experience to figure this out, but I think it became clear to me because of my son getting sick and everything that happened afterward, and how I was treated. That really shaped me. It was the sticking point that made me say, 'No, I'm not going to be treated this way anymore.'

This account describes a wrong that led to a change in her attitude toward her work, a process whereby work became "number two" in her life, and her private sphere became "number one."

During the 32 years of her experience working in retail, Jansen describes another process of change: the devaluation of her profession. As I have mentioned above, in the former GDR clerks enjoyed a privileged social position because of their access to scarce goods, which they could exchange through an unofficial barter economy (see Hofmann & Rink 1999). Being a clerk meant sitting in a key position that conferred a measure of power. In Jansen's narration, the devaluation she experienced consisted mainly in the loss of respect taking place on a societal level in a reunified Germany. In contrast to Swing's narrative, in which organizational changes to the industry give rise to disrespectful treatment of supermarket clerks by supervisors and bosses, Jansen's narrative centers on the general loss of social status for salesclerks:

> Today as a clerk, you are the lowest on the totem pole. That's how I see it. Not all customers think this, but many do. I mean, the rudeness of people, talking on the phone at the sales counter. And if I don't talk to them out of politeness and respect, because they're talking on the phone, they complain about me not serving them. I mean, what the heck? I have thought about taking my cell phone along and each time a customer stands in front of me with a cell phone, taking out my phone and

making calls myself. Or people have their headsets on, chatting, and then they say: 'Just a moment. A hundred grams of special sausage. Yes, I'm talking to you – what do you have for lunch?' Then to the headset: 'O, yes, I'm here!' Respect. It's a simple matter of respect, which I pay to them by looking at them while serving them and greeting them politely with 'Good day,' 'Good morning,' or 'Good evening.' I think their behavior shows no respect. Or as I mentioned, every other customer uses the informal form of address with me.[1] I wasn't aware that we'd gone out for a coffee together! In former times, people wouldn't have dared to act that way. Not even when I was 18 or so, but today they are standing in front of you saying 'Hey you [informal *du*], give me 500.' 'Uh, excuse me? Do we know each other?' But that's how society has become, simply no respect.

It is probably much more difficult and requires a lot of energy to maintain an affirming work attitude while one's profession undergoes a devaluation. In such situations, the strength of the working subject becomes crucial. Jansen demonstrates a process of coming to terms with her job in which she does not lose interest but develops the ability to depend less on others. Two important sources of her strength in the workplace are her union membership and participation in the workers' council. Just as she started in sales with commitment and engagement, so too did she begin her work as an elected union workers' council member with a high level of motivation. Once a month, for a whole day, professional workers' council members would meet to discuss current topics. This day is also paid for by the nonprofessional workers' council activists. Her supermarket chain has been bought by another one, and her store is now privately owned.

> I had to fight about it with my employer, how much and when and where. And this was a hard fight. So, for example we have had a weekly meeting of two hours, which were not always sufficient, because there are so many things we would like to do as a workers' council, or should do ... And I negotiated with the employer that afterward I or my deputy when I was on holiday always had one more hour for paperwork, to follow up and prepare the next meeting.

With pride, Jansen talks about dismissals she could prevent. But she also experiences disillusionment in relation to colleagues for whom she wanted to improve working conditions through a bargaining agreement.

> I had two issues I wanted to work out with him about the store agreement. It always failed in the end because the coworkers said, 'Oh, no, that's not necessary.' So. And I then had to pay my dues in the beginning of my work with the workers' council, and by now, in my branch, I tell them where they can find what, where they could google something. And they need to become active themselves. I'd be glad to go with them. And I will do what I did in the beginning: someone coughs and I take off. And if the boss asks, my colleague says I had a scratchy throat. These are the apprenticeship dues one has to pay. And so I have. 'What you always want. It's not as bad.' And since then I say, 'If the shoe really pinches, then, if you want to go, I'll

accompany you gladly, I'll back you up, but I'm not going to go work out for you in advance what you don't take advantage of. That won't happen again.'

Despite her disillusionment, Jansen is still a workers' council member and still finds her work in the council important. Overall, though, she has gone through tough times. There was a time when she suffered from temporomandibular joint inflammation caused by bruxism. She could not stop thinking of work, and it even kept her awake at night. She decided to run for the workers' council in a team and finally "worked hard to get my place in the shop, fought for it." She went through a process of adjusting her activity to her working context and colleagues' way of treating her that resulted in achieving a satisfactory work life for herself. She constantly and actively enacts this process. "And today I take care for this, that I am satisfied with myself and my work. And this was a long road." Asked what an ideal workplace would look like, Jansen thinks for about ten seconds and finally answers, "I am actually satisfied the way it is." This reply demonstrates how deep and profound her activity is, having worked hard to attain a conscious and self-determining attitude toward her job. Jansen's subject formation is a result not only of the occupation and the job she carries out, but on another level a result of her conscious deliberation and grappling with her job. Personal reconstruction or reconfiguration ("Umbau") as part of activity is especially visible in her subject formation.

I now turn to the final example of a clerk who has undergone a process of change in his work activity. In his case, an additional factor to the ones already presented, boredom, plays a crucial role in this change.

### Markus Willert

Markus Willert is 44 years old at the time of the interview. He was born in the former GDR, in a small town dominated by a chemical company that was shut down after reunification. He grew up with his mother, who worked in retail too, and his father, who was employed as a driver for the company. When Willert was ten years old, his sister was born. Soon afterward, his father died. Willert experienced the collapse of the GDR at the age of 14 or 15. He was attending the polytechnic secondary school, which usually ends after the tenth grade, but because of the shutdown of the chemical company and the difficult labor market, he continued school and graduated from a baccalaureate program. After school, he joined the army for one year. Upon his return, there were still no jobs or apprenticeships available, so he entered the job center's job creation program for a while. Finally, he obtained an apprenticeship at an electronics retail company. Having completed his baccalaureate, he was able to finish his apprenticeship in two years instead of three. He was one of the top

100 of his cohort, and immediately after having finished his apprenticeship he found a job with the help of a mentor.

This was the beginning of his career path to becoming shop manager at Netto. While the path was steep, his motivation declined over the years. Two years after starting his job, he became floor manager. Unfortunately, his company was sold several times, and sales declined. Willert was worried and asked a friend working in food retail for a job. In 2003, he started working at a discount grocery chain as store manager. Now he was managing a shop, mainly taking care of scheduling staff. About five years later, this company was sold to another one, and he continued to work as shop manager for the new chain. During this time, he met who would later become his wife, and through her he connected with the union. Here is where a second career started for him. He became a member of the workers' council, and at the time of the interview he was working as a professional workers' council member, dedicating himself full time to the council and being paid for it.

Concerning the trajectory of his motivation curve, there was a distinctly downward trend. Willert describes himself as an employee with high expectations concerning his own performance. "In principle, I always assume that I will do a good job because that's what I set out to do. How does the expression go: 'I'm obliged to turn in C work?' Instead, I make the obligatory standard B+ work." Willert describes his work expectations as normal, as a matter of course.

> Yes, it's "reasonable" in the sense that I do good work that will satisfy my boss, the customer, and certainly myself too. Yes, of course I'm not just throwing stuff down and saying, 'I don't give a shit.' It's not like that. Maybe it's because I need to perform at a level that makes others say 'Wow!' For me, that goes without saying. Because as a store manager, I need to uphold a higher standard than a lower-level employee throwing something together. If I make something, it has to be appealing and look good. That's just normal for me.

In the interview he offers three factors that influence his high expectations of his own work performance. The first is his socialization, which instilled in him a strong work ethic. The second is his military service, which got him in shape. The third is his vocational education, in which he was taught that in his profession, work expectations had to be high. He carried out the practical part of his dual-system vocational education in a small electronics retail shop, and as a result, he "was optimized in that direction all the time so that I was only focused on doing things very well or well. I didn't even give a thought to other considerations. If I hadn't done something well, I needed to do it again, and since then, I've done things properly." Over the course of about 20 years of work experience, his motivation to apply his strong work ethic declined. Echoing Kerstin Jansen's narrative, he also reports on deteriorating working conditions and a decline of the social status of his profession. But in contrast to Jansen, he seems less focused on these circumstances, and they don't appear to strongly impact his motivation. His decreasing motivation levels appear to stem mainly from the way his work became routinized and lacked new content. He began working with much less engagement.

> I take what I'm entitled to and they only give me what I am entitled to – end of story. I don't give any more thought to whether I did something really well or beautifully. I don't really give a damn. I've become so jaded and indifferent to the work in the shop because everything's become so automatic, I just don't think about it. Every day is the same. If you know how things will go for one week, you know how they'll go for the other 51 weeks of the year. And it's the same from year to year. Sometimes the packaging changes or the shelves, or some technological aspect, but the work stays the same. It's not exciting any more. Not at all.

Another source of his lack of motivation is the lack of praise and appreciation from his boss. In former times, when he still worked at the electronic goods shop, his boss praised him: "'You have done a fantastic job!'" Increasingly, his bosses cared less, and he would pick up on that and care less himself. He no longer praised his colleagues. To describe his relation to his own activity and the process of coming to terms with his job, he uses notions such as "reconciling," "accepting," or even "capitulating." To look at his career in a positive light, one could point out that he achieved a manager's position and a relatively high income. He himself admits to a level of comfort in his present position and notes that he does not want to risk losing income by changing jobs. He also points to his age, "I'm too old for that. I only want to be left alone and be able to care for my family, and then it's fine. I've arrived, if I may say so." But Willert is not content. In contrast to Jansen, his way of dealing with disappointments in his job is through passivity. "That's why I don't think about it. I just surrender and take things as they are – I just make peace with it." Even his work as a workers' council member reflects a rather passive attitude. He does not seem to fight for better working conditions because current legislation has tied the hands of the workers' council, but he does see a role for himself in teaching his colleagues to differentiate strictly between work and leisure, by not taking work home (e.g., printing price tags outside of work hours). Willert has reached a state of disillusionment in which he is convinced that there is no such thing as an ideal workplace. From this perspective, the meaning assigned to work is limited: work appropriation restricts work to a contract in which one sells one's own labor for a certain period of time in exchange for a wage. Possibilities of self-realization and personal development take place exclusively in the private sphere.

These five cases featuring change show different ways in which work activity contributes to subject formation. All five cases are characterized by strong emotional responses to various kinds of change in the workplace. While Simone Koch stays on the job but suffers while the process of deprofession-alization transforms her occupation, Swing leaves his profession because of the lack of respect he experiences. In his case, a college degree has given him alternatives. Papadopoulos is overworked and treated badly but has no better prospects, while Jansen grapples with and to some degree overcomes the personal hurt of getting no support from her workplace during the time when her child was sick. Eventually, she manages to find a path to relative satisfaction through her work. In Willert's case, the process of change in going from being highly committed to becoming indifferent and bored offers still another variety of subject formation through activity.

## PROCESSES OF CONTINUITY

The second prevailing pattern among the interviewees is that of continuity and coming to terms with their jobs. Their steady attitudes toward their work and work activities are characterized by perseverance and a willingness to endure the hardships of low-wage employment.

### John Williams

John Williams is a 52-year-old white man at the time of the interview. He grew up in a neighborhood of X. His father was a steelworker who addition-ally worked half-time at a meat market at night. His mother cared for eight children. At the age of 20, Williams was an X firefighter for two weeks before being laid off because the city was cutting jobs. He remembers this job wist-fully and notes that he would love to go back there, but that is impossible due to age restrictions. Later, he worked in a bank for about five years but was laid off when his bank was bought up by another one. After a time of unemploy-ment, he started working at Roch's Brothers, where he has now worked for more than 20 years. He is married to a woman who works for the town as an event coordinator. They have three children, of whom two are in college and the youngest is in high school.

"That's the way things are" is a phrase Williams uses several times during the interview. He has developed an accepting attitude toward his work. Yes, he would like to work elsewhere, as an electrician or moving around outside and earning more, but despite his weekly online applications, he receives no invitations for an interview. Actually, apart from automatic response emails he gets no responses at all, which is of course frustrating. He assumes that he would do better if he could present himself personally. "I'm confident, I feel like I can sell myself." But most applications are online only, and he continues to apply. But in the meantime, he likes his job. "Yes, I like it. On a scale of one to ten, seven. I'm not going to tell you I love it, I don't, I'd rather be with my family, but it's okay, I don't hate it, it's not like that." Not only does he not resist working there, he even enjoys parts of his job.

> Yeah, I like helping customers, I like helping people, I'm a people person. There's a lot of times an elderly woman might not be able to reach the top shelf, 'I need that can of soup up there,' and just simply getting it for them, you know, which is not a problem whatsoever but they appreciate that so much and it just kind of makes you feel good that part, customer service that's what that is.

Of course, liking his job and enjoying special parts of it such as helping customers contributes to accepting his job despite wishing he were working elsewhere. In addition, he feels well-treated by his bosses and customers. Williams started working in a supermarket when he was unemployed, and that lowered his expectations, making him happy to have a job of any kind. The training he received was on the job, as is typical in the U.S. He notes that he learned how to do it by "just watching others." Williams recalls his start.

> It's pretty much the store manager will on the first day, you know, will tell you, you'll come in and say okay, you're going to go with Joe and Joe is going to show you around, yeah they don't just throw you into the fire, they'll show you around and then maybe you're with them for a week, now you're on your own. So maybe a week's training and then the next week when you're on your own if you have any questions, you do have your coworkers or your store manager to go to if you have any questions.

In the U.S., training for jobs is carried out to a large part by colleagues and coworkers instead of vocational schools or instructors who are trained to instruct and supervise apprentices. Learning by watching others means learning the status quo. This is different from textbook learning where models and ideal concepts are explained. Learning the status quo orients expectations toward practice. It probably leads much more to an accepting attitude, in contrast to one in which workers and employees develop expectations of how they should carry out their work. For formally trained workers, product brochures and work outcomes are studied in combination with theoretical and abstract concepts.

Williams's way of working comes with a measure of acceptance.

> I'm willing to work hard, I'm willing to work any hours, I'm willing to work every day of the week if you need me, I'll be there. You know, when you get some young, let's say and I say youth because they, you know, college kids they still like to go out and drink and party and stuff and they're not going to come to work on some days and that's not good for a company, that's not me, you know, I'm reliable.

The core of his work ethos, his reliability, has not faded over the years. Due to seniority rules, he is entitled to choose his shift, which is the 7 a.m. to 3 p.m. morning shift, which he prefers, "but if they need me, let's say the person relieving me at 3:00 that's going to do the 3:00 to 11:00 shift, let's say they called in sick, now they need somebody to cover that, I'll do it on overtime, I can't do it every night, but I'll do it a couple of nights. And then there's 16 hours extra there." His physical strength has decreased over the years, but to the extent that he is able, he is committed to working hard. Being able to choose his shift and take a short break when needed enables him to work steadily.

> I'm on my feet a lot, sometimes my knees might bother me a little bit at this age, but that's, you know, it's part of the job. I can take a rest, you know you find your ways. You know, after you've been there so long and I've proven myself to be a good worker, if I sit down for a few minutes, I'm not going to sit down out on the floor where customers will see you (laughing), but there's a backroom you can hide in for a few minutes, so that's my around it. I'm just taking a break and as long as you do your work it's, you know, nobody's, you know, they're not [slave-drivers], you know.

Williams works under conditions in which he can address his needs creatively and find ways of taking needed breaks, securing his ability to remain in his job. A strong factor in Williams's permanence at work is his contribution to his family's middle-class lifestyle. "I have a mortgage to pay." His hourly wage is $21 with benefits. For him, the significance of work is that,

> it enables us to live a good life, we're okay, it pays the bills. I have two kids in college, my wife works too, we're not rich by any means, we're far from it but just middle class, but everybody is good, we get to go on vacation, we don't all fly somewhere but we'll drive to the beach in the summertime and rent a house for a week, and that's what we do. I mean the last time we flew somewhere was in '04 I think, so that's [..] years ago, we flew to I think Aruba, we went to Aruba, and went on a big vacation, but we can't do that all the time, that's too pricey. Especially, I have five airfares, I have three children, so it would be myself, my wife, and three kids, five airfares, along with the hotel – it's a lot of money, so I can't afford that.

Getting three kids through college, paying off a house, vacations, and other elements of a middle-class life like helping his youngest to buy a car – these are only possible if he works without disruption and over a long period of time. He plans to work until he is 72. Securing a middle-class lifestyle focuses him on the present and the daily routine; it creates a repetitive continuity. "I'm only supporting my wife and children. I'm supporting my family that's right here and yeah, I'd like to move on but I don't know at this point. I just, you know, week to week, you know try to save some money and that's what I'm doing,

I'm just paying the bills and just trying to live life." Williams does not give hints that he suffers from this restriction. For him, this is the essence of life. His environment is composed of people with similar lifestyles. He is not close with his colleagues as everybody is busy with work and family. Apart from some sports events he attends and a couple of retirement parties during the year, his social life centers on home and work. A homogenous environment is not fertile soil for the creation of new ideas and rather contributes to his constancy and steadiness.

**Thomas Berry**

In contrast to John Williams, Thomas Berry, born in 1979, does not enjoy his work. His main narrative centers on complaints about bad working conditions, low pay, and a lack of respect at work. He has a sense of betrayal because he works hard and efficiently, but his managers promote people from the outside. In general, though, he has praise for the company: "It's a good company, you know, but it's just that a few things they do lack and I just, I don't know, I just speak to my coworkers and just hope for the best, you know?" Berry is a 37-year-old black man at the time of the interview. He was born in X and has lived there his whole life. "When I was growing up, you know, we didn't have a lot of food and I always used to say I'm going to have my own coffee shop, I'm going to have my own store, you know, and so like I like to meet people so I decided to work there and I haven't looked back, you know?" Berry has worked full time for four and a half years in merchandising and on the loading dock. He earns $13 per hour. He has two children, eight and 17 years old. At the time of the interview, his company announced it was hiring for $16 per hour, and according to Berry this would mean laying off staff. His company is unionized, and he mentions coworkers deliberating about going on strike. He might follow if they go. In reality, he does not protest, but works steadily. Recalling his start at the company, when every day someone new took him around, he says:

> I just followed orders, I didn't complain, you know, because nobody's perfect, you know, and like a Stop & Shop chain or just a supermarket chain alone is very confusing, you know, and like you have all these kids and people in their thirties and people in their fifties so I just said fine so if I'm working with you today I tend to do how you like it, if I'm working with him today I do it how he likes it so I was adapting to the situation.

He proved to be very flexible in the way he worked with various colleagues. Berry describes himself as a fast learner who is able to multitask and "make your customer experience good." However, like Williams, he mostly just keeps his head down and keeps to himself. "I like you as a manager to not bother me, you know what I'm saying, so I'm working by myself, you know, all day every day, the only time I see you if there's something wrong or there's something missing or there's something that is not priced right." But with some colleagues, he is quite close:

> Some people care, you know, because we've been working together for so long so we have a bond, you know, we go out to eat, we have parties and stuff so like we do care about our job but we don't care about it as in … we care about the job but it's more of a family, you know, like 'Oh my god, he's leaving oh fuck,' like you know, 'Oh, he's dead,' or you know? It's not really about the job, job, job, you know?

The second feature, which he refers to several times, is his way of working dutifully but not happily, continuing without initiating changes. Berry sums up with the words "I do what I'm supposed to do just to get by."

## Pedro Sousa

Pedro Sousa is another clerk whose activity is characterized by a process of continuity. In contrast to Williams, he does not secure a middle-class life with continuity, but instead finds himself stuck in an exploitative work relationship.

Pedro Sousa is 48 years old at the time of the interview. He emigrated from Portugal to the U.S. in 1989, when he was 21 years old. In the U.S. he lived in a small bay area in eastern Massachusetts, where he worked as a bus boy, offering food to customers on trays and cleaning their tables. Later, he worked as a prep cook in a restaurant and became a grill cook. He left the restaurant because the constant smell of food made him feel sick. In X, he started working in 7-Eleven for two and a half years and now works at the same chain again, after several interruptions to work at other jobs. He works at two branches, for 25 hours a week and 21 hours a week, respectively. In one branch he earns $11 per hour and in the other he earns $10 per hour. Most of his shifts are in the afternoon and at night. Sousa studied for nine months to be a nursing assistant at a distance-learning institute. He got into trouble with the police and was not employed as a personal care attendant.

At the supermarket, he started out stocking and was then asked whether he was interested in learning to work the register, which he welcomed. The shop was very busy at the time. From the way Sousa describes the customers, it becomes clear that he observes them closely in order to figure out their needs and to sell them as much as possible. He states:

> Ringing customers – I call it taking care of customers. Always looking for their needs because they walk in and they buy one or two items but they might have other things in mind that they don't know is in the store. Or they want to buy and they just

look around and, 'It's not here.' But if you ask me, then I will get you and you will not lose the sale. You've got to know what's in their mind.

What might seem at first sight a way of job crafting (Wrzesniewski & Dutton 2001) is in fact a deep company-oriented work ethos that increases sales. Sousa's empathy goes far as he grasps even nonverbal messages by customers that might indicate what they are looking for without declaring it and thus willing to buy. He likes "looking for their needs. Where they're going; what they're doing you know?" Concerning his own needs, he locates them close to management's needs. "The reason why I said there has to be a relationship is because he [the boss] wants your help and you want his help. So you have to help him to help you. And he has to make money for you to make money." In another sequence, Sousa is very conscious about the reason why he is employed part time in two shops instead of full time in one: it saves the company money in benefits he would otherwise be entitled to. "It will benefit them more than me actually if I'm part-time." Another way of saving money is the practice of high turnover. "To hire someone for a lower pay. It's called rotation. They want to rotate employees, because they want to pay a lower rate to someone that's new, that's not experienced." He continues his account:

> I've seen things happen like that because of little mistakes and stuff like that. They suspend you and [do] not call you back. And if you go after them they lie, but they were really doing rotation. Trying to hire new employees for a lower rate. Because I earn $11 but they can start someone from $9. They can start someone from $9 or $8.50.

Still, Sousa is not a union member, he would not organize his interests in opposition to management, but instead works continuously. In his spare time, "I read and go to church. And cook." He goes to many different churches and attends "conference meetings for people that are in need of things. They give you an extra instruction how to get there. And then they can sign you up for conference and you join together and talk about your needs and what's going on." In addition, "I read spiritual things. How you benefit yourself; how you associate with things and people. It teaches you a lot." Often, Sousa cannot sleep; he sometimes lacks energy and is tired. He has no plans for the future. "It's hard making changes. My biggest call is earning the most money I can to make a change because I'm not planning to stay all this – not even half of my life with this work. I'm really trying to get all my money to make a change." He dreams of owning a gym to improve his health. Meanwhile, he works "side by side together and observing, you learn a lot." Asked whether he started working immediately, or shadowed first, he answers:

> No, immediately. But how you respond to people, this is what he [the supervisor] watches. You don't want to turn a customer away or disrespect a customer by not selling a product because you know, you're not appreciative; you're not welcoming a person in; he watches that. He will decide if he wants you too. You've always got to not to lose a customer. One guy taught me, it's like food on our tables. You don't want to lose a customer. Customers are our food on our tables.

Here it becomes clear that Sousa also practices tight control at work. He observes customers to figure out their needs in order to sell as much as possible to stay employed and be able to maintain himself. It seems to be a circle he is stuck in.

## COUNTRY DIFFERENCES

"Society produces the activity of its constituting individuals," writes Leontjew (2012 [1975]: 81). Following him, people do not simply adjust to exterior conditions. They need to appropriate them. This means that societal conditions encompass the motives and aims of activities whose means and processes they convey. Activity is work when it contributes to societal production and repro-duction, following Holzkamp-Osterkamp (1981 [1975]). In order to explain the differences between countries along processes of change and continuity in the job of supermarket clerk, we must take into account the social status of the occupation as a profession in Germany and as just a job in the U.S. An occu-pation that is a recognized profession (albeit a low-level one) is able to raise expectations. Within two or three years of vocational education, expectations in relation to the profession are taught in work and task concepts, and they form part of a vocational socialization. Later, these images and ideas of how to work and which ways of working are best meet with reality, and that reality is itself changing. Working conditions in supermarkets have mainly deteriorated over recent years. Raised expectations often cannot be met. This leads to disil-lusionment, as I have described above. The sales personnel interviewed in this study find different ways to deal with the disappointment of a career path that does not live up to expectations. Taken together, these are complex processes of changes in activities.

In contrast, the dominant pattern I found among long-term employed clerks in the U.S. was continuity. Working in a job that is not considered a profes-sion and enjoys little in the way of social prestige creates low expectations. A lack of career options within the occupation keeps those expectations low. Precarious working conditions in part-time and easily terminated positions create constant pressure that leads to an accepting attitude as clerks find themselves stuck: they are (barely) able to pay their bills, but still they cannot leave their jobs.

The two U.S. clerks whose activities I have categorized in terms of changes differ from the German ones. They, too, went through a process of disillusionment, but it was initiated more through feelings of being treated badly by managers and less in terms of the job's content expectations. Peter Swing and Vasiliki Papadopoulos had strong work ethics and expected fair treatment. This could be interpreted as a stand-in within the U.S. context for having a recognized profession. Instead of a socially institutionalized profession that regulates activities, the U.S. has low-level occupations such as salesclerk that are more oriented toward personal relationships between employees and bosses. As long as these workers feel they are treated fairly and receive recognition for their efforts, their work ethos remains strong, but a lack of personal recognition may result in weaker standards. There is no institutionalized structure that accords recognition independent of bosses' treatment of their staff.

## NOTE

1.    In German, the formal pronoun used to address adults one doesn't know well or to accord respect is "Sie." "Du" is the more familiar form for "you," used with friends, acquaintances, and family members as well as among young people.

# Conclusion to *Work Appropriation of Low-Wage Workers in the Service Sector*

To conclude, I first summarize my study and then explain the significance of my findings before suggesting possibilities for further studies.

## SUMMARY

This study's overall aim was to reveal how supermarket clerks perceive their work. Supermarket clerks form a large part of the workforce, and therefore from a purely quantitative perspective their work perceptions are important. As service workers, supermarket salesclerks receive relatively low wages, and that makes them a typical employee group of neoliberal societies of the Global North. During the last few decades, as these societies transformed from predominantly agricultural to industrial to service-dominated, the number of supermarkets increased, and supermarkets became the main providers of food for these societies' populations. The important role of supermarkets only fully reached the consciousness of the general public during the COVID-19 pandemic. Recently, food shortages and increased prices for food items as a result of climate change and armed conflicts added to supermarket clerks' key roles in the workforce. In sharp contrast to their societal significance, the level of recognition and wages they receive remain low. This discrepancy between importance to society on the one hand and social standing and level of remuneration on the other makes a study on supermarket clerks' perceptions of work a particularly pertinent case study for understanding labor under neoliberal conditions in the Global North.

For this reason, I have selected two countries, the U.S. and Germany, as representatives of different systems with regard to the vocational education of supermarket clerks. One of my initial research questions was whether the existence or lack of vocational education for the tasks carried out makes a difference in work perceptions and evaluations due to differences in vocational socialization, professional status, and identity that may impact perceptions of work. I found that this was, indeed, the case. Largely in the U.S., a system that offers no systematic vocational education for salespeople and therefore no professional status, supermarket clerks' narrations mapped out stories of an unsettled workforce. Despite being employed in many cases for a number of years, these workers emphasized the temporary nature of their jobs and the necessity of finding something better. Many gave the impression that there was no legitimate reason for staying at the job. Only interviewees who classified themselves as occupying the very bottom of the workforce (e.g., because they were disabled or marginalized for other reasons) referred to their occupation as a permanent one. In contrast, in Germany, supermarket clerks felt their jobs had social legitimacy and often planned on working many years in their profession. Even though their wages and working conditions left room for improvement, most of these workers were settled in their jobs.

I interviewed 55 supermarket clerks from a large variety of stores, from large-chain retailers to a nonprofit cooperative grocer, in both the U.S. and Germany. Equipped with a guided questionnaire, I asked about their socialization, life course, apprenticeship or training on the job, tasks they perform at their jobs, and working conditions. I also asked them to talk about especially memorable high or low points at the job, experiences with coworkers, and future plans. The sample was diverse in terms of age, working experiences, life circumstances, and national, racial, and ethnic backgrounds. Reading the transcriptions of the interviews again and again, I realized that their narrations were dominated by three areas: the social status of the occupation, the utility of their work, and the nature of their work activity. The social status of the occupation was in many cases a factor in the decision to become a supermarket clerk. Some described the job as suited to their place in life or the only one available, while others had completed a specialized vocational education for the profession. The overall picture mirrored the hierarchy of occupational classes in both societies. The interviewees' narratives about the utility of their tasks related mainly to serving customers, either directly by informing and advising, or more generally by ordering and stocking. These were the core areas they focused on when talking about the meaning and significance of their work. Their accounts of their activity, daily practices, and strategies for coming to terms with their work experiences – in some cases over many years – brought to light certain patterns. Overall, these employees' experiences of the activity of their work were highly dependent on life circumstances such as caring for children or being immigrants, and the impacts of these circumstances on work and labor in turn affected their life trajectories.

These three dimensions of status of occupation, use value, and activity form the basis of my redefinition of work appropriation. As I started with empirical data and not a fixed concept of work or labor, my notion of work appropriation does not contain a normative dimension of successful or joyful work. Following my definition, appropriation takes place whether or not the worker or employee enjoys working and even when suffering is involved. The more general nature of the term as I define it makes work appropriation a useful concept for analyzing work across a spectrum of experiences. The notion used here of work appropriation, which partly follows a grounded theory method, is therefore itself a result of this study in addition to being a theoretical concept used in the interpretation of the data.

A striking finding of this study is that a strong work ethos was widespread among supermarket clerks in both countries. While the strength of the work ethos among German and American employees did not differ noticeably, the content of that ethos did. Among vocationally educated professional super-market clerks in Germany, work ethos consisted in concrete expectations around using one's knowledge to advise customers on products, whereas in the U.S. many supermarket clerks were guided by a more abstract work ethos around serving customers generally. In both countries, the strong work ethic was highly linked to the employees' use value orientation. Good performance meant doing one's best to serve customers and their needs. But I also found a diverging pattern in the case of the U.S. supermarket salespeople. Several of them had developed a strong work ethos and spoke of their high performance on the job in relation to their own self-esteem. To sustain their dignity in a social context in which their labor is regarded as simple, routine, trivial, unskilled, dangerous, and underpaid, several U.S. supermarket clerks developed a strong work ethos as a kind of shield against their social devaluation. Instead of organizing politically and demanding better pay, more recognition, and improved working conditions, they worked hard and performed their best, unconsciously contributing to their own exploitation by not only meeting their customers' needs, but also satisfying their exploitative employers.

Finally, work appropriation appears to take similar forms across the two countries despite the significant contextual differences. One explanation for this may be the strong use value orientations of the workers and employees described in this study. A strong use value orientation serves people's needs to connect to others, building ties and communities for organizing social repro-duction. This need holds for all societies, independent of the specific designs of educational, labor, and welfare institutions.

## SIGNIFICANCE OF THE STUDY'S MAIN FINDINGS

My three main findings of this study are politically, societally, and scientif-ically relevant. The first main finding from the empirical data is that social institutions such as vocational education impact socialization, the formation of a vocational identity, the sense of belonging within a professional group, and the opportunity to acquire specific expertise. These are crucial elements for social recognition. The differences in the social status of sales personnel in the two countries demonstrate the significance of belonging to a profession for workers' and employees' well-being. The findings suggest the need for the professionalization of supermarket clerks in the U.S. and for a halt to the de-skilling process in Germany. Instruments such as collective agreements, which contribute to making workers' and employees' positions more secure, can allow collective stakeholders to alleviate the financial and social pressures on individual workers. Political actions through unions, professional associations, and government action can help to diminish corporations' power to exploit their workforces, including especially personnel at food retailers, who help supply food to the population but often go unrecognized and struggle to secure their own livelihoods.

The second main finding, i.e., that a strong work ethos is widespread among supermarket clerks in both countries, is immensely encouraging on a societal level. It points to the enormous power of a human workforce aiming at collectivity. The fact that, for the most part, people without recognition or a living wage nevertheless work hard could be interpreted as an anthropological feature of humans, a need to be constructively active, independent of working conditions. This knowledge points to the need for societal deliberations concerning social objectives and the deployment of this potential for aims apart from private corporations' bottom lines. The fact that many people's motivations and objectives for working are directed toward serving others emphasizes the social nature of human beings, which in itself is a great resource for societies. The desire to meet others' needs, echoed often throughout the interviews, reflects a fundamental impulse toward cooperation and mutual well-being. The pattern of exploitation aimed at the willingness of workers to perform quality work despite low pay or prestige is a feature of service-oriented jobs in the food system and also in other sectors, such as care and health. Relying on workers' and employees' motivations to work well without being appreciated has endured for years and often serves as a basis for exploitation and abuse. A societal discussion on recognizing and valuing those who perform essential work might raise consciousness on this issue and lead to solutions that could reduce the role of corporate profits in supplying food, potentially contributing to a better life for many.

In the case of some interviewees, the expression of a strong work ethic served as a means of maintaining their own self-esteem. This pattern seemed to arise in response to the perception of being devalued or treated poorly by bosses and sometimes customers too. In some cases, poor working conditions impeded good performance, but in others, self-motivation and high performance allowed the interviewees to preserve their self-respect in the face of dehumanizing conditions. This pattern differs from Wrzesniewski and Dutton's (2001) "job crafting" in that instead of improving or tailoring work tasks, the workers firmly stick to the same tasks despite the difficult working conditions. This kind of practice could be interpreted as a defensive form of resistance that is limited because it does not change conditions. In fact, by perpetuating the status quo, it acts as a form of self-exploitation. The position of the interviewees who hold up an image of empowerment and emancipation, ignoring their own obvious vulnerability, is characterized by the ambivalence of self-maintenance that becomes self-undermining. As long as corporations continue to prohibit unions and make huge profits based on low-wage workers operating in conditions of precarity, without offering perspectives and careers to underprivileged and migrant workers, we can expect this pattern to continue.

The third main finding is that by developing the notion of work appropriation on an empirical basis rather than a normative one, we can avoid restricting the understanding of appropriation as applying to a particular concept, content, or sector associated with work and instead focus on workers' and employees' views of their work in any context. In addition, the notion of work appropriation takes into account the interrelation of social structures and subjects' perspectives, enabling a better understanding of subjectification as well as societies on the whole. Therefore, even though work appropriation is not a normative concept, it can still inspire a normative outlook on how work might contribute to a more democratic, egalitarian society in the future.

## PROSPECTS FOR FURTHER STUDY: UTILITY OF WORK AS A KEY CATEGORY FOR A SOCIAL THEORY OF A BETTER SOCIETY

I conclude by underlining utility's importance as a category of work. In most parts of unpaid work (i.e., volunteering), utility is clearly a major objective. But its role in paid work is too often neglected, suppressed, or omitted. Inspired by Axel Honneth (2010), who asks how the category of societal work might be included into the framework of a social theory that goes beyond utopian perspectives and seeks qualitative improvements, I suggest that the notion of utility or use value can be of help. While Honneth follows Hegel's argument on the need for complexity in work and relates this claim to Durkheim's assertion that complexity leads to the "organic" solidarity of mutual recognition, and thus social integration through conditions of recognition linked to the exchange of deliverables ("Leistungen"), I argue that a major focus on the utility of work is key for any theory aimed at creating a better society. Of course, the complexity and division of labor that lead to interdependency, and thus social integration, are important aspects of work, especially in highly specialized societies. But utility is linked to content that serves people, that meets people's needs. It is therefore important for societies to discuss what they consider useful. Communities that put utility rather than deliverables at the center of the objectives of work are more egalitarian, ecological, and caring.

As I have pointed out, tailoring one's work to satisfy others' needs by producing items or offering services constitutes a social activity. Therefore, utility is a fundamentally social category. What is considered useful cannot be decided by one person but instead arises from communication and consensus. Since utility is linked to needs, it is grounded in and directed toward basic, fundamental elements of life that can be physical, social, emotional, or cognitive. Thus, work carried out to meet needs necessarily contributes to the social reproduction of human beings and societies. On a subjective level, such work can be perceived as highly rewarding, satisfying, and life-affirming. Since human life is dependent on nonhuman life, utility is also an ecological category. Interdependence goes beyond human beings, taking into account the natural world. Putting utility more at the center of work – and deciding as a society what work is most useful and how to organize it – has the power to potentially strengthen democracy. Deliverables and the division of labor might have been motors of modernization, but far too often they have been used for the benefit of a few individuals at the expense of positive change in living conditions and integration for much of the population. Obviously, utility cannot be the sole objective of work, placing functionality at the center of life at the expense of games, leisure, and creativity. However, it is time to put utility at the center of society-wide discussions on how people wish to live and design their communities and societies.

# References

Allmendinger, Jutta. (1989). Educational systems and labor market outcomes. *European Sociological Review, 5*(3), 231–250.

Anderson, D. Augustus, & Laughlin, Lynda. (2020). *Retail workers. 2018* (American Community Survey Reports, ACS-44). U.S. Census Bureau, Washington, DC. https://www.census.gov/content/dam/Census/library/publications/2020/demo/acs -44.pdf

Baethge, Martin. (1991). Arbeit, Vergesellschaftung und Identität – Zur zunehmenden normativen Subjektivierung der Arbeit. *Soziale Welt, 42*(1), 6–19.

Bahl, Friederike. (2018). Kompetenzprofile und berufliche Identität in Dienstleistungsberufen – zwei Säulen der Professionalisierung. In Rolf Dobischat, Arne Elias, and Anna Rosendahl (Eds.), *Das Personal in der Weiterbildung. Im Spannungsfeld von Professionalitätsanspruch und Beschäftigtenrealität* (pp. 137–157). Springer Verlag.

Beck, Ulrich, & Brater, Michael. (1976). Grenzen abstrakter Arbeit: Subjektbezogene Bedingungen der Gebrauchswertproduktion und ihre Bedeutung für kritische Berufspraxis. *Leviathan, 4*(2), 178–215.

Beck, Ulrich, & Brater, Michael. (1978). *Berufliche Arbeitsteilung und soziale Ungleichheit. Eine gesellschaftlich-historische Theorie der Berufe.* Campus-Verlag.

Beck, Ulrich, Brater, Michael, & Daheim, Hansjürgen. (1980). *Soziologie der Arbeit und der Berufe. Grundlagen, Problemfelder, Forschungsergebnisse.* Rowohlt.

Becker, Karina, Dörre, Klaus, & Reif-Spirek, Peter. (2018). *Arbeiterbewegung von rechts? Ungleichheit – Verteilungskämpfe – populistische Revolte.* Campus Verlag.

Becker-Schmidt, Regina. (1980). Widersprüchliche Realität und Ambivalenz: Arbeitserfahrungen von Frauen in Fabrik und Familie. *Kölner Zeitschrift für Soziologie und Sozialpsychologie, 32,* 681–704.

Becker-Schmidt, Regina. (1983). Entfremdete Aneignung, gestörte Anerkennung, Lernprozesse: Über die Bedeutung von Erwerbsarbeit für Frauen. In Joachim Matthes (Ed.), *Krise der Arbeitsgesellschaft? Verhandlungen des 21. Deutschen Soziologentages in Bamberg 1982* (pp. 412–426). Campus Verlag.

Becker-Schmidt, Regina, Brandes-Erlhoff, Uta, Rumpf, Mechthild, & Schmidt, Beate. (1983). *Arbeitsleben – Lebensarbeit. Konflikte und Erfahrungen von Fabrikarbeiterinnen.* Verlag Neue Gesellschaft.

Böhle, Fritz, Voß, G. Günter, & Wachtler, Günther (eds.). (2018 [2010]). *Handbuch Arbeitssoziologie: Vol. 1: Arbeit, Strukturen und Prozesse* (2nd ed.). Springer.

Boltanski, Luc, & Chiapello, Eve. (2003 [1999]). *Der neue Geist des Kapitalismus.* Universitätsverlag.

Bolte, Karl Martin. (1983). Subjektorientierte Soziologie – Plädoyer für eine Forschungsperspektive. In Karl Martin Bolte und Erhard Treutner (Eds.), *Subjektorientierte Arbeits- und Berufssoziologie* (pp. 12–36). Campus Verlag.

Bosch, Gerhard, & Lehndorff, Steffen (eds.). (2005). *Working in the service sector. A tale from different worlds.* Routledge.

Bosse, Steffen. (2022). *"Übermenschlich": Lidl-Mitarbeiter berichtet über Arbeitspensum bei Discounter.* https://de.finance.yahoo.com/nachrichten/%C3%BCbermenschlich -ehemaliger-lidl-mitarbeiter-berichtet-064700526.html?_fsig=MjX7CNCdigN4 AcwzKm0r2A--%7EA&guccounter=1&guce_referrer=aHR0cHM6Ly93d3c uc3RhcnRwYWdlLmNvbS88&guce_referrer_sig=AQAAAJwKs1BBu wpgJOoMO5EZQruraIrVo_SPzNlyD7nhCxhAIS57IEIHCC3JJJA-T-GvODHghLp _3fIFo1KU-axTYmyy1nl6lwzzSeMG2Q59A0T4CcuDwxKGS15_eL -McQmkdWxhpSGQ_Y6BEbjNPlrTud8CeZyeUgIPOoIhEDuZ3VWt

Bourdieu, Pierre, & Boltanski, Luc. (1977). Formal qualifications and occupational hierarchies: The relationship between the production system and the reproduction system. In Edmund J. King (Ed.), *Reorganizing education: Management and partic-ipation for change, Sage Annual Review of Social and Educational Change, Vol. 1* (pp. 59–69). Sage Publications.

Bozkurt, Ödül, & Grugulis, Irena. (2011). Why retail work demands a closer look. In Irena Grugulis and Ödül Bozkurt (Eds.), *Retail work* (pp. 1–21). Palgrave Macmillan.

Brand, Ulrich, & Wissen, Markus. (2021 [2017]). *The imperial mode of living. Everyday life and ecological crisis of capitalism.* Verso.

Brock, Ditmar, & Vetter, Hans-Rolf. (1982). *Alltägliche Arbeiterexistenz. Soziologische Rekonstruktionen des Zusammenhangs von Lohnarbeit und Biographie.* Campus-Verlag.

Bröckling, Ulrich. (2007). *Das unternehmerische Selbst. Soziologie einer Subjektivierungsform.* Suhrkamp.

Brose, Hanns-Georg. (1983). *Die Erfahrung der Arbeit. Zum berufsbiographischen Erwerb von Handlungsmustern bei Industriearbeitern.* Westdeutscher Verlag.

Bryman, Alan. (2016). *Social research methods* (5th ed.). Oxford University Press.

Bundesgesetzblatt. (2021). *Gesetz über die unternehmerischen Sorgfaltspflichten in Lieferketten.* https://www.bgbl.de/xaver/bgbl/start.xav?startbk=Bundesanzeiger _BGBl&jumpTo=bgbl121s2959.pdf#__bgbl__%2F%2F*%5B%40attr_id%3D %27bgbl121s2959.pdf%27%5D__1668772065325

Bundesregierung. (2022). *Corona-Virus in Deutschland.* https://www.bundesregierung .de/breg-de/themen/coronavirus/corona-regeln-und-einschrankungen-1734724

Burawoy, Michael. (1979). *Manufacturing consent: Changes in the labor process under monopoly capitalism.* University of Chicago Press.

Bureau of Labor Statistics. (2022). *Employment by major industry.* https://www.bls .gov/emp/tables/employment-by-major-industry-sector.htm

Carré, Françoise, & Tilly, Chris. (2017). *Where bad jobs are better. Retail jobs across countries and companies.* Russell Sage Foundation.

Clark, Michael et al. (2022). Estimating the environmental impact of 57,000 food products. *PNAS, 119*(33). https://www.pnas.org/doi/full/10.1073/pnas.2120584119

Club of Rome. (2022). *The limits to growth + 50. Global equity for a healthy planet.* https://www.clubofrome.org/

Congressional Research Service. (2022). *Section 307 and imports produced by forced labor.* https://crsreports.congress.gov/product/pdf/IF/IF11360

Connell, R. W. (1997). Why is classical theory classical? *American Journal of Sociology, 102*, 1511–1557.

Demszky, Alma, & Voß, G. Günter. (2018). Beruf und Profession. In Fritz Böhle, G. Günter Voß, and Günther Wachtler (Eds.), *Handbuch Arbeitssoziologie. Vol. 2: Akteure und Institutionen* (2nd ed., pp. 477–538). Springer.

DiMaggio, Paul, & Powell, Walter. (1983). The iron cage revisited: Institutional iso-morphism and collective rationality in organizational fields. *American Sociological Review, 48*, 147–160.

Dixson-Declève, Sandrine et al. (September 2022). *Earth for all. A survival guide for humanity.* https://www.earth4all.life/book.

Dörre, Klaus, Happ, Anja, & Matuschek, Ingo (eds.). (2013). *Das Gesellschaftsbild der LohnarbeiterInnen. Soziologische Untersuchungen in ost- und westdeutschen Industriebetrieben.* VSA.

Du Gay, Paul. (1996). *Consumption and identity at work.* Sage Publications.

Durkheim, Emile. (1977 [1930]). *Über die Teilung der sozialen Arbeit.* Suhrkamp Verlag.

EHI Retail Institute. (2022). *Nur Supermärkte mit Umsatzplus.* https://www.ehi.org/presse/nur-supermaerkte-mit-umsatzplus/

Ehrenreich, Barbara. (2011 [2001]). *Nickel and dimed. On (not) getting by in America.* Picador.

Esping-Andersen, Gøsta, & Korpi, Walter. (1987). From poor relief to institutional welfare states: The development of Scandinavian social policy. In Robert Erikson, Erik Jørgen Hansen, Stein Ringen, and Hannu Uusitalo (Eds.), *The Scandinavian model. Welfare states and welfare research* (pp. 39–74).

Esping-Andersen, Gøsta. (1990). *The three worlds of welfare capitalism.* Polity Press.

Estébez-Abe, Margarita. (2005). Gender bias in skills and social policies: The varieties of capitalism perspective on sex segregation. *Social Politics, 12*(2), 180–215.

European Union. (2022). *Proposal for a directive of the European Parliament and of the Council on Corporate Sustainability Due Diligence and amending Directive (EU) 2019/1937.* https://eur-lex.europa.eu/legal-content/EN/TXT/?uri=CELEX%3A52022PC0071

Evangelisches Gesangbuch. (1994). *Für Gottesdienst, Gebet, Glaube, Leben.* https://www.evangeliums.net/lieder/lied_ich_ruf_zu_dir_herr_jesu_christ.html

Federal Foreign Office. (2022). *Germany and Somalia. Bilateral relations.* https://www.auswaertiges-amt.de/en/aussenpolitik/somalia/209162

Federal Reserve Economic Data (FRED). (2022). https://fred.stlouisfed.org/release/tables?rid=331&eid=211#snid=867

Frey, Michael. (2009). *Autonomie und Aneignung in der Arbeit. Eine soziologische Untersuchung zur Vermarktlichung und Subjektivierung von Arbeit.* Rainer Hampp Verlag.

Friedrichsen, Jana. (2020). *Die Fleischindustrie und Corona.* https://www.wzb.eu/de/forschung/corona-und-die-folgen/corona-und-die-fleischindustrie

Fürstenberg, Friedrich. (1969). *Die Soziallage der Chemiearbeiter. Industriesoziologische Untersuchungen in rationalisierten und automatisierten Chemiebetrieben.* Hermann Luchterhand Verlag GmbH.

Giegel, Hans-Joachim. (1989). Der Lohnarbeiter als Subjekt. Von der Analyse des Arbeiterbewußtseins zur Biographieforschung. In Dietmar Brock, Hans Rudolf Leu, Christine Preiß, Hans-Rolf Vetter (Eds.), *Subjektivität im gesellschaftlichen Wandel. Umbrüche im beruflichen Sozialisationsprozeß* (pp. 100–128). Weinheim und München, Juventa.

Giegel, Hans-Joachim, Frank, Gerhard, & Billerbeck, Ulrich. (1988). *Industriearbeit und Selbstbehauptung. Berufsbiographische Orientierung und Gesundheitsverhalten in gefährdeten Lebensverhältnissen.* Opladen, Leske + Budrich.

Gilson, Erinn, & Kenehan, Sarah (eds.). (2019). *Food, environment, and climate change.* Rowman & Littlefield.

Glaubitz, Jürgen. (2019). Preiskrieg im Einzelhandel. *Ver.di Handel NRW*. https://handel -nrw.verdi.de/einzelhandel/++co++773ba932-b1cf-11e9-ad76-525400423e78

Goldthorpe, John H., Lockwood, David, Bechhofer, Frank, & Platt, Jennifer. (1971 [1968]). *The affluent worker. Industrial attitudes and behaviour*. Cambridge University Press.

Graf, Patricia, & Kupfer, Antonia. (2015). Geschlechterverhältnisse in ausbeutenden Arbeitsbeziehungen. *Aus Politik und Zeitgeschichte (APuZ)* 50–51/2015, 29–34.

Grenz, Frauke, & Günster, Anne. (2022). Who is relevant? And to which system? The re/production of power relations during the debate about "system-relevant" professions from a discourse analytical perspective. In Antonia Kupfer and Constanze Stutz (Eds.), *Covid, crisis, care and change. International gender perspectives on re/production, state and feminist transitions* (pp. 45–58). https://www.ssoar.info/ssoar/ bitstream/handle/document/79219/ssoar-2022-kupfer_et_al-Covid_Crisis_Care _and_Change.pdf?sequence=1&isAllowed=y. Verlag Barbara Budrich.

Greve, Bent. (2009). Can choice in welfare states be equitable? *Social Policy and Administration, 43*(6), 543–556.

Grugulis, Irena, & Bozkurt, Ödül. (2011). *Retail work*. Palgrave Macmillan.

Guillén, Mauro F., Collins, Randall, England, Paula, & Meyer, Marshall. (2002). The revival of economic sociology. In Mauro F. Guillén et al. (Eds.), *The new economic sociology. Developments in an emerging field* (pp. 1–32). Russell Sage Foundation.

Hall, Peter, & Soskice, David (eds.). (2001). *Varieties of capitalism: The institutional foundations of comparative advantage*. Oxford University Press.

Handelsblatt. (2022). *Nur noch etwas jeder zweite Beschäftigte in Deutschland arbeitet nach Tarif*. https://www.handelsblatt.com/politik/deutschland/arbeitsmarkt-nur -noch-etwa-jeder-zweite-beschaeftigte-in-deutschland-arbeitet-nach-tarif/25825570 .html

Handelsverband Deutschland. (2023). *Beschäftigungsstruktur im Einzelhandel*. https:// einzelhandel.de/beschaeftigungsstruktur

Handelsverband Deutschland. (2023). *Zahlenspiegel 2022*. https://einzelhandel.de/ zahlenspiegel

Hardering, Friederice, & Will-Zocholl, Mascha. (2020). Zwischen Sinngestaltung und Sinnbewahrung – Aneignungsweisen hochqualifizierter Dienstleistungsarbeit. *Berliner Journal für Soziologie, 29*, 273–298.

Hofmann, Michael, & Rink, Dieter. (1999). Frauen, die "Mitmischen" wollen. Eine Verkäuferinnenstudie. In *Tertiarisierung und Wandel sozialer Milieus in Ostdeutschland*, Forschungsbericht an die DFG, Bonn.

Haug, Frigga. (1999). Gebrauchswert. In Wolfgang Fritz Haug (Ed.), *Historisch-Kritisches Wörterbuch des Marxismus, Vol. 4, Fabel bis Gegenmacht* (pp. 1259–1289). Argument Verlag.

Hochschild, Arlie Russell. (2016). *Strangers in their own land: Anger and mourning in the American Right*. The New Press.

Hodson, Randy. (2001). *Dignity at work*. Cambridge University Press.

Holzkamp, Klaus. (2006 [1973]). *Schriften IV. Sinnliche Erkenntnis. Historischer Ursprung und gesellschaftliche Funktion der Wahrnehmung. Schriften IV Im Auftrag des Instituts für Kritische Theorie – InkriT, Herausgegeben von Frigga Haug, Wolfgang Maiers und Ute Osterkamp*. Argument Verlag.

Holzkamp-Osterkamp, Ute. (1981 [1975]). *Grundlagen der psychologischen Motivationsforschung*, Vol. 1 (3rd ed.). Campus Verlag.

Honneth, Axel. (2010). Arbeit und Anerkennung. Versuch einer theoretischen Neubestimmung. In *Das Ich im Wir. Studien zur Anerkennungstheorie* (pp. 78–102). Suhrkamp.

Honneth, Axel. (2023). *Der arbeitende Souverän.* Suhrkamp.

Hürtgen, Stefanie. (2017). Der subjektiv gesellschaftliche Sinnbezug auf die eigene (Lohn-) Arbeit. Grundlage von Ansprüchen auf Gestaltung von Arbeit und Gesellschaft. In Brigitte Aulenbacher, Maria Dammayr, Klaus Dörre, Wolfgang Menz, Birgit Riegraf, and Harald Wolf (Eds.), *Leistung und Gerechtigkeit. Das umstrittene Versprechen des Kapitalismus* (pp. 210–227). Beltz Juventa.

Hürtgen, Stefanie. (2018). Arbeitssubjekt und gesellschaftliche Handlungsfähigkeit – Denkweisen und Alltagspraxen von Arbeiter*innen in ihrer politischen Dimension verstehen. *SPW – Zeitschrift für Sozialistische Politik und Wirtschaft, 4*(2018), 45–50.

Hürtgen, Stefanie. (2021). Meaningful work and social citizenship. In Antonia Kupfer (Ed.), *Work appropriation and social inequality* (pp. 107–122). Vernon Press.

Hürtgen, Stefanie, & Voswinkel, Stephan. (2014). *Nichtnormale Normalität? Anspruchslogiken aus der Arbeitnehmermitte.* Edition Sigma.

Ibisworld. (2023). *Supermarkets and grocery stores in the U.S. – Employment statistics 2002–2028.* https://www.ibisworld.com/industry-statistics/employment/supermarkets-grocery-stores-united-states/

International Labour Office (ILO). (2012). *International Standard Classification of Occupations. Structure group definitions and correspondence tables,* Geneva. https://www.ilo.org/wcmsp5/groups/public/@dgreports/@dcomm/@publ/documents/publication/wcms_172572.pdf

Jacobsen, Heike, & Hilf, Ellen. (2019). Beruf als Fiktion. Wandel von Berufsfachlichkeit im Einzelhandel unter flexibilisierten Beschäftigungsbedingungen. In Wolfgang Dunkel, Heidemarie Hanekop, and Nicole Mayer-Ahuja (Eds.), *Blick zurück nach vorn. Sekundäranalysen zum Wandel von Arbeit nach dem Fordismus* (pp. 255–289). Campus Verlag.

Jaeggi, Rahel. (2005). *Entfremdung. Zur Aktualität eines sozialphilosophischen Problems.* Campus Verlag.

Jaeggi, Rahel. (2016). Nachwort zur Taschenbuchausgabe. In *Entfremdung. Zur Aktualität eines sozialphilosophischen Problems* (pp. 255–289). Suhrkamp.

Kern, Horst, & Schumann, Michael. (1977 [1970]). *Industriearbeit und Arbeiterbewußtsein. Eine empirische Untersuchung über den Einfluß der aktuellen technischen Entwicklung auf die industrielle Arbeit und das Arbeiterbewußtsein.* Suhrkamp.

Kern, Horst, & Schumann, Michael. (1984). *Das Ende der Arbeitsteilung? Rationalisierung in der industriellen Produktion, Bestandsaufnahmen, Trendbestimmung.* Beck.

Kleemann, Frank, & Voß, G. Günter. (2018 [2010]). Arbeit und Subjekt. In Fritz Böhle, G. Günter Voß, and Günther Wachtler (Eds.), *Handbuch Arbeitssoziologie* (pp. 15–57). VS.

Knapp, Gudrun Axeli. (1981). *Industriearbeit und Instrumentalismus: zur Geschichte eines Vor-Urteils.* Verlag Neue Gesellschaft.

Korczynski, Marek. (2009). Understanding the contradictory lived experience of service work: The customer-oriented bureaucracy. In Marek Korczynski and Cameron Lynne Macdonald (Eds.), *Service work. Critical perspectives* (pp. 73–90). Routledge.

Kratzer, Nick, Menz, Wolfgang, Tullius, Knut, & Wolf, Harald. (2015). *Legitimationsprobleme in der Erwerbsarbeit. Gerechtigkeitsansprüche und Handlungsorientierungen.* Nomos.

Kruse, Jan. (2015). *Qualitative Interviewforschung. Ein integrativer Ansatz.* Beltz Juventa.

Kunz, Malou. (2022). *Auswirkungen der COVID-19 Pandemie auf die psychische Gesundheit von Kindern und Jugendlichen aus benachteiligten Verhältnissen.* Unveröffentlichte Masterarbeit, Technische Universität Dresden.

Kupfer, Antonia. (2021). Introduction. In Antonia Kupfer (Ed.), *Work appropriation and social inequality* (pp. xv–xxiv). Vernon Press.

Kupfer, Antonia. (2023). Liaison of climate change and social inequality. In Sabin Bieri and Christoph Bader (Eds.), *Transitioning to reduced inequalities* (pp. 45–61). MDPI.

Kupfer, Antonia, & Stutz, Constanze. (2022). Continuity not change. The unequal catastrophe of the Covid-19 pandemic: An introduction. In Antonia Kupfer and Constanze Stutz (Eds.), *Covid, crisis, care and change? International gender perspectives on re/production, state and feminist transitions* (pp. 7–27). Barbara Budrich Publishers. Open access: DOI 10.3224/84742541.

Kupfer, Antonia, Eckert, Falk, & Krause, Ina. (2019). Beruf(en) im Verkauf – Soziale Positionierung und subjektive Bedeutung von Arbeit. *Österreichische Zeitschrift für Soziologie, 44*(1), 43–63.

Kurtz, Thomas. (2002). *Berufssoziologie.* Bielefeld: transcript.

Leontjew, Aleksej N. (1975 [1959]). *Probleme der Entwicklung des Psychischen* (5th ed.). Volk und Wissen Volkseigener Verlag Berlin.

Leontjew, Aleksej N. (2012 [1975]). *Tätigkeit, Bewusstsein, Persönlichkeit,* Vol. 40, International Cultural-historical Human Sciences. Lehmanns Media GmbH.

Lucius-Hoene, Gabriele, & Deppermann, Arnulf. (2004). *Rekonstruktion narrativer Identität. Ein Arbeitsbuch zur Analyse narrativer Interviews, Wiesbaden.* Verlag für Sozialwissenschaften.

Macdonald, Cameron L., & Merrill, David. (2009). Intersectionality in the emotional proletariat: a new lens on employment discrimination in service work. In Marek Korczynski and Cameron L. Macdonald (Eds.), *Service work. Critical perspectives* (pp. 113–133). Routledge.

Macdonald, Cameron L., & Sirianni, Carmen. (1996). The Service Society and the Changing Experience of Work. In Cameron McDonald and Carmen Sirianni (Eds.), *Working in the service society* (pp. 1–26). Temple University Press.

Macdonald, Keith M. (1995). *The sociology of the professions.* Sage Publications.

Marschelke, Jan-Christoph. (2015). Moderne Sklavereien. *Aus Politik und Zeitgeschichte (APuZ)* 50–51/2015, 15–23.

Marx, Karl. (1988 [1890]. *Das Kapital. Erster Band.* Dietz Verlag.

Matuschek, Ingo. (2010). *Konfliktfeld Leistung: Eine Literaturstudie zur betrieblichen Leistungspolitik.* Edition Sigma.

Menz, Wolfgang, & Nies, Sarah. (2018). Methoden der Arbeitssoziologie. In Fritz Böhle, G. Günter Voß, and Günther Wachtler (Eds.), *Handbuch Arbeitssoziologie.* Vol. 1: *Arbeit, Strukturen und Prozesse* (2nd ed., pp. 265–318). Springer VS.

Meyer, John, & Scott, Richard. (1977). Institutional organizations: Formal structure as myth and ceremony. *American Journal of Sociology, 83*(2), 340–363.

Meyer, John, & Scott, Richard. (1992). *Organizational environments: Ritual and rationality.* Sage.

Miani, Céline, Wandschneider, Lisa, Batram-Zantvoort, Stephanie, & Razum, Oliver. (2022). Covid-19 pandemic: A gender perspective on how lockdown measures have affected mothers with young children. In Antonia Kupfer and Constanze Stutz (Eds.), *Covid, crisis, care and change. International gender perspectives on re/production, state and feminist transitions* (pp. 75–93) https://www.ssoar.info/ssoar/bitstream/handle/document/79219/ssoar-2022-kupfer_et_al-Covid_Crisis_Care_and_Change.pdf?sequence=1&isAllowed=y. Verlag Barbara Budrich.

Mikl-Horke, Gertraude. (2007). *Industrie- und Arbeitssoziologie* (6th ed.). R. Oldenbourg Verlag.

Mikl-Horke, Gertraude. (2011). *Soziologie. Historischer Kontext und soziologische Theorie-Entwürfe* (6th ed.). Oldenbourg Verlag.

National Retail Federation. (2020). *The economic impact of the US retail industry.* https://cdn.nrf.com/sites/default/files/2020-06/RS-118304%20NRF%20Retail%20Impact%20Report%20.pdf

Newman, Katherine S. (2008 [2006]). *Chutes and ladders. Navigating the low-wage labor market.* Harvard University Press.

Newman, Katherine S., & Tan Chen, Victor. (2007). *The missing class. Portraits of the near poor in America.* Beacon Press.

Nies, Sarah. (2015). *Nützlichkeit und Nutzung von Arbeit. Beschäftigte im Konflikt zwischen Unternehmenszielen und eigenen Ansprüchen.* Nomos.

Orloff, Ann Shola. (2009). Gendering the comparative analysis of welfare states: An unfinished agenda. *Sociological Theory, 27*(3), 317–343.

Oxfam. (2019). *Supermarkt-Check.* https://www.oxfam.de/system/files/supermarkt-check_2019_international.pdf

Pongratz, Hans, & Voß, G. Günter. (1998). Der Arbeitskraftunternehmer. *Kölner Zeitschrift für Soziologie und Sozialpsychologie, 50*(1), 131–158.

Popitz, Heinrich. (2010 [1957]). Einleitung: Grundlegende Fragestellungen der Soziologie: Fünf Problemkreise. In *Einführung in die Soziologie. Herausgegeben und mit einem Nachwort von Jochen Dreher und Michael K. Walter* (pp. 11–20). Konstanz University Press.

Popitz, Heinrich, Bardt, Hans Paul, Jüres, Ernst August, & Kesting, Hanno. (1972 [1957]). *Das Gesellschaftsbild des Arbeiters. Soziologische Untersuchungen in der Hüttenindustrie* (4th ed.). Mohr (Paul Siebeck).

Powell, Martin, Yörük, Erdem, & Bargu, Ali. (2019). Thirty years of the *Three Worlds of Welfare Capitalism*: A review of reviews. *Social Policy Administration, 54,* 60–87. DOI 10.1111/spol.12510.

Rosenthal, Gabriele. (2008). *Interpretative Sozialforschung. Eine Einführung.* Juventa.

Ross, Dorothy. (1991). *The origins of American social science.* Cambridge University Press.

Sallaz, Jeffrey J. (2013). *Labor, economy, and society.* Polity Press.

Scaturro, Ruggero. (2021). Modern slavery made in Italy – Causes and consequences of labour exploitation in the Italian agricultural sector. *Journal of Illicit Economies and Development, 3*(2), 181–189.

Sennett, Richard. (1989). *The corrosion of character. The personal consequences of work in the new capitalism.* W. W. Norton & Company.

Shipler, David K. (2005). *The working poor. Invisible in America.* Vintage Books.

Soric, Miodrag. (2020). *'Modern slavery' at the heart of slaughterhouse outbreak.* https://www.dw.com/en/coronavirus-modern-slavery-at-the-heart-of-german-slaughterhouse-outbreak/a-53396228

Staab, Philipp. (2014). *Macht und Herrschaft in der Servicewelt*. Verlag des Hamburger Instituts für Sozialforschung.

Statista. (2022). *U.S. Food retail industry statistics and facts*. https://www.statista.com/topics/1660/food-retail/#topicHeader__wrapper

Statistisches Bundesamt. (2020). *Berufliche Bildung. Auszubildende nach Ausbildungsberufen*. https://www.destatis.de/DE/Themen/Gesellschaft-Umwelt/Bildung-Forschung-Kultur/Berufliche-Bildung/Tabellen/liste-azubi-rangliste.html

Statistisches Bundesamt. (2022a). *Berufliche Bildung. Auszubildende nach Ausbildungsberufen*. https://www.destatis.de/DE/Themen/Gesellschaft-Umwelt/Bildung-Forschung-Kultur/Berufliche-Bildung/Tabellen/liste-azubi-rangliste.html#111984

Statistisches Bundesamt. (2022b). *Entwicklung der Reallöhne, der Nominallöhne und der Verbraucherpreise*. https://www.destatis.de/DE/Themen/Arbeit/Verdienste/Realloehne-Nettoverdienste/Tabellen/liste-reallohnentwicklung.html#134646

Stein, Mark. (2019). Modern slavery in agriculture. In D.M. Kaplan (Ed.), *Encyclopedia of Food and Agricultural Ethics*. Springer. https://link.springer.com/referenceworkentry/10.1007/978-94-024-1179-9_627

Strohschneider, Tom, & Gerlof, Kathrin. (2019). *Slaves in Europe's fields. On the exploitation of migrants during the harvest and grassroots union resistance in Italy, Austria, and Spain*. https://www.rosalux.de/en/publication/id/41102/slaves-in-europes-fields

Tagesschau. (2020). *Erntehelfer kommen im Sonderflieger*. https://www.tagesschau.de/wirtschaft/erntehelfer-einreise-101.html

Terkel, Studs. (2004 [1972]). *Working. People talk about what they do all day and how they feel about what they do*. The New Press.

Thompson, Paul. (1983). *The nature of work. An introduction to debates on the labour process*. Macmillan Press.

Thompson, Paul. (2021). Foreword. In Antonia Kupfer (Ed.), *Work appropriation and social inequality* (pp. ix–xiii). Vernon Press.

Turner, Stephen P., & Turner, Jonathan H. (1990). *The impossible science: An institutional analysis of American sociology*. Sage.

U.S. Census Bureau. (2023). *A profile of the retail workforce*. https://www.census.gov/library/stories/2020/09/profile-of-the-retail-workforce.html

U.S. Department of State. (2022). *U.S. relations with Somalia*. https://www.state.gov/u-s-relations-with-somalia/

Vallas, Steven. (2012). *Work. A critique*. Polity Press.

Vallas, Steven, Finlay, William, & Wharton, Amy S. (2009). *The sociology of work: Structures and inequalities*. Oxford University Press.

Veltman, Andrea. (2016). *Meaningful work*. Oxford University Press.

Voss-Dahm, Dorothea. (2008). Low-paid but committed to the industry: Salespeople in the retail sector. In Gerhard Bosch and Claudia Weinkopf (Eds.), *Low-wage work in Germany* (pp. 253–287). Russell Sage Foundation.

Voss-Dahm, Dorothea, & Lehndorff, Steffen. (2003). *Lust und Frust in moderner Verkaufsarbeit. Beschäftigungs- und Arbeitszeittrends im Einzelhandel*. Graue Reihe des Instituts für Arbeit und Technik.

Voswinkel, Stephan. (2005). *Welche Kundenorientierung? Anerkennung in der Dienstleistungsarbeit*. Edition Sigma.

Voswinkel, Stephan. (2012). Arbeit und Subjektivität. In K. Dörre, S. Sauer, and V. Wittke (Eds.), *Kapitalismustheorie und Arbeit. Neue Ansätze soziologischer Kritik* (pp. 302–315). Campus Verlag.

Voswinkel, Stephan. (2015). Sinnvolle Arbeit leisten – Arbeit sinnvoll leisten. *Arbeit*, *24*(1–2), 31–48.

Voswinkel, Stephan. (2019). Entfremdung und Aneignung in der Arbeit. In F. Böhle and E. Senghaas-Knobloch (Eds.), *Andere Sichtweisen auf Subjektivität* (pp. 167–197). Springer.

Voswinkel, Stephan. (2021). *Arbeitssoziologie und Gesellschaftstheorie. Perspektiven der Arbeitssoziologie 2*, IWS working paper #14. Institut für Sozialforschung. http:// www.ifs.uni-frankfurt.de/wp-content/uploads/Voswinkel-IfS-Working-Papers.pdf

Voswinkel, Stephan, & Wagner, Gabriele. (2013). Vermessung der Anerkennung. Die Bearbeitung unsicherer Anerkennung in Organisationen. In Axel Honneth, Ophelia Lindemann, and Stephan Voswinkel (Eds.), *Strukturwandel der Anerkennung. Paradoxien sozialer Integration in der Gegenwart* (pp. 75–120). Campus Verlag.

Voß, G. Günter. (1983). Bewußtsein ohne Subjekt? Zur Differenzierung des Bewußtseinsbegriffs in der Industriesoziologie. In Karl Martin Bolte and Ehrhard Treutner (Eds.), *Subjektorientierte Arbeits- und Berufssoziologie* (pp. 324–359). Campus Verlag.

Voß, G. Günter. (2018). Was ist Arbeit? Zum Problem eines allgemeinen Arbeitsbegriffs. In Fritz Böhle, G. Günter Voß, and Günther Wachtler (Eds.), *Handbuch Arbeitssoziologie. Band 1: Arbeit, Strukturen und Prozesse* (2nd ed., pp. 15–84). Springer VS.

Williams, Mark, Gifford, Jonny, & Zhou, Ying. (2022). Social stratification in meaningful work: Occupational class disparities in the United Kingdom. *The British Journal of Sociology*, 1–18. DOI 10.1111/1468–4446.12941.

World Food Programme (WFP). (2020). Rapport PAM Analyse des Vulnérabilités, Régions du Liptako-Gourma: Conflits Persistans, Pertes des Terres Agrigoles et Insécurité Alimentaire Récurrente, July 2020. https://docs.wfp.org/api/documents/ WFP-0000117788/download/

World Food Programme (WFP). (2022). *Somalia*. https://www.wfp.org/countries/ somalia

Wrzesniewski, Amy, & Dutton, Jane E. (2001). Crafting a job: Revisioning employees as active crafters of their work. *Academy of Management Review*, *26*(2), 179–201.

Yeoman, Ruth, Bailey, Catherine, Madden, Adrian, & Thompson, Marc (eds.). (2019). *The Oxford Handbook of Meaningful Work*. Oxford University Press.

# Index